ROYAL HISTORICAL SOCIETY
STUDIES IN HISTORY
SERIES
No. 18

# THE SHADOW OF THE BOMBER
The Fear of Air Attack and
British Politics 1932-1939

## Recent volumes published in this series include

| | | |
|---|---|---|
| 12 | Preachers, Peasants and Politics in Southeast Africa 1835-1880: African Christian Communities in Natal, Pondoland and Zululand | *Norman Etherington* |
| 13 | Linlithgow and India: British Policy and the Political Impasse in India 1936-1943 | *S. A. G. Rizvi* |
| 14 | Britain and her Buffer State: The Collapse of the Persian Empire, 1890-1914 | *David McLean* |
| 15 | Guns and Government: The Ordnance Office under the Later Stuarts | *Howard Tomlinson* |
| 16 | Denzil Holles: A Study of his Political Career | *Patricia Crawford* |
| 17 | The Parliamentary Agents: A History | *D. L. Rydz* |

For a complete list of the series please see p. 166

# THE SHADOW OF THE BOMBER
The Fear of Air Attack and British Politics
1932-1939

Uri Bialer

LONDON
ROYAL HISTORICAL SOCIETY
1980

© Uri Bialer 1980
ISBN 0 901050 78 4

The Society records its gratitude to the following, whose generosity made possible the initiation of this series: The British Academy; The Pilgrim Trust; The Twenty-Seven Foundation; The United States Embassy bicentennial funds; The Wolfson Trust; several private donors.

Printed in England
by Swift Printers (Sales) Ltd
London E.C.1.

# CONTENTS

|   | Acknowledgements | vi |
|---|---|---|
|   | Introduction | 1 |
| 1 | Air Disarmament (1931-1933) | 7 |
| 2 | Air Power and Early Rearmament (1934-1935) | 41 |
| 3 | Security by Convention (1934-1936) | 76 |
| 4 | Air Warfare Rules (1936-1939) | 101 |
| 5 | The Bomber vs. the Expeditionary Force (1935-1937) | 127 |
| 6 | Epilogue to an Obsession | 151 |
|   | Index | 161 |

# ACKNOWLEDGEMENTS

I am grateful to Professor Donald C. Watt who first drew my attention and interest to the subject of this book and whose advice and encouragement throughout the various stages of its writing have been invaluable.

I am indebted to H.M. Stationery Office and the libraries of Cambridge University, Kings College; and the British Museum for permission to consult and quote from sources in their possession.

For allowing me access to private papers I owe gratitude to Lord Caldecote, Lady Liddell-Hart, the Rt. Hon. David Marquand, Professor Temple Patterson and Lady Vansittart. Mr Haslam of the Air Historical Branch of the Air Ministry, Mr John Motun, the Director of the British Air League and Dr. Patrick Fridenson allowed access to some valuable studies. Mr John Barnes, Dr. Brian Bond, Mr. Stephen Brooks, Sir Michael Creswell, Dr. Noble Frankland, Professor Norman Gibbs, Dr. Martin Gilbert, Professor Tom Harrison, Professor Michael Howard, the Rt. Hon Philip Noel-Baker, Professor Michael Postan, Dr. Norman Rose, Captain Stephen Roskill and Viscount Samuel greatly helped with valuable information and advice.

My great institutional debts are to the Hebrew University of Jerusalem, The Friends of the Hebrew University in London and the Leonard Davis Institute for International Relations for their moral and financial support during the years I have been engaged in this study. I would also like to express my thanks to the Editors of the *Journal of Contemporary History and War and Society* for permission to use some material which first appeared in their journal and yearbook (vol. 13 and vol. 1 respectively).

I am especially grateful to Dr. Stuart Cohen for his criticism and help in revising the draft and to Mrs J. Deutsch for typing the successive manuscripts. Last but at the same time first my deep thanks are to my wife Rachel for her support.

The multiplicity of my debts to others require me to emphasize that the responsibility for interpretations contained in this study lie solely with myself.

Uri Bialer<br>
Jerusalem<br>
January 1980

# INTRODUCTION

During the First World War, Britain's basic strategic posture was revolutionized. Hitherto, command of the oceans had been the overriding necessity, and its attainment had conferred upon the country two essential advantages. First, sea power — in its classic form — had guaranteed the maintenance of uninterrupted communications between Britain and her various Imperial outposts. Second, naval superiority had protected the British Isles themselves against invasion, and had thus *ipso facto* ensured the security of the foundations of national power.[1] The appearance of the aeroplane affected both considerations. Air power threatened the inviolability of imperial communications; worse still, it undermined the immunity of the mother country to hostile penetration. The makers of British defence and foreign policy could no longer rely upon the navy to preserve the nation's invulnerability to invasion. They were forced to adjust their traditional strategic concepts to the possibility that a potential enemy might employ a new weapon with which to overcome and subdue the country.[2] For the first time, the heart of the empire was endangered by the threat of aerial bombardment.

The British Government had first begun to take serious note of the possible strategic implications of the aeroplane as soon as flights were initiated in Britain, early in 1908. A Home and Ports Defence sub-committee was then appointed to examine the dangers to which the country might be exposed 'by development of aerial navigation'. Within two years, that body had concluded that airship attacks on Great Britain should be regarded as *'possible* operations of war'.[3] Late in 1917, after German aeroplanes launched their first daylight raids on London, the emphasis of the warning had been significantly altered. Now, the Cabinet was informed, 'the day may not be far off when aerial operations with their devastation of enemy towns and

---

[1] For the 'invasion scares' which swept Britain at the end of the 19th Century, and which were largely due to the new wave of technological changes, see Howard Moon, 'The Invasion of the United Kingdom: Public Controversy and Official Planning' (unpublished Ph.D. thesis, University of London, 1968.)

[2] See B. Powers, *Strategy Without Slide Rule, British Air Strategy 1914-1939* (London, 1976). For a general analysis of this revolution, see D. Smith, 'A Comparative Study of the Influence of Air Power on the National Policies of Germany, Great Britain, the United States and the Soviet Union' (unpublished Ph.D. dissertation, The Catholic University of America, 1951), pp. 133-65; and G. Quester, *Deterence Before Hiroshima* (New York, 1966).

[3] W. Raleigh and H. Jones, *The War in the Air* (London, 1922). Vol. I, pp. 71-72. Italics added.

destruction of industrial and populous centres on a vast scale may become the *principal* operation of war'.[4]

Ultimately, it took twenty-two years for that day to come. Nevertheless, throughout the intervening period, and increasingly so towards its end, the Government was particularly sensitive to this defence issue. The establishment of the Royal Air Force (itself the first independent air arm in the world)[5] in April 1918, signified no more than a preliminary accommodation. Between the two World Wars the threat of a 'bolt from the blue', in the form of an air attack, merited increasing attention. By the early 1930s, when the Government began to realize that Britain's involvement in a European war was credible as well as possible, the danger of aerial bombardment appeared to have become frighteningly real. The need to counter 'the peril from the sky' then became a prominent consideration, which preoccupied the minds of the men who formulated Britain's defence and foreign policy.

The fear of aerial bombardment in inter-war Britain was unprecedented and unique. It differed in both nature and extent from the apprehensions to which other contemporary problems of defence gave rise. In general terms this was due, firstly, to the novel objectives of the weapon itself. Hitherto, military weapons had conventionally been directed primarily against rival armed forces. The prominent targets of aerial bombardment, by contrast, were the enemy's urban centres of dense civilian habitation; his morale was to be broken by the destruction of his towns and the infliction of heavy losses on their inhabitants. This feature was of particularly crucial significance for Britain, whose civilian population had hitherto been largely protected by the island nature of their country. Henceforth, it seemed, aerial bombardment would deprive them of the security bestowed by geographical insularity, just as air warfare would itself contract the distance between the civilian hinterland and the military theatre. Consequently, concern that the civilian population would form a likely target in future war was both widespread and deeply felt.

This was especially so since air warfare was virtually untried. There were few instances of air bombardment anywhere between the two World Wars. Consequently, there was little substantial evidence

---

[4]Report by General J.C. Smuts to the War Cabinet on Defence Arrangements for Home Defence Against Air Raids, 17 August 1917. H.A. Jones, *The War in the Air* (London, 1937), Vol. VI, pp. 11-12. Italics added.

[5]On the background to that decision see A. Ranson, 'The Politics of Air Power — A Comparative Analysis' in C. Friedrich and S. Harris (eds.), *Public Policy* (Cabridge, 1958), pp. 353-76.

on which to base a reasoned estimate of its potential in a full-scale conflict.[6] In any case, what was known itself supplied sufficient grounds for apprehension. The advance of aircraft technology was considerable and tangible, and gave rise to lurid predictions of the effect of air power on 'the next war'. Indeed, the danger of air attack was often described in Britain in almost apocalyptic terms.[7] Subsequent events were to prove that the fears of professionals and amateurs alike had been exaggerated. Yet in the light of previous experience, slight as it had been, their estimates did not seem totally unreasonable. On the contrary, the First World War had itself fostered the acceptance by the British Air Staff of a strategic doctrine which emphasized the potentially decisive effect of a strategic bombing offensive on the nature of a future conflict. During the interwar period, the members of that body became persistent and influential prophets both inside and outside Government circles, and their prophecy was of destruction by an aerial 'knock-out blow'.

Much has been written about the serious apprehensions of aerial bombardment in inter-war Britain. Particular attention has been paid to the awareness of the danger during the late 1930s, when the threat of war advanced from the realm of military and professional speculation to that of an immediate political concern. However, most of the historical literature deals with the issue as a background element, albeit an important one, in the account of British air rearmament and the strengthening of air defence during that period. It does not discuss the important extent to which the need to counter the air peril influenced various defence and foreign policy considerations. This study accordingly attempts to fill a gap; it aims to focus on the fear itself, and to discover the extent to which it was shared by those responsible for shaping national policy. In the first, third and fourth chapters, it attempts to trace the influence of this apprehension on some of the key decisions in British foreign policy. It is suggested that the fear of a 'knock-out' blow from the air largely impelled the British Government's constant and continuous search for an international air disarmament agreement throughout the 1930s. From 1932 until 1939 the Cabinet devoted much effort to securing various forms of such an agreement, which was regarded as an important means of minimizing the 'air peril'. Throughout this period, and in the face of virtually insuperable difficulties, the Government persistently — and not

[6] On the general influence of technical changes on military thought between the Wars, see E. Emme, 'Technical Changes and Western Military Thought 1914-1945', *Military Affairs* 24 (1960), 6-19.

[7] For a general analysis of this issue see E. Emme, 'Some Fallacies Concerning Airpower', *Annals of the American Political and Social Science Association* 299 (May 1955), 12-24.

merely intermittently — tried to secure international conventions which would provide for limitations on aircraft production, the abolition of the bomber, prohibitions of the act of bombing, a guarantee against air attack and a convention regulating the conduct of air warfare. The quest started even before the emergence of German air power and ended only when its futility became unquestionably clear to the last of its proponents in the British Government.

Historians did not fail to recognize the great sensitivity of the makers of British defence policy to the danger of aerial bombardment and the considerable attention they gave to this issue in their discussions on rearmament and defence plans during the second half of the 1930s. Thus, in his unpublished *Prewar Evolution of Bomber Command,* Professor Wernham, referring to the general discussions on rearmament, noted that 'before the end of 1936 the idea that Germany might attempt a knock-out blow by air against the United Kingdom had already come to dominate British planning'.[8] Robert Rhodes James observed, in his study of Churchill's career in the interwar period, that 'the debate on rearmament between 1933 and 1938 was principally on air rearmament as a deterrent'.[9] Correlli Barnett, in *The Collapse of British Power,* put it more forcefully:

> rearmament in Britain was dominated throughout its course by an obsession with air power. . . . to the British Government rearmament came to seem almost a question of air power alone. Cabinet discussions tacitly assumed that the next war, if it came, would take the form of a direct, almost a private duel between the British and German Air Forces.[10]

It is clearly beyond the limits of this book to substantiate these claims in detail and to evaluate the influence of 'air anxiety' on British rearmament and strategic planning in this period. What we shall concentrate on in the second and last chapters is the effect of this anxiety on two cardinal elements in the history of British rearmament. The purpose is to show that the fear of a knock-out blow by air attack played a crucial part in the early debates on rearmament and resulted, in 1934 and 1935, in decisions to base rearmament largely on the air arm. It was also of significant importance to the understanding of British decision late in 1937 to enfeeble her ability to invervene by land in a continental war. This decision, known as the 'limited liability' formula, prevented any military preparations made in peace

---

[8]R. Wernham, *The Royal Air Force in Bombing Offensive Against Germany, Prewar Evolution of Bomber Command 1917-1939* (Ministry of Defence Air Historical Branch, 1947), p. 15.

[9]R. James, *Churchill: A Study in Failure 1900-1939* (London, 1970), p.435.

[10](London, 1972), p. 494.

time with a view to large scale military operations in Europe. These decisions were important stages in the long debate on priorities in British rearmament. It is my contention that it was the argument that tackling the 'air peril' must take priority which held sway in this debate and was of critical importance.

On the whole, the records now available support the conclusion that Britain pursued a single objective by simultaneously employing conflicting means. While paying considerable attention throughout this period to the issue of air rearmament, the Government devoted much effort to achieving an international air disarmament agreement. There can be no doubt that the spectre of air attack had a material influence on the making of both defence and foreign policy.

In what follows I present an approach to national behaviour which focuses on the process of decision-making. I underline the fact, too often neglected, that in no area is one calculating decision-maker, entirely responsible for the formulation of government policy, and show that authority is distributed amongst a conglomerate of departments and politicians who may differ substantially about what their government should do on any particular issue, and who compete in attempting to influence its decisions and actions. Close study of the department files which have become available in Britain, owing to the reduction of the fifty-year rule to thirty years, has brought to light some of the infrastrusture of the policy-making process. One particulary important contribution these newly opened records made to historical research is well expressed by Professor Dilks: 'It is not for the revelation of cardinal facts hitherto unsuspected, but for a new perspective, a fresh rating and balancing of evidence that the new archives are invaluable'.[11]

The analysis of British policy making during this period indicates that decision-makers do not always determine their policies in accordance with a consistent set of strategic objectives, but according to idiosyncratic conceptions of national security, and various interests of a departmental, domestic and personal nature which also come into play. The identification and examination of these elements can make a greater contribution to the historian's understanding of the motivations underlying policy than can a more rigid methodology which binds analysis to definitions of national interest. Admittedly during the mid-1930s, at least one Permanent Secretary of the Air Ministry considered the pulling and tugging of the Service departments in the process of policy-making to be 'a petty departmental prejudice, a

---

[11] 'Appeasement Revisited' *Leeds University Review* (May 1972), p. 33.

centrifugal vice in the life blood of the Services'.[12] Nevertheless, a retrospective analysis of the policy-making process in these terms is of great help for an examination of the formulation of British strategy during this period.

Admittedly this book concentrates on one single aspect of the factors involved in the making of policies most of whose cardinal features are by now well known. It is, however, based on certain evidence which has hitherto been largely overlooked; it suggests a new perspective which, I hope will contribute to the better understanding of British defence and foreign policy during the 1930s.

---

[12]Sir Christopher Bullock in a personal letter to Lord Weir, 25 November 1935, *Weir Papers* (Cambridge) 13/3.

# 1
## AIR DISARMAMENT

> Reading the histories of primitive clans, we have thought men were savages who cut the throats of another's family when they had dealt (or failed to deal) with him. But that's nothing to what a bombing aviator may do. A strange thought — that to this senseless wickedness has the western world been brought, by the collaboration of the 'nice boy' aviator, the mild-mannered, laboratory-minded man of science, the peace-protesting politicians, the herd-like multitude! At none of these can we point and say 'that is the criminal!' The crime is in the total lack of international control which people have allowed to grow up: mankind is Frankenstein: science, especially the science of aviation is his monster. Can we learn to control it? (P.M. Swanwick, *Frankenstein and His Monster: Aviation for World Service* (London 1934), p.5).

The danger of a knock-out blow by air attack was a grave concern which critically affected the making of British defence and foreign policy during the 1930s. The Government, indeed almost the entire nation, expected a devastating bombardment against vital parts of the country, and above all against the capital, to be a decisive blow in any future war against Britain. This belief was reflected in the discussions of the important subjects of disarmament and rearmament which preoccupied British decision-makers during the period. Moreover, concern with the danger was a major reason for the Government's continuous efforts, from the early years of the decade onwards, to reach an international air disarmament agreement. This study begins, therefore, with an examination of the manifestations of anxiety about bombardment and their influence on the making of British air disarmament policy at the international Disarmament Conference which sat in Geneva from 1932 to 1934.

The issue of air disarmament cannot be divorced from the basic framework of problems confronting the British Government in its policy towards the Conference.[1] Many influences worked upon the

---
[1] For a good general discussion on this subject, see E.B. Segal, 'Sir John Simon and British Foreign Policy: The Diplomacy of Disarmament in the Early 1930s' (unpublished Ph.D. thesis, University of California, 1966), to which I am indebted for some of these general remarks. R.A. Chaput, *Disarmament in British Foreign Policy* (London, 1935), is a good general analysis of the subject. A.C. Temperley, *The Whispering Gallery of Europe* (London, 1938) and A. Eden, Earl of Avon, *Facing the Dictators* (London, 1962) are useful for the decision making process in the Government. See C. Loosli Usteri, *Geschichte der Konferenz fur die Herabsetzung und die Begrenzung der Rustungen 1932-1934, Ein politischen Weltspiegel* (Zurich, 1940), and especially E. Bennett, *German Rearmament and the West 1932-1933* (Princeton, 1979) for international politics of the period.

framing of that policy: the financial exigencies produced by the economic crisis; the reluctance of the Dominions and of the United States to be drawn into any European commitment; the perilous state of Britain's own armaments (which weakened her negotiating hand); and the British Government's opposition to proposals for first-rate reductions which made no allowance for those cuts already effected. Unfortunately, not all of these influences pulled in the same direction; rather, their combined effect was to place the Government in a state of considerable tension and paradox. The general effect of various diplomatic, economic, military and imperial factors was to impede the taking of any bold line or risks abroad; yet internal political pressures demanded a Government success, particularly in the field of disarmament.

Ideally, the British Government would have liked a successful disarmament conference, culminating in a binding disarmament convention. From the perspective of British defence, such an outcome could only improve the relative position of Britain's armed forces. Convinced of the futility and waste of modern war machines and committed, in the words of Article Eight of the League Covenant, to the reduction of armaments 'to the lowest point consistent with national security', both Labour and Conservative Governments had already pegged British arms to a level below that attained in 1914. The fact that this example had not been emulated by the other Powers, with the exception of those forcibly disarmed at Versailles, had already placed Britain at a decisive disadvantage. From the perspective of British defence, therefore, all-round disarmament could not but improve Britain's relative strategic position. There were, in addition, more particular reasons to seek such an outcome. One was that the avoidance of any disruption to the existing international order was a cardinal principle of Britain's inter-war foreign policy. A disarmament convention would have facilitated this and by reducing the dangerous tension between France and Germany, it would help to reconcile the German demand for *Gleichberechtigung* — entitlement to equal rights — and the French desire (in any case excessive in Britain's eyes) to preserve intact the Treaty of Versailles. Furthermore, and especially after the successful conclusion of the Washington Naval Treaties of the previous decade, a new disarmament agreement would have a favourable effect on Anglo-American relations; indeed, it might contribute towards American cooperation on debts and other issues. Finally, the Government faced a widespread and extremely vociferous domestic public campaign for disarmament, which had itself been stimulated by the lengthy preparations for the Geneva Conference, and gained in strength once the proceedings commenced.

The appeal of disarmament to the British public was rooted in many causes. Foremost among them was the belief, itself never seriously questioned that the First World War had been caused by massive armaments: disarmament was thus seen as a panacea. Members of the Labour Party and the League of Nations Union were particularly vocal advocates of this line, and they launched an impressive public campaign designed to press the Government to take a lead at the Disarmament Conference. The National Government, which took office after the 1931 general elections, proved to be particularly sensitive to such pressure.[2] Notwithstanding the sharp decline in the Labour Party's fortunes in 1931, the part played by the disarmament issue in the Conservative defeat in 1929 was not forgotten. The public campaign, and the by-elections of 1933 and 1934, imparted to the Government a deep sense of electoral insecurity. The Cabinet felt that a considerable vote-catching success was necessary to ensure its continued tenure of office. Failure to substantiate Britain's adherence to the cause of disarmament, by securing a binding convention, was considered to be an eventuality pregnant with grave domestic political consequences. A Cabinet Committee, appointed in January 1932 to define Britain's attitude towards the Conference, agreed that 'the failure of the Disarmament Conference would be a disaster the [political] effects of which can hardly be measured'.[3]

The problem, of course, was how to bring about a disarmament agreement. The difficulties were sufficiently formidable — as, indeed, they still are — when only two states were involved. The essential prerequisites were a stabilization of the armed forces of the contracting parties for a prearranged period at an agreed level, proportionate to their respective defence requirements. The complexities of the objective and subjective calculations involved were significantly multiplied when the goal was a general disarmament treaty, involving several states. As much had already been discovered throughout the 1920s, when the founders of the League of Nations unsuccessfully attempted to gain universal fulfilment of Article Eight of the Covenant. By 1932, at least one British Foreign Secretary had sardonically suggested: 'The verb to disarm should be classified by

[2]See J.P. Kyba, 'British Attitudes Towards Disarmament and Rearmament 1932-1935' (unpublished Ph.D. dissertation, London School of Economics, 1966), for a useful analysis of public opinion, and also James K. Thompson, 'Great Britain and the World Disarmament Conference 1932-1934' (unpublished Ph.D. dissertation, University of North Carolina, 1961). On the myth of the "Merchants of Death" in Britain, see C. Trebilcock, "Legends of the British Armament Industry 1890-1914," *Journal of Contemporary History*, V, 4, (1970), pp. 3-21.

[3]19 January 1932, Cabinet Records, Public Record Office, London (hereafter Cab.), Cab. 24/227.

grammarians as a defective verb, you can say you will disarm but you can't say we disarm.'[4]

Fundamental to the success of any attempt to achieve disarmament at Geneva during the 1930s, was the reconciliation of the French demand for security and the German demand for equality of rights.[5] It was the latter which the British found to be of crucial importance. The analysis presented by Alexander Cadogan of the Foreign Office early in 1932, was typical:

> All the difficulties of the Conference turn on one fundamental question — are we to try to keep the present Europe by force, by maintaining the restrictions imposed on Germany by the peace treaty, or are we to bring to an end the 'post war' period, allow Germany to resume her place and rights as a great power on equal footing with the others, and trust that the reluctant removal of her grievances coupled with the security afforded by the Covenant of the League will initiate a period of real peace? French policy plainly cannot be maintained for ever, the French seem determined to hold on to it till it breaks while to us it seems more hopeful to take the chance now of conciliatory methods . . . If no concession is made to Germany now she will wait until she is strong enough to take everything at one blow in defiance of the others and in a spirit of hostility to them. The problem of the disarmament conference is to satisfy Germany.[6]

Britain's most obvious contribution would have been to make a further commitment to French security. But to have done so would have run counter to the essentially defensive nature of her policy at the time of the Conference; British statesmen firmly and consistently took the line that in no circumstances could they increase the nation's commitments abroad. They possessed neither the capability to implement such a commitment, nor the will to strengthen their own armed forces. Ramsay MacDonald, the Prime Minister, admitted the essential paradox as early as July 1931: 'if we get France to agree to reductions, it would be impossible to guarantee any assistance to France which would be of sufficient value to enable them to make such reductions. We would seem to be faced with rather a vicious circle'.[7]

[4]John Simon, *Retrospect* (London, 1952), p. 185.

[5]For a general analysis of this problem, see A. Wolfers, *Britain and France Between the Wars* (New Haven, 1940).

[6]From a personal letter to H. Smith, 5 May 1932, Foreign Office Records, Public Record Office, London (hereafter FO) FO 800/390 CF/3211.

[7]Cab. 21/346.

By the early part of the following year, the full implications of the situation had already produced a sense of considerable pessimism within the Government about the possibility of reaching successful agreement at Geneva.[8] The outbreak of the Manchurian crisis in February 1932, and the consequent creation of what proved to be perpetual dangers and difficulties in the Far East, in any case rendered the prospect of a Convention visionary.[9] Thus, even before the Conference opened, the Government had been reduced to a feeling of paralysis, the dangers of which were clearly expressed by Sir Robert Vansittart, the Permanent Under-Secretary of State for Foreign Affairs. 'The result of breaking no eggs', he warned, 'is admittedly not an omelette, but may well be a mess'.[10] Since public expectations and enthusiasm were still high, the Government could not, for obvious political reasons, abandon the search for a formula which might provide a basis for agreement; neither could it admit defeat even though failure was apparent. Samuel Hoare, at the time Secretary of State for India, was stating what was apparent to many of his colleagues when he privately informed the Prime Minister: as to the Conference 'if we cannot get on with it, we cannot get on without it'.[11]

The result had been continuous efforts to find what Anthony Eden, who led the British delegation at the Conference, called 'intermediate positions'.[12] These were designed to still the criticism of silence and to provide some basis for negotiations without tackling the basic problem.

In addition to such pressures of a general nature, the internal process whereby Britain's air disarmament policy was decided was further influenced by three elements of specific importance. All three were connected with the concept of the aerial knock-out blow. They were: public opinion on the specific subject of air disarmament; the personal views of some prominent decision-makers on the danger of air attack; and the attitudes and opinions of some departments of state on this matter.

A distinction can properly be made between public opinion on air disarmament and the general attitude towards disarmament as a

[8]This pessimism led, in January 1932, to efforts to delay the opening of the Conference. See Cab. 63/44.

[9]For an expanded analysis of the crisis, see C. Thorne, *The Limits of Foreign Policy* (London, 1973,).

[10]1 January 1932, Cab. 27/476.

[11]MacDonald Papers, (London), 2/6.

[12]Eden, *Facing the Dictators,* p. 29.

whole. This is because the problem of air disarmament has its own specific characteristics. The danger threatened by air bombardment to the civilian population seems to have been far more apparent to the British public than the dangers of other means of warfare. Ordinary citizens were aware that air warfare tended to nullify the distance between the military battleground and the civilian hinterland. The short but impressive experience of the aerial bombardment of London in the First World War, and the rapid and tangible progress of aircraft technology, were grist to the mills of popular writers on the subject of air warfare, who specifically stressed the immense destructive capability of air bombardment. In this respect, there seems to have been little to distinguish between the professional analysis of the impact of air attack in a future war and its portrayal in contemporary science fiction.

Military analysts in Britain often enlarged on the air menace in cataclysmic terms. One of them defined it as 'a brain child born in the early years of the century and turned into a Frankenstein in the early 1930s'.[13] Their views were shared by other professionals, among them architects. Thus, one of the latter wrote:

> We are entering upon a new age of architecture: future civillizations may call it the Funk-hole Age. It may be the prelude to another Dark Age in which our children and grandchildren and great grandchildren will live amid ruins, and will be compelled to endure ... shortage of the bare necessities of life. We have an obligation to consider and prepare national schemes of some kind which will enable at least a nucleus of civilization to be preserved in the event of a general breakdown. Is it too futuristic to suggest that we should create special shelter cities, either adjacent to existing cities or situated in different parts of the country?[14]

In his fascinating first effort to analyse the popular image of the 'next war', I.F. Clarke observed that the scene of a devastating air attack was a common theme in the fiction of the 1930s.[15] This appeared to be particularly true of Britain.[16] It is therefore not surprising to read that

---

[13] L.E.O. Charlton, *War from the Air* (London, 1935), p. 7. See also A.E. Blake, 'The Future of Warfare' in *Fortnightly Review* September 1930, pp. 29-40, and 585-598.

[14] John Gloag, 'The Funk Hole Age' *The Building,* 8 May 1937.

[15] See I.F. Clarke, *Voices Prophesying War 1763-1984* (London, 1966), p. 170.

[16] See Wyndham Lewis, *The Danger of Youth* and *Filibuster in Barbary* (London, 1932), as well as M. Helders, *War in the Air* (London, 1932), for reflections in the fiction of the period.

Kingsley Martin, editor of *New Statesman,* regarded these apocalyptic views as 'very characteristic of the thought of the period'.[17]

The vision of a devastated city and its mutilated inhabitants, common to all these writings, underlined the widespread belief that air bombardment could destroy such conurbations as London within a matter of hours. It would appear that the main reason for the intense interest shown by the British public in the subject of air disarmament was the awful realization that their island existence would no longer protect them from direct and intense involvement in a war in which their country was a participant. It is therefore hardly surprising that air peril constituted a prominent refrain in the campaign launched by various organizations at the time of the Disarmament Conference. Indeed, the necessity to arouse the public to the consequences of future air warfare before it was too late,[18] even gave rise to deliberate attempts to specify the horrors which such a conflict might entail. An article published in the *New Statesman,* which consistently and fervently advocated disarmament, was typical. It stressed the horrors of attack by gas bombs, which it labelled a 'synthetic earthquake' that 'could only be equalled by one of nature's worst convulsions'. It drew attention to the impracticability of any means of defence, and concluded with a warning that this vision of destruction had to be considered seriously 'if we are refused international measures of disarmament to safeguard this matter'.[19]

The League of Nations Union, one of the most powerful pressure groups in the campaign, showed itself particularly aware of the sensitivity of the public to the issue.[20] Writing to Lord Cecil of Chelwood, one of the leaders of this organization, in August 1931, Philip Noel-Baker,[21] stated:

> The existence of the Air Force obviously creates the danger which they are supposed to guard against, if they did not exist the danger would be non-existent. I suggest it should be well to admit that *the air danger is the only one that shakes Great Britain*

---

[17] Kingsley Martin, *Editor: A Second Volume of Autobiography 1931-1945* (London, 1968), p. 193.

[18] Clarke, *Voices Prophesying War,* p. 172, analysed this theme as expressed in the fiction of this time.

[19] 'The Next War' *New Statesman and Nation,* 30 January 1932.

[20] For the activities of this organization during the inter-war period, see Ernest Bramstead, 'Apostles of Collective Security: The League of Nations Union and its function', *Australian Journal of Politics and History* 13 III (1967), pp. 347-64.

[21] A pacifist and a participant in the foundation of the League of Nations. He was one of the Union's most fervent advocates of disarmament. He became Arthur Henderson's private Secretary when the latter was Chairman of the Disarmament Conference.

> *close at home, i.e., we have for it a vivid interest in Air Disarmament.*[22]

Cecil himself gave eloquent expression to similar sentiments in an article which he wrote for the *New Statesman* in May 1932:

> Behind all these schemes and several others are the terrible memories of aerial bombardment, the knowledge that the power of aircraft to destroy dense centres of population has immensely increased and . . . there can be no adequate protection of a great city against aerial attack . . . If the Conference of Geneva were to eliminate certain weapons of Land-Sea warfare and even reduce the armies and navies considerably and yet leave untouched the national air forces, 'security' would not be adequately provided for . . . and people would continue to be obsessed with the nightmare of destruction from the air.[23]

In elaborating the reasons for the public campaign for the abolition of military aircraft in the House of Lords at the end of November 1932, Cecil pointed out another important element of the anxiety about aerial bombardment — the effect the threat of the air weapon was having on international relations.

> A peculiarity of bombardment from the air is that it falls upon the civilian population, but I should never advocate the abolition of bombardment from the air on that ground . . . The only ground on which it seems to me that you may reasonably put it forward as part of a disarmament proposal is . . . that the blow which may be struck by a sudden air bombardment would be so serious as to possibly decide the whole future of the struggle . . . which is the great cause of international unrest in the world of the present time.[24]

Winding up the Commons' debate on disarmament on 10 November 1932, Stanley Baldwin, then Lord President of the Council, provided the air disarmament campaigners with particularly valuable ammunition. 'No power on earth,' he sombrely prophesied, 'can protect the man in the street from being bombed. Whatever people may tell him, the bomber will always get through'. One effect of this declaration was to strengthen the Union's arguments. In Cecil's words, Baldwin had 'said more vehemently everything that we

[22]Cecil Papers, (London) Vol. 51107, 31 August 1931. Italics added. Cecil's correspondence with Noel-Baker throughout the period of the Conference provides many other letters referring to the importance of air disarmament as an element in the Union's campaign. See Vol. 51107 and 51108 of the Cecil Papers.

[23]'The Riddle of the Air', *New Statesman and Nation,* 7 May 1932.

[24]86 Lords Col. 111, 29 November 1932. See the same motif in M. Garnett, 'Freedom of the Air', *Contemporary Review,* May 1933, p. 545.

have been saying from Union platforms for the last months and indeed for years[25]. Another, was to concentrate the public's gaze almost exclusively on the particular problem of the air menace. In general, Baldwin's speech was favourably received in the press. Clive Wigram, Private Secretary to the King, wrote to Simon on 14 November that 'the King was much interested in the leader in *The Times,* 'The Menace from the Air' and feels that abolition of the bomber would be a valuable contribution towards disarmament'.[26] As John Kyba's analysis of British attitudes towards disarmament has already shown, the abolition of bombing and the internationalization of civil aviation now became the *one* disarmament proposal upon which the whole country was united.[27]

Only in style did *The Times* leader of 11 November, 1932, differ from the *New Statesman* pronouncement of 18 November; in principle both agreed that 'the supreme menace and the supreme horrors of war come from the air and unless Mars can be dethroned in the sky, there will be small gain in pinpricking him on the earth and sea'. By the end of 1932, the need to reach an air disarmament agreement was regarded as an urgent and prime national need. When the Earl of Halsbury said in the Lords that the way to tackle the danger of air attack was, paradoxically, to make civil aviation bigger, 'so that people can understand that they can get here, there and everywhere directly before anybody can stop them . . .',[28] he only showed how popular was the concept which had been expressed by Baldwin.

The League of Nations Union and other pacifist organizations were not the only groups to be aware of the public's interest in the problem of air disarmament. Early in 1933, when the Labour Party started to use the alleged failure of British policy at the Conference as a major weapon of attack in Parliament, it was air disarmament which Labour members chose as their central theme. One of their favourite accusations was that the Government's refusal to outlaw the right to use air bombardment for police action in the East was the main reason for the failure to reach an air disarmament agreement at Geneva.

Baldwin's phrase about the bomber always getting through was exploited constantly in the Parliamentary campaign, not least scathingly by Clement Attlee. Speaking in the Commons in June 1933, the

---

[25] Cecil to Noel-Baker, 15 November 1932, Cecil Papers, Vol. 51107. See also Gilbert Murray's letter to Sir John Simon, 14 November 1932, FO 800/287.

[26] FO 800/287.

[27] Kyba, *British Attitudes,* p. 173.

[28] 85 Lords, Cols. 1279-1286, 14 November 1932.

future Labour Prime Minister drew on Baldwin's native background for a parallel: 'It is as if the Lord President knew of the terrible danger threatening the County of Worcester from the ravages of the musk-rats but said, "I must keep musk-rats because then I should get a cheap fur for my wife',"[29]

Moreover, the criticism did not come exclusively from Labour members:[30] Some Conservatives stressed the same points. One was the maverick back-bencher, Vyvyan Adams, who, when moving a motion calling for the eradication of bomber aircraft, conjured up a prophetic picture:

> If in the course of some future catastrophe, a gas-filled bomb, owing its survival to our own predilection for the principle of air bombing, was to crash through the delicately illuminated ceiling of this chamber . . . let them [the elder statesmen] remember that they alone are responsible for the terrors that have fallen upon the earth.[31]

Another Conservative who used the same line of attack was one of those very elder statesmen whose blood Vyvyan Adams was bent on chilling: Austen Chamberlain, foremost architect of the Locarno Treaty.[32] As hope of reaching an agreement at Geneva receded, it was this particular aspect of the air problem — the vulnerability of the British Isles to a knock-out blow — that helped to keep the disarmament issue alive in British politics and the Press in 1933.[33]

It is difficult to measure accurately public opinion during the inter-war period. Even such apparently unmistakable indications as the East Fulham by-election of 1933, when a wave of pacifist emotion swept the Labour candidate to victory, and the house-to-house Peace Ballot conducted by the League of Nations Union in 1934-5, remain open to debate.[34] This is not to suggest that a historical study of the

[29] 270 H.O.C. Col. 34, 13 June 1933.

[30] It should be noted that this line of attack continued well into the late 1930s, thus as late as March 1937, the Labour Party released a pamphlet entitled 'Labour's Immediate Programme' which, while attacking the Government for its failure to work for international disarmament, declared that the Party would do everything within its power to check the arms race by following *inter alia* the policy of substituting 'an international air policy force for national air forces'. *The Times*, 8 March 1937.

[31] 270 H.O.C.,Col. 88.

[32] See Chamberlain's speech on 5 July 1933, 280 H.O.C., Col. 354.

[33] See, *inter alia*, *Manchester Guardian* leaders, 24 June and 4 August 1933; *Daily Herald* leader, 29 May 1933, and *Economist* leader, 3 June 1933. *The Times*, *The Observer* and the *Saturday Review* were among the few that did not take part in this campaign.

[34] M. Ceadel, 'Interpreting East Fulham' in C. Cook and J. Ramsden (eds.), *By-Elections in British Politics* (London, 1973), pp. 118-140. See K. Middlemas and J.

reasons for the movement of public opinion on the issue (retrospectively, a misconceived movement) is of secondary importance, nor must the importance of a historical study of public opinion itself be belittled. Rather, the difference is one of perspective.

For a study of *decision making,* more important is an analysis of the evaluations which decision makers themselves gave to opinions publicly held on various subjects. Such evaluations may not necessarily have reflected what seems in retrospect to have been the true state of affairs; but insofar as they influenced decisions, they must be given due weight. Whether or not disarmament was a decisive influence in the East Fulham by-election, for instance (and recent research suggests that it was not), is not at issue; the result still had considerable influence on the issues of disarmament and rearmament. Baldwin's personal evaluation of what this election indicated, rather than what it did in fact imply, had a critical influence on his conclusion that it was politically inadvisable for Britain to start rearming.

There can be little doubt that public opinion had an important influence on the making of British policy at the Disarmament Conference. In formulating that policy, decision makers aimed, *inter alia,* at satisfying, or at least not contradicting, what seemed to them to be a very firm public advocacy of disarmament.

MacDonald, the lifelong Socialist who attempted to remain an unrepentant idealist in foreign affairs, was particularly susceptible to this pressure. This was especially so since he was, in any case, ostracised by his former friends in the Labour Party and isolated from his new Liberal and Conservative colleagues in the Government.[35] In domestic issues, his personal views were increasingly overridden by an unsympathetic Cabinet; in foreign affairs, however, his failing health notwithstanding, he attempted to assert a commanding influence. The 'weary Titan', as he was once described by Geoffrey Dawson of *The Times,* [36] who wrote in his notebook that the national Government 'is nae my ain hoose',[37] appears to have attached

Barnes, *Baldwin: A Biography* (London, 1969), p 744, and Kyba, *British Attitudes,* Ch. 9 for one interpretation of the East Fulham by-election and Richard Heller 'East Fulham Revisited', *Journal of Contemporary History* 6 III (1971), 172-96 for another. See also C. Stannage, 'The East Fulham By-Election of 25th October 1933', *Historical Journal* 14 (1971), 165-200. For a recent study of public opinion during this period see P. Waley, *British Public Opinion and the Abyssinian War 1935-1936* (London, 1975).

[35] See D. Marquand, *Ramsay MacDonald* (London, 1977), pp. 671-730.

[36] M. Cowling, *The Impact of Hitler, British Politics and Policy 1933-1940* (London, 1975), p. 128.

[37] July 1934, quoted in Marquand, *Ramsay MacDonald,* p. 678.

overriding importance to carrying an individual programme in international questions, and especially to attaining a great triumph in that of disarmament. The Cabinet minutes leave no doubt of his persistent pressure for a successful issue to disarmament negotiations and of his deep personal sensitivity to public opinion on the issue. Thus, despite his failing eyesight, he used to read many of the letters which the public addressed to him on the subject,[38] and was profoundly concerned at the attack on him by Labour supporters over matters of policy at the Disarmament Conference.[39]

MacDonald's idealism expressed itself in his continuous interference in international affairs. This was hardly true of Baldwin; he was said to have closed his eyes when foreign matters were discussed in the Cabinet during the 1920s; and to have asked to be woken up 'when you are finished with all that'.[40] What did particularly engage his interest was the domestic political position of the Government, and of the Conservative Party in particular. In this context, it is significant that Baldwin considered the public advocacy of disarmament during the early 1930s to have been an important, perhaps decisive, factor in the making of British policy. The private correspondence he received from various pacifist groups during that period indicates that his responsiveness to public opinion was widely felt; his own, sometimes crucial, intervention in the formulation of the Cabinet's policy towards the Disarmament Conference, itself shows that this feeling was not misplaced. Indeed, the entire controversy surrounding Baldwin's famous speech in the House of Commons on 12 November 1936, in which he admitted that he had not campaigned for rearmament in 1933 for fear of not being able to win a General Election on the issue, in fact underscores one factor — his deep personal conviction of the strength of British public feeling on disarmament in 1932-4. As he said: 'At that time [when] the Disarmament Conference was sitting in Geneva . . . there was probably a stronger pacifist feeling running through the country than at any time since the war'.[41]

Sir John Simon, the anti-militarist and almost pacifist Liberal who had resigned office rather than agree to conscription during the First

[38] See minutes of meeting he had with a deputation of various public bodies headed by the Archbishop of Canterbury on 11 November 1933, FO 371/19379, W 12899/46/98.

[39] He wrote to Simon on 11 August 1932, that 'you cannot underestimate the evil work of that combination [Noel-Baker and Henderson]', quoted from Simon Papers in Segal, *Sir John Simon,* p. 265.

[40] G. Young, *Stanley Baldwin* (London, 1952), p. 63.

[41] Middlemas and Barnes, *Baldwin,* p. 970. See, on this controversy, Barbara C. Malament 'Baldwin Re-restored?' *Journal of Modern History* 44.1. (1972), 87-96.

World War, is a third case in point. His personal views on foreign policy were essentially moral, rather than strategic. In 1932, he admitted that 'I as a Foreign Secretary do not really see Great Britain involved in any war for many years to come, probably the next fifty years', and believed that 'this is the sort of attitude a Foreign Secretary has to adopt'.[42] His preoccupation with disarmament at the time was basically a function of his reading of public opinion on the matter. Late in 1932, Lord Irwin (later Lord Halifax) assured Simon that he was 'right in feeling the weight of public opinion in this sense . . . I have no doubt that you are on the spot when you judge this disarmament business to be vital to the Government certainly in the long sense'.[43] A year later, Simon himself disclosed his personal apprension as to the consequences to the National Government of a failure of the Conference. In a private letter to Vansittart, he wrote:

> The loss of credit which the British Government will suffer in the eyes of the public if there is no international agreement which can be called a Disarmament Agreement will be something tremendous. Henderson may be stupid but he is quite clever enough to make a great deal out of that and it is not the Socialists merely who will denounce us, it is a vast body of opinion in all parties. I feel in my bones that we are digging the grave of the elder statesmanship if we cannot do better than that.[44]

The clear consensus among key decision-makers regarding the intensity and importance of the pro-Disarmament campaign at the time of the Conference, was thus hardly questionable. As Samuel Hoare, himself a shrewd observer of politics, remarked in his memoirs: 'the combination of all these forces, moral, political and religious, created so strong a volume of opinion in favour of disarmament that no government, right, left or centre, could resist it'.[45]

Within the context of this study, particularly significant is the fact that British decision-makers appear to have been in no doubt that public feeling on the question of *air* disarmament was especially strong. One of the first to appreciate the political importance of this mood was Hankey, Secretary to the Cabinet, whose lengthy administrative experience had enabled him to make particularly acute

[42] In a conversation with Group-Captain Babington on 23 July 1932, Air Ministry Records, Public Record Office, London (hereafter Air), Air 8/140.

[43] 16 October 1932, quoted in Segal, *Sir John Simon,* p. 327.

[44] 23 December 1933, Cab. 21/387.

[45] Viscount Templewood, (formerly Sir Samuel Hoare), *Nine Troubled Years* (London, 1954), p. 114.

judgments of the opinions which influenced decisions. Writing to Simon in May 1932, he noted: 'Compared with bombing aeroplanes the public interest in such matters as heavy guns or whether a battleship should be 35,000 or 25,000 tons is almost negligible'.[46]

The need not to disregard the popular demand to abolish the bomber constituted an important element in discussions on air disarmament. MacDonald expressed his concern 'lest public opinion might become restive if we adopted a purely negative attitude to the one form of disarmament which might affect the man in the street in this country'.[47] Simon and Baldwin shared these views and, on various occasions, referred to the importance of satisfying, and not countering, this specific public demand.[48]

The opinions held by some of the decision-makers on the essence and significance of the danger of air bombardment are highly relevant to an understanding of the extent of the Government's concern about a knock-out blow from the air. This was perhaps the most important element behind the efforts to reach an air disarmament agreement at this time.

Much has been written about Baldwin's obsession with the danger of air attack.[49] The public had no knowledge of his opinions on the subject until his speech in the House of Commons on 10 November 1932; but the Cabinet and the Cabinet Disarmament Committee had been fully aware of his fears for many months. Baldwin believed that a future war involving Britain would open with a devastating air bombardment on densely populated areas. His obsession with Britain's vulnerability to air attack and his deep revulsion against war turned him into the most fervent advocate of air disarmament within the Government. He was one of its first members to warn of the specific danger of the German air force. As early as March 1933, long before the formal announcement of the creation of the Luftwaffe, he warned the Cabinet Disarmament Committee that an air force would be the first corps the Germans would start to develop. 'There were two things', he said, 'that frightened him more than anything else. The first was the liability of this country to air raids and the second was the rearming of Germany. The latter contingency if it arose was a terrible

[46] 6 May 1932, FO 800/286.

[47] At a meeting of the Cabinet Disarmament Committee, 5 April 1932, Cab. 27/505.

[48] See above minutes and discussions of the British delegation in Geneva on 27 April 1932, Air 8/151. Also Simon's private letter to MacDonald on 18 July 1932, FO 371/16431 W/8178/10/98.

[49] Middlemas and Barnes, *Baldwin,* p. 732.

thing. The air was the first arm which the Germans will start to build up . . . We must have a convention prohibiting bombing'.[50] That was why he persistently pressed his colleagues to continue to strive for such a convention, even after their informal recognition that such an agreement could not be achieved at Geneva.[51]

Baldwin's was not a solitary voice; on the contrary, his views were shared by many of his colleagues. The Cabinet records reveal that although other ministers might have expressed their fears over aerial attack more reservedly, they felt them no less deeply. Thus when, in October 1932, Baldwin predicted in the Commons that 'the bomber will always get through', he did not merely summarize a theory which the Air Staff had held for more than a decade; he gave public expression to what had hitherto been an unmentioned, but widely shared apprehension within the Government as a whole. MacDonald, for instance, had long given an air disarmament convention priority over any other agreement at Geneva. As he explained in June 1932, 'it might prevent a full-blown offensive being developed at zero hour, which was in fact the real danger to which London might be exposed'.[52]

Simon, who won his reputation more as an analyst than an effective decision-maker, had been alive to this threat to British security at an equally early date. In a private letter to the British Ambassador in Paris, also in June 1932, he wrote: 'It would be the ending of a *nightmare* if the great powers had the sense to agree to abolish military and naval aviation'.[53] Moreover, Simon defined in characteristically clear terms one of the basic elements of the fear of a 'bolt from the blue' by air attack, the fact that it constituted what might be called a 'progressive unknown'. In his own words:

> The fact remained that until something was done to stop the menace, the prospect of a future war . . . was appalling, particularly to civilians in crowded places. *If civil and military aviation were in a position to do what they could do after fifteen years of evolution, what were the prospects by 50 years hence?* This in fact was the big issue which was making them all so much concerned to get some remedy.[54]

Sir Herbert Samuel, leader of the Liberal Party, who had been greatly influenced by his experience as chairman of the Air Raids Pre-

[50] 7 March 1933, Cab. 27/505.
[51] See below, pp. 45, 77, 79n.
[52] In the Cabinet Disarmament Committee, 5 April 1932, Cab. 25/505.
[53] On 9 June 1932, FO 800/287. Italics added.
[54] In the Cabinet, 1 June 1932, Cab. 23/71. Italics added.

cautions sub-committee of the Committee of Imperial Defence (C.I.D.), shared this anxiety about an aerial knock-out blow.[55] So, too, did Samuel Hoare who had been under the strong personal influence of Lord Trenchard, the first Chief of Staff of the R.A.F., and perhaps the Government official most dedicated to the R.A.F.'s strategic bombing concept.[56]

In analysing the decision-making process whereby British air disarmament policy was fashioned, the consistency of the opinions held by some departments of state as to what this policy should have been remains to be discussed. All based their conclusions on a common concern about the country's vulnerability to a possible air attack. Yet, they differed as to the means whereby Britain could be protected. The strategic thinking of the Air Staff was prominently oriented towards deterrence, and emphasized what today could be classified as a 'balance of terror' concept.[57] Christopher Bullock, the Permanent Under-Secretary of State for Air, succinctly summarized this line of thought in a private letter of November 1931:

> If we really want to work towards the abolition of war we should make it as brutal as possible. I am not sure that a dispassionate and logical review of the problem does not lead one to suggest that if you give the civilian population immunity you are likely not only to precipitate wars but to prolong the one started.[58]

Other departments of state, however, had decidedly different views.

Throughout the period of the Disarmament Conference, the Foreign Office was pressed to formulate concrete policy suggestions of its own; it consistently advocated acceptance of substantial air disarmament, which it regarded as the greatest contribution Britain could make to ensuring the desired outcome — an international disarmament convention. The office was anxious to extricate itself from the difficult position in which it had been placed by the Cabinet's reluctance to undertake any further commitment to French security.[59] It

---

[55] See Samuel's speech in the Cabinet Disarmament Committee on 6 June 1932, Cab. 21/354.

[56] For Hoare's interest in this subject, see Templewood, *Nine Troubled Years,* p. 117. J.A. Cross, *Sir Samuel Hoare: A Political Biography* (London, 1977), pp. 83-125, and B. Powers, *Strategy Without Slide Rule, British Air Strategy 1914-1939,* (London, 1976), p. 134.

[57] For an analysis of the formative years of the Air Staff's concepts of aerial warfare, see B. Powers, *Strategy Without Slide Rule,* pp. 107-58, and H. Montgomery Hyde, *British Air Policy Between the Wars 1918-1939,* (London 1976), pp. 1-189.

[58] However, Bullock concluded that 'this ... is not a doctrine which I think it would be wise to formulate publicly at the present time'. Weir Papers, (Cambridge) 13/3.

[59] Vansittart failed, in January 1932, the persuade to Cabinet to accept his comprehensive

was also very conscious of the popularity in Europe of the proposal to abolish air bombing.[60] Furthermore, and even before the Conference was properly under way, the Permanent Under-Secretary —for one — had become fearful of German air rearmament. Thus, Vansittart drew the attention of the Government to this danger as early as February 1932, when he commented:

> they [the Germans] are likely to rely for their military power still more on the mechanical weapons of the future such as tanks, big guns and *above all* military aircraft. The appointment of the egregious Goering is an earnest of this. Aviation in particular offers Germany the quickest and easiest way of making her own power effective. With her industrial system and her already flourishing civil aviation she will have no difficulty and no insurmountable expense in proceeding to the creation of one of the leading air forces of Europe.[61]

During the course of the year, Vansittart's fears grew apace, and a letter he wrote to Hankey in January 1933 sounded an even more urgent note:

> I feel myself that the *real crux is air disarmament* and I know you share this view. If no serious progress can be made with this, I think it does not matter much what happens to the rest of the disarmament programme since this is the arm in which we are likely to be faced in the future with the most bitter armament race . . . *The speed and ease with which new types are being developed makes it a far more formidable danger than anything in the way of naval or military armaments.*[62]

Simon accepted this assessment, and in a paper submitted to the Cabinet just over a month later, he warned that 'Germany will rely for her military power above all on military aircraft'.[63]

As long as there remained any hope of achieving a substantial air disarmament agreement, the Foreign Office continued to advocate its original policy. When that hope faded, in March 1933, it was air rearmament in which this department seemed to become most

---

plan for British policy at the Conference. This included a 'Mediterranean Locarno' agreement as a British counter to French disarmament. See Cabinet meeting on 15 December 1931, Cab. 23/69, and Vansittart memorandum dated 1 January 1932, Cab, 27/476. For a thorough biography see N. Rose, *Vansittart* (London, 1978).

[60] See analysis of this point written in Foreign Office minutes of 27 April 1932, FO 371/16429, W 4550/10/98.

[61] FO 371/17380, W 2322/117/08. Italics added.

[62] 18 January 1933, Cab. 63/46 M(33)6. Italics added.

[63] 27 February 1933, Cabinet Paper (hereafter C.P.), C.P. 52 (33).

interested. Submitting a report to the Chiefs of Staff Sub-Committee, the Foreign Office warned that 'Germany will proceed to the building of a formidable armament on land and *especially* in the air'; it urged that the Air Force begin 'in all seriousness' to rearm, in order to be able to defend Great Britain against a renascent German air force.[64]

Throughout this period, the Admiralty and the War Office also informed the Cabinet and the Disarmament Committee of the advisability of abolishing the bomber. Neither department could accept the Air Staff's theory that counter-attack offered the best means of defence against bombardment from the air.[65] Instead, they advanced three main arguments against this strategic doctrine. First, they claimed, the construction of a British bomber force would direct attention away from the supposed common aim of all the services, namely, the defeat of the enemy's armed forces. Second, the Air Staff was advocating in peacetime a form of action which no British Government would allow to be put into effect in case of a declaration of war. Finally, and above all, the Air Staff was gambling on the effect of air attack on an imponderable factor — the moral fibre of a potential enemy's civilian population.[66].

The Admiralty, in particular, gave unrestrained vent to its feelings. One internal memorandum contained the following coriating passage: 'Air bombing is very aggressive and in no way defensive... The Army and Navy do not want [bombers]. Only the Air Ministry wants to retain these weapons for use against towns, a method of warfare which is revolting and un-English.'[67]

The material consequences of a disarmament convention prohibiting bombing were too obvious to be overlooked by the Air Ministry. This was put bluntly to Simon by the Ministry's representative in Geneva, Group-Captain Babington: 'We had assumed that if the menace of attack were removed by a paper "prohibiting" it would be impossible to justify maintenance of defence forces against a threat which (on paper) did not exist.'[68]

[64]C.I.D.paper 1112-B, 19 May 1933. The chiefs of Staff, however, did not share this assessment, as will be discussed later.

[65]See C.P. 164(32) for the Admiralty's attitude, and C.P. 176(32) for that of the War Office.

[66]For an admirable analysis of these arguments, see Air 2/675 No. 832335. British air power theory was unique in denying the classical principle of the necessity of defeating the 'enemy air force in being', see M.S. Smith 'The R.A.F.and Counter-Force Stategy Before the Second World War', *Journal of the Royal United Services Institute* (June 1976), pp. 68-73.

[67]Admiralty Records London, Public Record Office (hereafter Adm.) Adm.116/2827/PDO 800/04058/32, 13 April, 1932.

[68]23 July 1932, Air 8/140.

For obvious reasons, the Air Ministry vehemently opposed the general trend in the Cabinet and the Disarmament Committee, and constituted one of the great obstacles to any British initiative on air disarmament at Geneva. Some of its criticisms of the practicability of various air disarmament plans raised difficult problems for the Cabinet. Ministers could not deny, for instance, that to outlaw bombing would be tantamount to robbing Britain of the cheapest means of military control in the East, 'police bombing'.[69] However, the Air Ministry's main, and irrefutable, argument concerned civil aviation. It would be impossible to prevent the misuse of civil aircraft by an international air disarmament agreement abolishing the bomber or the act of bombing. The Ministry kept hammering away at the ease with which civil aircraft could be transformed into military planes.

British reluctance to accept any international control of civil aviation (not to speak of a League of Nations air force) was another reason for what proved to be a permanent deadlock. The various air disarmament proposals all failed to meet these arguments and this strengthened the point made constantly by the Air Ministry: the only international agreement which could grant true security against air attack was one which outlawed flying altogether.[70]

Prior to 2 February 1932, the day on which the Disarmament Conference opened, the Government's deliberations on the air question were characterized by an inability to define a policy line. In fact, not until the middle of the year was there more than superficial discussion of anything that could be called a plan for air disarmament. Primarily, this was because the Government originally intended the Conference to base its work on the Draft Disarmament Convention which had been agreed to in 1930. This was a very general framework for the future discussion of principles and actual guarantees of various categories of armaments. Although the Draft Convention could not possibly be regarded as a solution of the basic problems of the Conference, it did offer an easy answer to Britain's search for a policy on the matter of air disarmament. It proposed limitations according to numbers and horse power of aircraft, and thus provided some sort of basis, albeit a rather narrow and technical one, for the deliberations at Geneva.[71]

[69] See E.B. Scovill, *'The R.A.F., the Middle East and Disarmament'* (unpublished Ph.D. thesis, Michigan State University, 1972).

[70] For general analysis of the problem of civil aviation in the context of air disarmament, see D. Carlton, 'The Problem of Civil Aviation in British Disarmament Policy 1919-1934', *Journal of the Royal United Services Institute,* 664 (November 1966), pp. 307-316.

[71] See Chaput *Disarmament in British Foreign Policy,* pp. 339-343.

A three-party committee appointed in March 1931 had by July reached only very general and vague conclusions about a policy at the forthcoming conference.[72] Referring to these conclusions, Simon wrote to MacDonald: 'I confess I do not see light at present on disarmament policy at all. If the government considerations are technical, neither our fighting forces nor any other will declare themselves able to reduce. The political aspects are more difficult but less hopeless.'[73] However, one of these conclusions referred specifically to the subject of any disarmament agreement as the removal of the danger of a knock-out blow in the early stages of a future war.[74] What its formulators had in mind was aerial bombing.

In his memoirs, Hoare, who with Cecil and Lloyd George advocated accepting this principle, explained its underlying motive: 'The need as I saw it to prevent the defeat of a peaceful country by a sudden and overwhelming attack from the air.'[75] This conclusion, like the others of the time, was only a general suggestion, without any concrete proposals for its implementation.

The political and economic crisis of August 1931 delayed the formulation of a specific policy for several months. The plan eventually recommended by a special Cabinet committee on 11 January 1932 was based on the draft convention.[76] This was the first report to refer to the proposal to abolish military aircraft, and the matter was dealt with succinctly: 'Although the idea... is attractive, it will not be properly effective unless some satisfactory method can be found by which civil aircraft can be prevented from being used for offensive purposes.'[77] Sir John Simon explained the Government's attitude:

> We could not possibly say that we were in favour of preserving military aircraft, but at the same time we felt that as we lived in a practical world it was no good supporting a proposal to abolish military aircraft unless reasonable and practicable steps were forthcoming for dealing with civil aviation.[78]

[72] See Cab. 16/102.

[73] 19 December 1931, FO 800/285.

[74] Cab. 16/102 D.C. (P)50, Article 3.

[75] Templewood, *Nine Troubled Years,* p. 117 and discussion in the three-party committee, 22 July 1931, Cab. 16/102.

[76] This followed the defeat of the Foreign Office's 'political' plan in Cabinet. See above, p. 22n.

[77] Cab. 27/476.

[78] 1 January 1932, *ibid.*

The problem of civil aviation, one of the obvious and insurmountable obstacles to any air disarmament plan, was accepted as an unquestionable justification for halting exploration of the subject.

The supposition that the draft convention would provide the basis for discussions at Geneva was proved incorrect when the French made independent proposals, known as the Tardieu Plan, in February 1932. This recommended, *inter alia,* the prohibition of the bombing from the air and the creation of a League of Nations air force.[79] The British Government could no longer afford to delay the formulation of a plan of its own which would be recognized as a specific British contribution to the Conference. Pressed to provide a formula on which to base a plan, the Foreign Office suggested the principle of 'qualitative disarmament', of which certain concrete proposals for a measure of air disarmament were essential ingredients.

No sacrifice could of course be made of Britain's essential interests. In particular, the Foreign Office had to circumvent two pitfalls: the civil aviation problem and the British interest in keeping its airforce for police purposes in the East.

The Foreign Office proposal, put forward by A.W. Leeper of the League of Nations Department, therefore envisaged a plan calling for the prohibition of bombing from the air on the territory and shipping of another sovereign state, thereby excluding British territories in the East.[80] Nevertheless, a positive gesture did appear vital, for throughout the period, the Foreign Office was very much aware of the necessity to adopt an outstanding position on 'some big point' — especially air disarmament.[81]

'Our position in international politics' advised one official,

> will really become impossible if after demanding that bombing from the air be examined from all its aspects we have absolutely no concrete proposals to put up when the matter is considered in the committee. There is very little chance of our idea being accepted, [however] if it is not accepted we can say we have done our best and the foreigners have turned down our excellent proposal. What about public opinion here? The experience of the Department is that over the last 18 months or so every society like the League of Nations Union and the Womens

---

[79] See J. Wheeler Bennett, *Disarmament Deadlock,* (London, 1934), pp. 14-15.

[80] FO 371/16429 W 3359/10/98, 18 March 1932.

[81] See the discussion on this issue, in the Cabinet Disarmament Committee on 7 January 1932, Cab. 27/476.

Peace League has been demanding nothing else. These societies constitute a considerable body of public opinion.[82]

It was this essentially political need which induced the Cabinet, on 5 April 1932, to accept the Foreign Office formula, which was considered to be an important ingredient of the prospective general British plan.[83]

The Air Ministry, whilst aware of public pressure for disarmament, could not agree to the suggested plan. Indeed so vehement was its opposition that within a week the subject had to be reopened.[84] The discussions which followed were confined mainly to the advantages and disadvantages of substantial air disarmament plans from the point of view of Britain's vulnerability to air attack. Simon, the Foreign Secretary, emphasized his conviction that international acceptance of the formula would contribute towards Britain's security. He wrote:

> The danger of London being heavily and suddenly bombed by way of a knock-out blow must be our main preoccupation.... It [the Foreign Office plan] would minimize the danger of London being suddenly subjected to a heavy scale of air attack. i.e., the knock-out blow.[85]

The Admiralty and the War Office recommended the abolition of the bomber as the basis of the British air disarmament plan, agreeing with the Foreign Office that it would definitely be advantageous as far as the defence of the country was concerned.[86] The well-known Air Ministry arguments led to opposite conclusions.

The controversy prevented any clear decision in the Cabinet Disarmament Committee, and the problem was referred to the British delegation in Geneva. The delegation accepted Simon's argument as the criterion on which any air disarmament plan should stand or fall:

> There was one concrete problem, namely the safety of London. If London were to be exposed to increased danger by accepting prohibition, we obviously should not advocate it. On the other hand, if it were to make for the greater safety of London, we should endeavour to secure its acceptance.[87]

The matter came to a head at the Cabinet meeting of 4 May. The Prime Minister and the Foreign Secretary pleaded the urgency of a

[82]Howard Smith, Minutes, dated 27 April, FO 371/16428.
[83]Cab. 27/505.
[84]Cab. 23/71.
[85]Cable A.M. 719, 14 April 1932, Air 8/151.
[86]Adm. 116/2826/PD/04039/32, 29 March 1932.
[87]27 April 1932, Air 8/151.

decision on the matter in view of the need to implement the principle of qualitative disarmament by concrete air proposals. In the discussion which followed Baldwin put forward his own proposal: the best way to tackle the problem was to scrap all military aircraft and to abolish the subsidies to civil aviation. He had, he explained, been impressed by the forecasts of the appalling consequences of a future war conducted from the air; he hoped that his proposal would remove 'one of the main elements of fear that was such a disturbing feature in the international situation'.[88] Despite its drastic and seemingly absurd nature, Baldwin had clearly given much thought to his suggestion. Moreover, he seriously intended to implement it. Within four days he had included it in a seven-point plan which he presented, in the presence of Simon and with the latter's approval, to Hugh Gibson the principal United States delegate to the Disarmament Conference.[89] His motive and rationale for doing this were explained in a private letter to MacDonald a few weeks later: 'I am not at all sure that the shock that such a proposal, coming from us, would make, would not be a good thing for the statesmen of Europe.'[90] Baldwin's proposal and the Foreign Office formula had been referred to the Coast Defence sub-committee of the C.I.D., which had been called upon to consider them particularly from the point of view of the defence of London.

It is not difficult to understand the perceptible anxiety that permeated the Air Ministry during the early days of May 1932. Acceptance of even the relatively moderate Foreign Office formula would imply denial of the R.A.F.'s main strategic theory. The Ministry used a variety of tactics to delay, and if possible prevent, a final decision.[91] When these failed, it tried to prove that substantial disarmament plans would not secure London from air attack, and were therefore futile in themselves. It based its arguments on the traditional Air Force position, leading to two major conclusions. The first was that a devastating air attack was inevitable in any future war (thus justifying the existence of the R.A.F. itself); the second was that the only defence against air attack was counter-attack. The various arguments were minuted by the Chief of Air Staff as follows:

    (a)    The danger to London of being heavily and suddenly

---

[88] Cab. 23/71.

[89] Segal, *Sir John Simon,* p. 131

[90] 19 June 1932, MacDonald Papers.

[91] For the efforts to delay decision, see discussions in the Cabinet on 17 April 1932, Cab. 23/71. For the efforts to persuade the Admiralty to change its attitude see Adm. 116/2827/PD/04087/32. For the attempts to reach an unequivocal rejection of the whole plan by the government of India, see correspondence between the Air Ministry and the R.A.F. in India in Air 8/145.

bombed will always be in existence as long as aircraft existed;

(b) a moral knock-out blow might well be instantaneous if we were surprised with no effective defence;

(c) we could not secure London by means of Fighters alone.[92]

These well-expressed arguments, accompanied by many technical examples, could not but impress the C.I.D. sub-committee, which discussed the Foreign Office formula on 6 May. The fact that neither the Chief of the Imperial General Staff nor the First Sea Lord were members of this committee precluded any serious technical objection to the Air Ministry arguments.[93] In fact, the discussions turned into long monologues by Sir John Salmond, Chief of the Air Staff, and Lord Londonderry, the Air Secretary. Both men stressed the capital's vulnerability to air attack even after the hypothetical adoption of a formula, based on the overwhelming French superiority in army cooperation aircraft as well as in civil aviation.

> Can we let the fate of London (and the Empire) hang on the observance by nations far less scrupulous of an intrinsically *unreasonable* prohibition, when, if they act by way of reprisal against naval or other measures by us argued to be illegal, they can claim that the bombing of London is strictly permissible under the accepted principles of International Law, *whatever engagements they may have entered into at Geneva?*[94]

These views, perhaps not unexpectedly, carried the day. The Committee's conclusions were a victory for the Air Staff theses, implying *inter alia,* a conformation of the 'air menace' theory

> At first sight we expected to find that the security of London would be increased by a proposal to prohibit bombing on the territory and shipping of another sovereign state. This undoubtedly would be the case if we could be certain that the rule would be observed in times of war. . . . London will be by no means immune from air attack and it is estimated that one week's bombing will involve 18,750 casualties.[95]

---

[92] 3 May, air 8/139.

[93] The Treasury, which was not represented on this committee, had favoured the Foreign Office formula for its own reasons of economy and in a departmental minute expressed regret that neither the Admiralty nor the War Office had taken part in these discussions. Treasury Records London (hereafter T) T 161 S36666/06/2, box 661, 10 May, 1932. See also Hopkins' minutes on C.P. 226(32), T 175(28).

[94] Cab. 16/106.

[95] Cab. 16/106. The basis of the calculation was the experience of the 1917 bombardment.

The implications of the sub-committee's endorsement of the R.A.F. view, although not recognized at the time, were far-reaching. For various other disarmament proposals were even more susceptible to the counter-arguments of the Air Ministry than was the Foreign Office plan. Thus, the decision of 6 May 1932, was a major potential obstacle to any other substantial air disarmament initiative in Geneva.

While the Cabinet confirmed the Coast Defence sub-committee's recommendation on 11 May, 'considerable disappointment was expressed at the comparative meagreness of the contribution that it was proposed to offer to aerial bombardment'.[96] Accordingly, it was decided to submit Baldwin's proposals for the abolition of military aircraft and the restriction of civil aviation to a specially appointed Cabinet committee.[97] On 1 June, this body presented the Cabinet with a paper strongly recommending the acceptance of Baldwin's proposals.[98] Its view was supported by the War Office and the Admiralty who claimed that, from the broadest view of national defence, an effective total abolition could not but be advantageous.[99] Sir Herbert Samuel confirmed this assessment. As chairman of the Air Raids Precautions sub-committee of the C.I.D. he informed the Cabinet of his latest report which stressed the appalling consequences of future air raids to the civilian population. He urged the Cabinet not to be deterred by technical difficulties. Lord Hailsham, the Secretary of State for War, told the Cabinet that he personally considered that anything which would tend to reduce or eliminate that menace would be 'a tremendous relative gain for the British Commonwealth . . . and a great access of strength to us',[100] Sir Bolton Eyres Monsell, the First Lord of the Admiralty, also urged tackling 'the fear of being bombed out of the unknown [which] was one of the strongest causes of increase of armaments'.[101]

Faced with this opposition, Londonderry could not but warn the Cabinet that the publication of the proposal at Geneva was likely to have a deplorable effect on the morale of the R.A.F., which 'might

[96] Cab. 23/71.

[97] Cab. 23/71.

[98] Actually, only Baldwin himself and Simon took part in the discussions. The representatives of the three Services did not as had been intended, participate. See C.P. 164/32.

[99] See C.P. 176/32 and C.P. 183/32.

[100] Cab. 23/71.

[101] Cab. 23/71.

militate against the efficiency of the service'.[102] Nevertheless, and despite his obvious irritation with the 'failure of the Army and the Navy to recognize the potentialities of the air arm as a means of warfare',[103] he could not completely dissuade his colleagues.

Summarizing the three main arguments for acceptance of the latest air disarmament proposals, the Cabinet records emphasized three points.

(1) The dangers to great cities all over Europe, including London.

(2) The resulting apprehension and unrest among the people of Europe.

(3) The objective of the Government to make a serious effort to eliminate the danger of air attack. If no such efforts had been made at the Disarmament Conference it was suggested [probably by Samuel] that there would be serious reproaches when an attempt was made to educate public opinion on the need for air raid precautions which would otherwise be necessary in the near future.[104]

These considerations were well known, but so were the seemingly unanswerable arguments advanced by the Air Ministry. Civil aviation as a potential menace which could not be properly and efficiently controlled was presented as the major obstacle to the adoption of Baldwin's drastic proposals. The Cabinet could not therefore reach any definite conclusion, but authorized the Prime Minister and his colleagues to enter into private and informal conversations embracing the proposals with the French Prime Minister at their forthcoming meeting in Paris.[105]

The Foreign Office was sceptical about the prospects of these talks and Vansittart wrote to Simon that they 'stand or fall by the possibility of internationalization of civil aviation, favouring abolishment of military aircraft and reluctance to internationalization of civil aviation would not be accepted'.[106] That forecast materialized and the

[102] Londonderry to Simon, 11 July 1932, FO 800/287.

[103] FO 800/287.

[104] Cabinet Meeting, 7 June 1932, Cab. 23/71. The last point can be better understood in light of the pressure the Air Raids Precautions sub-committee had put on the C.I.D. to give certain publicity to its work. 256 C.I.D. Meeting 9 June 1932, Cab. 2/5 and C.I.D. Papers 188/A, 180/A.

[105] Cab. 23/71. See Simon's cable to Sir William Tyrrell, the British Ambassador in Paris, 9 June 1932, FO 800/287.

[106] FO 371/16462 W/7043/1466/98.

talks which took place in the second week of July proved to be fruitless. The French refused to accept any of Baldwin's propositions,[107] and this brought to an end the first stage of Britain's search for a substantial air disarmament plan. All initiatives seemed to be blocked by inherent difficulties in executing the proposals to abolish the bomber or the act of bombing, and by the opposition of the Air Ministry.

In the middle of June, the British delegation in Geneva discussed with the French the possibilities of achieving an air disarmament agreement based on restricting air bombardment to the battlefields.[108] These discussions ceased once the Americans launched the Hoover Plan on 22 June. One of the principal points of this sensational plan was its intention to abolish all bombers and prohibit any air bombardment.[109] In view of the wide public approbation given to these proposals, the British Government had no choice but to accord them its general support, despite its awareness of their impracticability. Thus, in a speech to the House of Commons, Simon declared:

> My fair conviction is that there is nothing in the whole disarmament discussions which is more vital than that Great Britain should play its own full part in seeing that steps should be taken effectively to stop this abominable practice of indiscriminative bombing which is threatening the whole future of the World.[110]

However, for practical reasons which by now were only too obvious, the Government could not give its unreserved backing to the American plan. On 20 July, in Geneva, Simon managed to evolve a formula which might serve as a basis for the continuation of the discussions, and a resolution to this effect was passed by the Conference on the 23rd. While the air disarmament section called for the prohibition of air bombardment,[111] there were some important qualifications. These aimed at securing British interests where police air actions were concerned, and scotching the French proposal for the internationalization of civil aviation.[112]

[107] FO 371/16462, W 7043/1466/98.

[108] Cabinet Meeting, 24 June 1932, Appendix III, Cab. 23/71.

[109] For details of the Plan, see FO 800/287.

[110] 268 H.O.C. Col. 1247, 12 July 1932.

[111] MacDonald backed Simon's efforts, which were not approved by the Air Ministry. See records of their cables correspondence for 11 July 1932, FO 371/16431, W 8178/10/98.

[112] Simon's letter to Baldwin, 20 July 1932, FO 800/287. For the full text of the 23 July resolution, see FO 371/16431.

Simon was convinced that bombing from the air must be outlawed and that the 'only statesmanlike policy for us is to join in the process'.[113] The need to avoid antagonizing the Americans was a distinct factor in the formula, which in some respects at least echoed the Hoover Plan. Simon put the matter bluntly in a private letter to MacDonald: 'After all if we have to pay £50,000,000 to America there won't be much money left over for the R.A.F. It would be better to meet this world wide demand and thereby preserve relations with Washington.'[114]

MacDonald, together with Baldwin, agreed, but neither they nor Simon himself had any illusions as to the likelihood of this new formula actually being implemented. Moreover, previous discussions within the Government made it impossible for the British themselves to present the Plan to the Conference. The air section of the resolution of 23 July, therefore, was nothing more than the expression of a general desire to find some new means of tackling the air peril by international agreement.[115] The real problem remained as intractable as ever.

The firm demand by the Germans for *gleichberechtigung,* and their threat not to return for any more meetings of the Conference should it not be seriously dealt with, led to the reconsideration of British policy on air disarmament in October 1932. After a succession of meetings during the end of that month and the beginning of November, the Cabinet drafted a plan which recommended a two-stage scheme: first, the leading powers would reduce their air forces to the level of the R.A.F., then, all nations, including Britain, would cut 33 per cent off what remained. This suggestion was found just as unacceptable by the other countries concerned, especially France, as all previous proposals.

But while working on the scheme for quantitative reduction, Britain had for the first time recognized and was shortly to advocate publicly, the ideal of a qualitative solution. The Government moved perceptibly closer towards the complete abolition of all military and naval aircraft, combined with the effective control of civil aviation.[116] Hitherto, this suggestion had been blocked by the decisions of June

---

[113] In this letter to Baldwin, 20 July 1932, FO 800/287.

[114] 18 July 1932, FO 371/16431.

[115] In his notes on 28 July, Simon described the 23 July resolution as a 'breathing space' designed to keep the machinery of the Conference going by providing a very loose and general frame of future work. See FO 800/287.

[116] See Cabinet Meetings, 19, 31 October and 2, 6 November, Cab. 23/72 as well as FO 371/16432, 10837/10/98. For the formal plan see Cmd. 4189.

1932, and the subsequent French refusal to countenance any such radical course. New factors, however, seemed to justify its adoption at this stage.

In formulating its 'qualitative' scheme, as an answer to Germany's demand for equality, the Cabinet Drafting Committee, which included Sir John Simon, Neville Chamberlain and Sir Philip Cunliffe-Lister,[117] gave three reasons why the Conference should accept the principle of total abolition.

1. The prevention of the knock-out blow.
2. Certain peculiarly terrible potentialities which recent experiments had shown the aircraft clearly possessed. *The only way to check such a development was to take the edge out of the national organization whose business it was to explore them intensively.*
3. The desirability of getting public opinion to realize the dangers of all the world from the developing military aviation.[118]

The wish to secure Germany's return to the Conference as well as to prevent her air rearmament were, however, the major reasons for publicly adopting this principle. As the Drafting Committee put it: 'If naval and military aviation were abolished Germany could gain complete equality of status without being allowed to rearm herself.'[119] At the same time, it is clear from the Cabinet minutes cited above and from the last part of Baldwin's speech in the Commons on 10 November, that a growing 'air anxiety' had exerted weighty influence on this decision. It gained a stronger hold following Hitler's advent to power two months later.

The crux of any proposals to abolish military and naval aircraft was the question of civil aviation. Before February 1933, the problem of how to tackle this obstacle was only superficially dealt with by the various committees and the Foreign Office.[120] The decisions reached during the previous summer had merely recognized the supposedly obvious futility of trying to control the development of civil aviation. They had not gone further and examined the technicalities of the problems involved. However, the advocacy of the principle of abolition of air forces and a working proposal which Britain submitted

[117]The Colonial Secretary, later (as Lord Swinton) to be Secretary of State for Air.
[118]Cabinet Meeing, 8 November 1932, Cab. 23/72. Italics added.
[119]Cab. 23/72.
[120]On various initiatives up to that time see FO 371/15705 W 8457/47/98, 9 July 1931; FO 371/16430, W 5916/1466/98, 24 May 1932.

to the Conference on 23 January 1933, confirming this principle, made such an enquiry now essential. On 17 February the Cabinet Disarmament Committee started to discuss these matters. The object, as defined — ironically — by a future Secretary of State for Air, Cunliffe-Lister, was 'to make the world safer from the terror of bombing. . . . The problem was now to prevent 100 tons of bombs per day being dropped on London'.[121] In view of his experience in dealing with international cartels and organizations, Cunliffe-Lister had been asked by the Cabinet Committee on 17 February to circulate a scheme for the control or internationalization of civil aviation. Such a scheme was to fulfil two basic conditions: it was to prevent the resources of civil aviation from being used for military purposes in the event of an outbreak of war; but it was not to hamper the fullest development of aviation in every country for civil and commercial purposes.

The scheme which Cunliffe-Lister presented on 22 February 1933, was the most serious effort which the British Government ever made to try to solve this persistent problem. As such it merits detailed examination. It should be borne in mind that the Government had traditionally opposed either the internationalization of civil aviation or an international air force.[122] What Cunliffe-Lister was trying to project was a form of international *control* of civil aviation.[123] His scheme was designed to form the basis for a convention providing for the complete prohibition of the use of all aircraft for military and naval purposes (subject to exemption for a limited number of machines in outlying places) and the progressive abolition of military aircraft by agreed stages. Military characteristics were to be forbidden in civil aircraft, and there were to be safeguards, in time of peace and war alike, against their adaptation for military and naval use. The scheme postulated the formation of an international company under the Charter of the League of Nations to take over and operate existing international civil aviation services and to supervise the operation of national civil air services working solely within the territory of one country. National companies were to be formed in each state in association with the international company.[124]

[121]Cabinet Disarmament Committee, 22 February 1933. Cab. 27/505. See also Londonderry's letter to MacDonald on 24 February 1933 in which he stressed Cunliffe-Lister's special interest in solving the problem by abolishing the bomber. MacDonald Papers 2/7.

[122]See reference of the Cabinet Disarmament Committee to this point in January 1932. Articles 69-74, Cab. 27/476.

[123]D.C. (M)(32)37, Cab. 21/379.

[124]D.C. (M)(32)37, Cab. 21/379.

This impressive and well-planned scheme did not satisfy the Cabinet Committee, whose members felt that it was unlikely to provide a really effective barrier to the employment of civil aviation for military purposes and that it was liable to hamper the expansion of imperial communications and the development of the aircraft industry. There were three main reasons for their objections to the scheme. First, they found it lacking in certain guarantees for preventing civil aircraft being used for warlike purposes. Second, because the physical conditions of the British Isles did not favour internal air travel, Britain was inevitably comparatively inferior to other countries in civil aircraft. Finally, the unwillingness of the United States to accept any restraint on its civil aviation put the British aircraft industry at a competitive disadvantage.[125]

The Cabinet Committee's rejection of the most drastic formula ever devised in Britain for countering air attack put an end to any hope that she might agree to the total abolition of military and naval aircraft. Further discussions designed to find some way of at least minimizing the danger produced the idea of an improvised force of civilian bombers manned by personnel untrained for war. At the same time the Cabinet Committee accepted the Air Ministry's argument that the only guarangee of reasonable immunity to bombing by civilian aircraft was the maintenance of a small force of military aircraft as an antidote.[126] But the obvious complications inherent in advocating such an idea, with its latent implication of a retreat from international control of civil aviation and complete abolition of military aircraft, prevented its final adoption.[127] The resultant setback at Geneva to British policy in general, and to the important air initiative in particular, led Eden to the conclusion that only a complete change of tactics could save the Conference. The result of his initiative was a new plan — the so-called MacDonald Plan — which was discussed in the Cabinet at the beginning of March.[128]

On 5 March the Cabinet Disarmament Committee decided to cease its search for a formula which would lead to the total abolition of military aircraft. The Government thus overtly admitted that it no longer saw any possibility of the Disarmament Conference being able to reach an agreement to abolish the dreaded bomber.

[125] *Ibid.*
[126] Cab. 21/379.
[127] Cabinet Disarmament Committee, 27 February 1933, Cab. 25/505.
[128] Eden's cable to the Foreign Office of 27 February, FO 371/11380, W 2100/117/98, L.N. 141, and Eden, *Facing the Dictators,* pp. 30, 33.

The records of the discussions at this stage, however, reveal a new element which seemed to make a substantial air disarmament agreement more necessary than ever. This was the growing concern with the failure of the Conference to halt German rearmament. For the first time the Cabinet's apprehensions concerning the particular danger which German air rearmament presented to Britain had been discernible.[129]

Having abandoned once and for all the hope of abolishing the bomber, the Government lowered its sights to a more limited objective: a convention prohibiting bombing from the air. But its realization that even this was unlikely to be attained at Geneva is reflected in the wording of a decision reached by the Cabinet on 8 March 1933:

> Among the measures for averting the breakdown of the Conference, international restriction of military and naval aviation takes a high place . . . owing to the exposed position of London. As a *matter of principle* it would be in the best interest of this country to attempt to secure the abolition of bombing from the air.[130]

The obstacles to such a convention were many, and the lack of any British initiative at Geneva on the problem of civil aviation made the possibility of any sort of air disarmament agreement all the more remote. Sir Alexander Cadogan summed up the atmosphere in Geneva to Eden: 'By talking of the possibility of the total abolition of military aircraft we had raised great hopes and our subsequent attitude at the Committee had dashed the hopes to the ground.'[131]

Nevertheless on 16 March the Government did put before the Conference another plan, whose air disarmament section contained the formula: 'The higher contracting parties accept the complete abolition of bombing from the air [except for police purposes in certain outlying regions].' It also proposed the complete abolition of military and naval air forces, 'which must be dependent on effective supervision of civil aviation'.[132]

In view of what had already transpired, the British delegation

---

[129] See C.P. 52(53) and the Cabinet Disarmament Committee discussion on 7 March 1933, Cab. 27/505.

[130] Cab. 23/75. Italics added.

[131] FO 371/17380, W 2401/117/98, 7 March, 1933.

[132] For the ful text see Cmd. Miscellaneous No. 2, 1933.

could have had no higher expectations of this proposal than of its alternative suggestion:

> should it prove impossible to ensure such effective supervision [the Permanent Disarmament Commission will determine] the minimum number of machines required by each High Contracting Party consistent with its national security and obligations...[133]

In his speech to the Conference, MacDonald did not attempt to hide his Government's increasing pessimism on the matter: 'It was a difficult problem, plan after plan... international control and so on... had been produced by the most expert minds. He would confess that the British Government had not been able to see a way out of this serious problem.'[134]

Further discussions in Geneva showed that MacDonald's pessimism was not misplaced; no agreement could be reached on the basis of the British formula, while the reservation as to police bombing was almost unanimously condemned.[135] Internal political considerations prevented Britain from openly admitting that she despaired of any air disarmament agreement being reached at Geneva; but the Cabinet Disarmament Committee's records show plainly that all hope had disappeared by the beginning of March 1933. Even though the Conference was provided, as it had been in the previous June, with a plan to argue over, nobody within the government seems to have had any illusions about the outcome.[136] In any case, once Germany withdrew from the Conference in October 1933, its meetings were deprived of any sense of reality. The formal continuation of proceedings until 1934 had no substantial influence on policy making.

A widely shared and very real apprehension about the air peril in the next war, whenever that might come, had influenced the British Government's struggle for air disarmament at Geneva in 1932-3. Its various proposals had predicated an international agreement either abolishing the bomber altogether or prohibiting the act of bombing. But even while formulating them, the Government had been conscious that they were useless as a means of tackling the problem of Britain's vulnerability to air attack. Nevertheless so strong was the fear of the knock-out blow that it continued to provide the principal momentum for efforts to reach some sort of international air disarmament agreement which were to continue right up to 1939.

[133]*Ibid.*, Art. 35b.
[134]16 March 1932, FO 371/17353, W 2883/40/98.
[135]Eden to the Foreign Office, 27 May 1933, FO 371/17381, W 6020/117/98.
[136]See FO 371/17382, W 6642/117/98, 6 June 1933.

Perhaps the most remarkable aspect of this dominating fear is that it should have manifested itself as early as 1932-3. The growing concern about air attack at this time was in no sense a reflection of any material development in the international situation, or any real change in the military map of Europe. Until the end of 1933, only the French air force could possibly endanger Britain — for the Luftwaffe had yet to come into being — and war with France had long been considered a very remote contingency. The discussions concerning the air peril throughout this period are notable for the absence of any mention of a potential enemy. But they prepared the way for, indeed perhaps biased, the discussions in the Cabinet and the Cabinet Disarmament Committee in 1934-5. As the following chapter will show, these discussions resulted in the decision to base early rearmament largely on air rearmament.

# 2
# AIR POWER AND EARLY REARMAMENT: 1934-1935

'One of the thoughts which continuously dominates the thoughts of ministers is the danger of the German air menace to England. What I am uncertain about is what is the air menace to this country from Germany and is it vital or not.'
(Admiral Chatfield, April 1934. (Cab. 21/388))

As from the end of 1933 two issues dominated official discussions of Britain's foreign policy: the breakdown of the Disarmament Conference and Germany's secret rearmament. Ultimately both were to become important factors behind the drive to re-equip Britain's own forces. In immediate terms, however, the effect of the gradual collapse of the Geneva talks was bound to be greater. As early as 1931 the members of the Cabinet had determined that should all attempts to achieve an international convention fail Britain would have to rearm. Conscious of the deterioration in the nation's defences, Ministers had in that year approved a highly significant resolution submitted by the Three Party Committee: 'any future reductions [in armaments] by us must be part of an international agreement . . . [and] that the possibility of keeping our armaments at their present low level may have to be reconsidered unless there are comparable reductions by other powers.'[1] Thereafter, the progress of the Disarmament Conference had necessarily been regarded as a crucial determinant of the future orientation of British policy. 'It is success in this conference or war', wrote Ormsby-Gore to Baldwin,[2] and his letter typified the mood of the Government (of which he was one of the younger members) as a whole. Admittedly, while the abortive Conference continued to work in Geneva, and as long as there seemed the slightest chance of reaching some international disarmament agreement, the Cabinet could ignore the signs of a prospective change in the military map of Europe. What it hoped for was a kind of convention which, while legitimizing part of Germany's secret rearmament, would put an effective control on its extent.[3] The search for a disarmament

[1] Article No. 6 of the Three Party Committee's Resolution, 15 July 1934, D.C. (P) 50, Cab. 16/102. On the Committee, see above p.

[2] 1 October 1933, Baldwin Papers (Cambridge), vol. 121, p. 76.

[3] On the effect of the German issue on Anglo-French relations at the time, see N.H. Waites, 'British Foreign Policy Towards France Regarding the German Problem from 1929 to 1934' (unpublished Ph.D. thesis, University of London, 1972).

agreement did not therefore cease when Germany left the Conference in October 1933; it remained a basic target of British foreign policy for years to come. But from that date the need to consider some measures of rearmament could no longer be ignored. As MacDonald noted early in 1934: 'For the moment we are continuing the policy which has been mine from the beginning but I am too well aware that at any moment it may be changed, not because this or any other Government wants it, but because it is forced upon us by the refusal of other nations to keep down their arms.'[4]

As is well known it took some time for consideration to be translated into action. Despite the weight of the factors impelling the Government to discuss rearmament, all deliberations on the subject were coloured by the strength of the arguments against adopting such a course. Thus, as historical research has already established, the trend of public opinion in 1934-5 exerted a powerful, and negative, influence on the Government's calculations as to the political advisability of launching large-scale rearmament.[5] Economic considerations had a similarly restraining effect.[6] As presented by the Treasury, the economic argument was simple: the only way to implement the rearmament plans proposed by the three Services, within the time considered necessary, was to place the entire economy on a semi-war footing. That course, however, according to the Treasury's reasoning, might endanger precisely the economic stability which was considered to be of primary importance in a prospective protracted war. Throughout the 1930s the Treasury's fundamental idea of 'business as usual' competed with the traditional demands of the Chiefs of Staff, who insisted that only all-out rearmament would prove that Britain 'meant business'.

Overriding all other factors operating against rearmament were the expectations which the policy makers entertained regarding probable future developments: they just did not believe in the imminence and inevitability of war. That disbelief, which persisted

---

[4]Quoted in David Marquand, *Ramsay MacDonald* (London, 1977), p. 752.

[5]See *inter alia* J. Robertson 'The British General Election of 1935', *Journal of Contemporary History* 9.1, (1974), 149-64, and Joseph Wightman, 'The Rearmament Issue in the British General Election 1935', *Proceedings of the Social Science Association,* 1963, pp. 23-29.

[6]See D.H. Aldcroft, *The Inter-War Economy* (London, 1971); F. Coghlan, 'Armaments, Economic Policy and Appeasement, Background to British Policy', *History* 57 (1972), 205-16; R. Parker 'Economic Rearmament and Foreign Policy before 1939: A Preliminary Study', *Journal of Contemporary History* (October 1975), pp. 637-47; R. Shay, *British Rearmament in the 1930's* (Princeton, 1978) and especially G.C. Peden, *British Rearmament and the Treasury 1932-1939,* (Edinburgh, 1979).

late into the 1930s, was particularly potent during the early part of the decade. Admittedly, the Manchurian Crisis of 1931 had led to a formal abrogation of the 'Ten Year Rule'; thereafter, the Services were freed from the need to base their budgetary plans on the assumption that no major war would occur for the next ten years. But even this alteration in outlook did not indicate a novel sense of urgency, as the Admiralty discovered when it attempted to take advantage of the supposed change of mind late in 1932.[7] Hankey, who, throughout these years, constantly tried to draw the attention of politicians to the country's military unpreparedness, was naturally fully aware of the dominant attitude of his Cabinet masters. In November 1933 he privately complained that 'one of the difficulties in dealing with the problem [of defence preparedness] is that in present political conditions it is rather a delicate matter to raise formally. I have occasionally spoken of it during the last years to politicians but have met with the same kind of reception, it was rather pooh-poohed. . . . ' When, in March 1934, Baldwin hinted to the Commons that Coastal Defence had been 'starved to death', Hankey reported to a friend that the implied prospect of rearmament produced 'a kind of chilling atmosphere in the House'.[8]

Until the end of 1934 the refusal to countenance the possibility of war was bolstered by the hope of reaching some international disarmament convention. In November 1933 Ramsay MacDonald assured his War Minister that 'if a reasonable agreement should be possible then the question of re-imposition of the Ten Year Rule might be contemplated'.[9] Eight months later, Neville Chamberlain stressed that 'every programme now adopted must be open, so that it could be accelerated or decelerated to suit later needs.'[10]

Not even the obvious signs of substantial secret rearmament in Germany affected the extent of disbelief in the possibility of war. When air rearmament measures were decided upon in the spring of 1935, the Prime Minister explained that it was 'not because war was anticipated'.[11] So slow, and so unwilling, were many in high places to recognize the danger that two years later, in 1937, a man as influential

---

[7] See T 161 S/18917/016/1 Box 560. An analysis of the impact of the 'Ten Year Rule' on rearmament is given in F. Cameron, 'Some Aspects of Diplomacy and Strategy 1933-1939' (unpublished Ph.D. thesis, Cambridge University, 1973), pp. 1-54.

[8] To the Earl of Selborne, 13 November 1933, Cab. 63/47, M.O. (33) 15. To 22 March, 1934, Cab. 63/48, M.O. 34(5).

[9] 23 November 1933, Cabinet Disarmament Committee, Cab. 27/505.

[10] 17 July 1934, Cab. 16/110.

[11] 20 May 1935, Cab. 27/508.

as Edward Bridges, Chairman of the Treasury Inter-Services Committee, felt impelled to criticize those members of the Government who were urging the completion of rearmament before 1939, when, according to British military intelligence, Germany would be ready for war. 'Is it not about time', he complained, 'that it was expressed that there is no particular magic about April 1939: Of course if we knew for certain that war was going to break out on that date we should all be arming more rapidly'.[12] But lack of certainty, as Donald Watt has shown, was at the root of the phenomenon of disbelief, which was especially prevalent in 1934-5: 'They [the British decision-makers] could see a threat but not a certainty, they could see peril of war but not the impossibility of avoiding it. It was on this point that the flow of paraphrastic memoranda with which Sir Robert Vansittart bombarded them failed to carry ultimate conviction.'[13]

This, of course, is not to imply that the Government was oblivious to the defence problems facing Britain, and especially to the danger of an air attack. On the contrary it was greatly influenced by the fear of a knock-out blow from the air and the accompanying apprehension about Britain's vulnerability to air attack. However, in order to understand the role of this 'air anxiety' in the development of the decision-making process in 1934-5, and the extent to which it influenced the Government's ultimate decision to commence rearmament, it is necessary to examine here the points of view of three groups: the decision-makers themselves; their professional advisers; and the general public.

As was seen to be the case in the formulation of British policy towards the Geneva Conference in 1932-3, the individual views of the leading Ministers exerted a particularly strong influence on the Government's combined assessment of the 'air danger' to Britain in 1933-5. Indicative, within this context, is the prominence which this particular concern attained in the mind of the influential Chancellor of the Exchequer, Neville Chamberlain. Although constantly repudiating all-out rearmament, Chamberlain gave evidence during this period of his particular sensitivity to the air danger. Addressing a C.I.D. meeting early in 1935 he presented a clear review of his own conceptions on the matter:

> To a layman imagination the new danger which had to be faced was that a country might think they could settle accounts by one single terrific knock-out blow on vital spots. If what he had

[12] Edward Bridges's notes in T 161, Box 1071 S/42580/1.

[13] D.C. Watt, *Personalities and Politics* (London 1965), p. 118. For a clear example, see Samuel Hoare's notes on January 1937 in Templewood Papers, Cambridge, Z/2.

suggested was right, surely it would be a new temptation to an ill-disposed country to strike a blow of this kind, much greater in fact than it would be to start a war by a slow process of mobilization and moving the army, that in any case must take some time but *it might be hoped that an air blow such as he had described would more or less end the war before it began*[14]

The temptation, he went on to point out, would be thwarted, 'when the aggressor realized that action of this kind would not be the end of war'.[15] What seems to have worried Chamberlain specifically was the possibility that 'conditions might arise in which Germany could use her air force on a much bigger scale than in the last war' and thus present the British Government with a menace of an air attack 'of formidable proportions and having a crippling effect'.[16]

Some Ministers advanced their growing concern with this threat as one of the main causes justifying Britain's embarkation on a rearmament programme; others, however, initially considered it a good reason to continue the search for an international air agreement.[17] Thus Baldwin was still pursuing the line he had adopted in May 1932 when he addressed the House of Commons in March 1934. Should the Disarmament Conference fail to achieve a General Convention, he announced, Britain would continue to work for an air pact. He emphasized that 'the great peril from the air is the attempt of any given nation, under any impulse, to get a knock-out blow early and to decide the War. . . . The real danger to peace is a very strong air power on the one hand and a defenceless city on the other.'[18]

By May Baldwin himself appeared to have abandoned his argument but Simon and MacDonald nevertheless continued to urge a bold British initiative in air disarmament as the main solution to the problem. Indeed, commenting on a proposal made by Simon on 14 May for a convention prohibiting bombardment from the air, MacDonald went so far as to ask, 'why have bombers at all?'[19] When their hopes were finally dashed, Simon and MacDonald turned their full attention to air rearmament. It is not surprising to find Simon explaining his reasons for giving priority to air rearmament in the allocation of defence expenditure in the following terms: 'Germany

[14]25 February 1935, 258 CID, Air 8/20. Italics added.

[15]*Ibid*.

[16]10 May 1934, Cab. 27/507.

[17]See references by Hailsham, Halifax and Hoare to the air danger as a decisive argument for rearmament on 19 April 1934 and 3 May 1934, Cab. 16/110.

[18]286 H.O.C. Deb. 8 March 1934.

[19]MacDonald Papers, 352/A.

was much closer to us physically, so that their [air] menace though not close to us in time was closer to our *hearts*.[20]

That the air menace was similarly close to the hearts of the British public had by now become abundantly clear to the decision-makers. As much is revealed in the records of the general discussions of rearmament in the Cabinet, and these also show that this consideration significantly affected the decision reached. But public opinion played a double-edged role in the shaping of those early plans, for it both impeded and stimulated the decision to rearm. The negative role is well known and has been much discussed. What is too often mininized is its positive effect as a catalyst in the timing of rearmament and in the choice of the form rearmament was to take.

The obvious signs of the breakdown of the Disarmament Conference in 1934 concentrated public attention in Britain on the problem of war. In public discussions on disarmament and rearmament, prominence was given to the issue of the air danger and its implications for British defence. The danger of air attack remained one of the important pivots on which propaganda for the disarmament campaign in that year turned, but it also became a central feature of the campaign for rearmament which began to gather momentum once the failure of the Disarmament Conference was manifest. Both 'disarmers' and 'rearmers' based their conclusions on the same well-known and widely-shared fears of an airborne knock-out blow. As John Kyba puts it in his analysis of British public opinion on disarmament and rearmament: 'The fear of attack from the air was a prevalent phobia throughout 1934'.[21]

The common grounds for anxiety were the popular assumptions about the nature of the 'next war', the destructive capability of the main instrument of that war (the air weapon), and its prospective effect on the civilian population, all providing common grounds for anxiety. Early in 1934 Liddell Hart described the resultant speculation as 'picturing another war as a process of launching vast aerial armadas at the enemy's cities ... seeing the war of the future as purely a war in the air in which the civilian population will serve as a massed target for the contending champions'.[22] Philip Noel-Baker, that most vocal

[20] 17 May 1934, Cab. 16/110. Italics added.

[21] J. Kyba, 'British Attitudes Towards Disarmament and Rearmament 1932-1935' (unpublished Ph.D. thesis, London School of Economics, 1966), pp. 214-15.

[22] 'War in the Air', *Heliocs,* January 1934, p. 235. He himself criticized this assumption, but found little support from other professional writers. It is interesting to note that his criticism was based mainly on the contention that the air forces of that time were not large enough to achieve what had been expected of them. At the same time, he did not seem to cast serious doubts on the prospective ability of large air forces to

leader of the disarmament campaigns sustained by the Labour Party and the League of Nations Union, declared early in 1935: 'In the next war our only hope of saving London will be to destroy Paris or Berlin before the enemy's attacks begin. And if this is true, can we resist the conclusion that the next war if it comes will obliterate the civilization in which we live?'[23]

The pacifists also often used the same motif. In his vision of the result of a single air raid on London, Major-General J.F.C. Fuller provided another fervent advocate of disarmament, Bertrand Russell, with one of the most spine-chilling of all his predictions:

> London for several days will be one vast raving bedlam, the hospitals will be stormed, traffic will cease, the homeless will shriek for help, the city will be a pandemonium. What of the Government at Westminster, it will be swept away by an avalanche of terror. Then will the enemy dictate its terms....[24]

J.L. Garvin, the editor of *The Observer,* was on the opposite side of this political debate, representing that section of the British public which in 1934 began to urge rearmament. His premise, however, was identical to that of the disarmers. In a leader which he published in December 1933, he pointed out that 'for air attack, Great Britain, full of cities and towns, is demarcated, laid out and exposed like no other country on earth. London, with its dense millions of human beings, is a target fifty miles broad.... The island in case of conflict can be savaged with terrific rapidity'.[25] He thus gave expression to the fear that in a war which seemed increasingly likely, Britain would no longer be able to rely on her traditional insular defence.[26]

Although agreeing on the cataclysmic nature of the threat, the two camps suggested diametrically conflicting methods of dealing with it. The disarmament campaigners demanded some form of drastic air disarmament agreement, basing their conclusion on Baldwin's famous phrase, 'the bomber will always get through'. Their favourite suggestion was the internationalization of civil aviation and the complete abolition of military aircraft.[27] Intensive air rearmament, they held,

---

achieve the knock-out blow. See *When Britain Goes to War* (London, 1935), pp. 49-50, and in his papers, (London) 11/1937/38b.

[23]'A National Air Force — No Defence', in Storm Johnson, (ed.) *Challenge to Death* (New York, 1935), p. 205.

[24]Bertrand Russell, *Which Way to Peace* (London 1936), p. 37.

[25]3 December 1933.

[26]See for example, P.C. Groves, *Our Future in the Air* (London 1935), p. 67.

[27]See, *inter alia,* H.M. Swanick, *Frankenstein and his Monster* (London 1934), pp. 20-22, and L.E.O. Charlton, *War from the Air* (London 1935), p. 183. The latter was

could not provide the desired security, especially since a stable equilibrium in the air could not be maintained for long and the temptation of a pre-emptive attack would always exist.[28] The strength of this feeling can be gauged from the fact that almost 10,000,000 out of the 12,000,000 persons who answered the questions of the National Peace Ballot in 1934-5 favoured the total abolition of military aircraft by international agreement.[29] The rearmament campaigners on the other hand constituted the protagonists of the deterrent theory. Their claim was that the only way to avoid aerial bombardment was the construction of a large air force capable of retaliation;[30] their programme was the intensive development of Britain's air power. A review of the press presented to the Cabinet late in December 1933 revealed that out of 62 London and Provincial morning and evening newspapers, 44 definitely supported a one-power standard in the air, to be achieved by an increase in British strength if other powers would not reduce.[31]

One proposal which generated support from many newspapers was that the Government should continue to strive for an agreement which would either abolish air bombardment altogether or would at least provide Britain with allies if attacked. *The Times* was the strongest supporter of this form of convention. Urging the Government to work for such a pact, one leader suggested: 'If this principle [bombing retaliation by parties to the agreement] were once to become firmly established, then the deterrent against any air swoop would be so tremendous that no Government in their senses would undertake it.'[32] Another was the suggestion that the Government attempt to implement the principle of qualitative rather than quantitative air disarmament. This suggestion could even be supported by some advocates of air rearmament, as was instanced by Winston Churchill, one of the most vocal of the latter. His idea was to limit the use of air weapons, rather than their number. This would not involve a delay in production; provided the other Power agreed, it would ensure

---

one of the prominent contributors to the air danger popular literature of the time. On this subject see R. Higham, *The Military Intellectuals in Britain 1918-1940* (New Brunswick, 1966).

[28] One of the prominent writers who seemed to be obsessed by the air danger was P.C. Groves, whose sensational *Behind the Smoke Screen* gave rise in 1934 to a considerable amount of writing on the subject in the Press. A useful collection of this material is to be found in Groves's papers, now deposited with the Liddell Hart papers.

[29] See A. Livingstone, *The Peace Ballot* (London, 1935).

[30] Kyba, *British Attitudes*, p. 137.

[31] See C.P. 305/33.

[32] Leader, 1 June 1934.

'the restriction of air warfare as far as you can to the zone of the armies or military objectives'.[33]

Manifestation of the public's growing apprehension was not restricted to the press campaign,[34] nor to the several deputations to Westminster by various peace organizations urging air disarmament.[35] The fear of aerial bombardment also, and most significantly, found expression in Parliament itself.[36] The danger of air attacks was the central theme of no fewer than three debates on disarmament and rearmament from November 1933 to July 1934, a period during which Parliament had not yet publicly admitted Germany's secret air rearmament. Furthermore, the first two debates took place before the Cabinet took its decision on rearmament. The first serious debate on rearmament since the opening of the Disarmament Conference took place on 28 March 1933, on a private motion which called attention to 'the inadequacy of the present provision made for the air defence of Great Britain';[37] the second, on 8 March 1934, centred on the adequacy of the Air Estimates to provide defence against air attack; the third, on 30 July 1934, dealt with the general subject of armaments. Prominent among the many Conservative M.P.s who began, during the course of these debates, to press for intensive air rearmament, was Winston Churchill. He was, at this time, evincing a particular interest in defence against the danger of an airborne knock-out blow, and in his campaign for air rearmament made use of estimates supplied to him by officials who disagreed with the Government's public estimates and policy.[38]

In formulating its response to the public's evident concern over Britain's air vulnerability, the Government's principal concern was to steer a course which might best meet the conflicting demands of those who campaigned for disarmament and those who pressed for rearmament. A rearmament scheme based specifically on air expansion

[33] 8 March 1934, 286 H.O.C. Deb.

[34] With the Rothermere press, the *Observer* and the *Saturday Review* urging air rearmament, and the *Manchester Guardian,* the *New Statesman* and the *Economist* disarmament. For an analysis of the British press in the 1930s, see F. Gannon. *The British Press and Germany 1936-1939* (London, 1971), especially pp. 32-89.

[35] See a record of these deputations in FO 371/17329, W 14437, 46/98.

[36] For a detailed analysis of the attention given to the subject by Parliament, see D.B. John, 'The Debate on British Military Air Policy 1933-9', (unpublished Ph.D. thesis, University of Kentucky, 1969).

[37] 283 H.O.C. Deb.

[38] On this issue see R.R. James, *Churchill: A Study in Failure 1900-1939* (London, 1970), p. 237; B. Liddell Hart, *Memoirs,* Vol. II (London 1965), p. 305; and especially Martin Gilbert, *Winston S. Churchill,* Vol. V, *1922-1939* (London, 1976), pp. 549-581.

appeared to meet this requirement: it would provoke minimal criticism from those who urged disarmament, whilst providing a satisfactory reply to those who called for rearmament. Baldwin had virtually dictated the orientation of British policy in this direction even before the Government committed itself to any formal decision on the issue. In a clear response to the growing anxiety concerning Britain's liability to air attack expressed by Conservative M.P.s, Baldwin made a statement to the Commons on 8 March 1934:

> This Government will see to it, [he declared] that in air strength and air power, this country shall no longer be in a position inferior to any country within striking distance of our shores.[39]

This significant and bold undertaking committed the Government to an emphasis on the air aspect of the yet undecided rearmament plan. It also dominated the debate on the subject as a whole for years to come. There can be no doubt concerning Baldwin's motives. Addressing the Cabinet two months later, he explicitly stated: 'If it was impossible to limit air force, public opinion might be willing to agree to anything which could prevent a foreign air force from getting any closer than they were today.'[40]

Ormsby Gore, the First Commissioner of Works, had already reached the same conclusion. Writing to MacDonald, he stated his belief that:

> public opinion will *readily* respond to, and welcome, any proposal clearly designed for the actual defence of the British Isles, particularly against air attacks. I hold therefore that *priority in action and presentation* ought to be given to the air defence of Great Britain.[41]

Both Vansittart and Warren Fisher, the Permanent Under-Secretary of the Treasury and head of the Civil Service, who took an active part in the discussions on rearmament at this time, appreciated the importance of this point. They even drew the Services' attention to the political aspect of the need to respond to the public concern, when the professional military advisers discussed the general subject of rearmament with a view to submitting specific recommendations.

---

[39] 286 H.O.C. Deb.
[40] 17 May 1934, Cab. 16/110.
[41] 6 March 1934, Prem. 1/175. Italics added.

The chiefs of the Service Departments had not themselves been immune to the manifestations of public feeling which appeared in the press during the early part of 1934. On the contrary, in their view many of the articles were both the result and the cause of a distinct feeling of panic, the effect of which would only increase the moral and material damage which an enemy might hope to attain. In order to minimize this possibility they had therefore urged the Government to launch an information campaign, designed to put the danger of air attack in what they described as 'the right perspective'.[42] They now received instruction on a different aspect of the issue. Thus, Warren Fisher explained in a private letter to Admiral Chatfield, the Chairman of the Chiefs of Staff Committee, that 'the public here is beginning to feel uncomfortable about the air and is therefore most educative in this sphere'.[43] Vansittart put the same point in a different manner: 'Ministers would expect to have something which they could show to the country. If the public were to be brought to the point of paying large sums for defence, then it was necessary that the air expansion should receive full treatment.'[44]

When the professional advisers' rearmament scheme was placed before the politicians for a decision on priorities, one decisive influence was the Ministers' apprehension about the prospective public response to the decision to rearm. Indeed, the decision reached in July 1934 to give priority to air expansion in terms of both action and presentation was to a considerable extent a response to the British public's growing apprehension. As Baldwin told the Cabinet Disarmament Committee:

> It was felt that at all costs we must put ourselves in a position to make it extremely difficult for Germany to attack us suddenly. *For the political point of view it was necessary to do something to satisfy the semi-panic conditions which existed now about the air and for obvious reasons. From the political point of view the air was the most important and decision could be taken.*[45]

A few days later, Hankey privately explained the political aspect behind the emphasis on the air arm during the early days of rearment to the Dominions High Commissioners.

> There had been a good deal of pressure in Parliament and outside on the subject of air defence and the necessity for an

---

[42] 342 C.O.S. Cab. 53/24.
[43] 11 July 1934, Cab. 21/404.
[44] 16 March 1934, Cab. 16/109.
[45] 2 July 1934, Cab. 16/110. Italics added.

earlier start on this side of the question was to a great extent due to this Parliamentary pressure.'[46]

The danger of an airborne knock-out blow and, more generally, the implications of British air inferiority, were at that time not only subjects of intense public debate but they were also constant subjects of discussion among various Departments of State. These held diverse views both on Britain's defence requirements and on the pace and strategic aims of Germany's air rearmament. The professional advisers tendered different conclusions on these issues to the Cabinet and its Disarmament Committee, and put forward different estimates, and the resultant controversy greatly influenced the Cabinet's own discussions on the rearmament question.

In this controversy, which theoretically was a matter exclusively for military judgment, the Foreign Office and, in particular, its Permanent Under-Secretary of State, played a prominent role. Vansittart's concern with the danger of German air rearmament as early as 1932 has already been noted. During 1934 and 1935 he appears to have given much further thought to the implications of Germany's growing air power in relation to British defence and foreign policy. The result was that in those years the Foreign Office placed great emphasis on this problem whenever the question of rearmament arose.

Vansittart's particular apprehension about the dangerous nature of British air inferiority stemmed from his profound conviction that the Nazis had been quick to discover the decisive military and *political* use which could be made of the knock-out capability of air power: 'The Kaiser — long out of date — said that Germany's future lay upon the water. The new regime have made it abundantly clear already that the future of Germany lies in the air, and a very formidable future too.'[47]

He was of the strong opinion that the Germans would use strategic air bombardment, or the threat of it, as one of the main weapons with which to exert international influence. As early as January 1934, he warned the Chiefs of Staff that 'the young spirits among the Nazis regarded air power as a means by which through threat of action or by action itself they would demand the colonial Empire back again'.[48] In May 1935, he wrote to Hankey that the German generals 'are convinced that no population could really stand more than a few days

[46] 6 July 1934, Cab. 21/389.
[47] 31 December 1935, FO 371/18852, C 8542/55/18.
[48] 30 January 1934, Cab. 16/109.

of intensive bombardment and at the end of that time they could impose any conditions they like'.[49] From what he knew of the mentality of the Nazi leaders he felt that they might take a gamble of this sort even before Germany was completely prepared, in military terms, for war. At a time when nobody in the British Government considered Germany to be militarily prepared for an all-out war, Vansittart warned that German aggression could not be assessed exclusively in terms of military preparedness. In April 1935 he wrote:

> In the triumvirate [Hitler, Georing and Geobbels] — even if they are increasingly falling under the influence of the General Staff and officials, we are not dealing with men who can be judged by ordinary standards, that [if] a serious economic and financial strain should become unbearable, the Nazi oligarchy might be tempted to precipitate a foreign crisis as a means of saving the regime from internal catastrophe. . . . For it may well be not the complete technical readiness of Germany which will decide, but rather certain psychological and non-military factors.[50]

Moreover, it was from the air, in particular, that trouble must be expected. In a memorandum he addressed to Hankey in May 1935, Vansittart stressed that 'the real danger is and will be for some years to come what an irresponsible man like Goering might do in and with such a moment'.[51]

Vansittart was further concerned with the effect of German air superiority in Europe on Britain's political position on the continent. In April 1935, he wrote:

> Air policy in its broadest aspects cannot now be divorced from foreign policy. In recent years we have been heavily handicapped by our loss of material weight. . . . To impose on us inferiority till 1939, will confirm it still further. Apart from the visibly growing German menace, any continued inferiority in the air will weaken our influence throughout Europe, where we are already considered to need more support than we can give, and the difficulty of conducting an independent and effective foreign policy will increase if this general estimate of us is allowed to continue.[52]

What Vansittart refused to accept — and this stemmed from his general view of Anglo-French relations — was the contention that France would always be ready to help Britain defend herself from air

[49] 22 May 1935, Cab. 21/540.
[50] 29 April, 1935, FO 371/18840, p. 114.
[51] 22 May 1935, Cab. 21/540.
[52] 24 April 1935, FO 371/18839, D.C. (m) (32)139.

attack.⁵³ Rather, he continuously urged the Government to undertake full-scale air rearmament, based on both civil defence and a striking air force as a 'deterrent to gambling' by Germany's air marshalls.⁵⁴ As early as the beginning of 1934, Vansittart and the Foreign Office started to cultivate their own sources of information on German air rearmament. Some of this intelligence originated from within the Government, in particular from officials who were alarmed by what they considered to be a dangerous neglect of Britain's national interest. Like senior officials at the Foreign Office, they were sceptical of the official assessment of German air power, which they attempted to change by a constant and continuous measure of co-operation. One such source was Charles Medhurst, Deputy Director of Air Intelligence, whose view of German air rearmament, as apprehensive as that of the Foreign Office, had not yet been accepted by the Air Ministry.⁵⁵ Another was Major Desmond Morton, the head of the British Industrial Intelligence Centre. From 1934 onwards he provided the Foreign Office with valuable information on German rearmament, and especially on air rearmament.⁵⁶ More significantly, he often sent detailed criticism of the Air Ministry estimates. Morton even risked his career by giving similar information to Churchill, who used it in order to maintain his pressure on the Government and to arouse public opinion.⁵⁷

The atmosphere within which Morton accomplished this task, and the personal and professional risks which he took in doing so, are clearly illustrated in a letter which he wrote to Liddell Hart in 1961:

> No one loved us [the Industrial Intelligence Centre] and no one gave us credit for prophesying with accompanying statistical proofs what turned out to be miraculous accuracy the military air and naval units each country would be able to put into the field in the first year of a world war.... No politician in power likes to be given information backed by facts and calculations which entirely upset his whole policy.... Our reports raised riot. Each time, neither Baldwin nor Chamberlain wanted to believe them.... In November, 1938, I was roughly warned by Neville

⁵³See his letter to Hankey, 2 March 1934, Cab. 21/434.

⁵⁴2 June 1934, Vansittart Papers, 1/11.

⁵⁵K. Strong, *Intelligence at the Top* (London, 1962), p. 18; D. Divine, *The Broken Wing* (London, 1965), p. 194; Liddell Hart, Papers, 11 (1935) 114, and Air Staff notes on 25 May 1935, Air 8/186.

⁵⁶Desmond Morton private letter to Liddell Hart, 9 July 1961, Liddell Hart Papers.

⁵⁷Gilbert, *Winston Churchill*, pp. 554-9. And Gilbert *Winston Churchill* companion document volumes *Wilderness Years* and *Coming of War* (London, 1980).

[Chamberlain] and his ministers that if a spot of it [report on German rearmament] leaked out, I would be hung.[58]

Other items of information were provided from sources which operated outside British official circles. Thus Colonel Malcolm Christie, who had served in the Royal Flying Corps in the First World War, worked closely with Vansittart in obtaining information about the German Air Force.[59] He had established valuable contacts with German officials and Nazi leaders, especially those connected with air affairs, during his service as British Air Attache in Berlin between 1927 and 1930. His later frequent business trips to Germany enabled him to produce a series of reports on the situation there, particularly in relation to foreign policy and war plans. The Foreign Office also used information which it obtained from German sources, among whom were Admiral Canaris and General Milch.[60] Intensive efforts were made in the office, especially by Michael Creswell, Allen Leeper and, above all, Ralph Wigram, head of the Central Department, to digest this information, to make the Minister's evaluations as accurate as possible, to cross-check every appreciation submitted by the Air Staff, and to warn against errors and wrong deductions.[61]

Sir Warren Fisher, who exerted considerable influence throughout the period, held views similar to those of the Foreign Office on issues of air rearmament. On numerous occasions he too warned that the most significant danger to confront Britain in a future war would be aerial bombardment in its initial stages. He also agreed with Vansittart's criticism of what he regarded as the complacency of the Service Departments, especially in matters of intelligence and assessment.[62]

In a private letter to Chamberlain after the Munich crisis, he accused the Air Staff of having misinformed the Government in their estimates of both German air power and the extent of the danger of air attack throughout the early stages of the debates on rearmament. They had, he said, provided the Government with 'soothing syrup'.[63]

[58] 9 July 1961, Liddell Hart Papers.

[59] T.P. Conwell Evans, *None So Blind* (London 1947), based on Christie Papers, Churchill College, Cambridge.

[60] A. Eden, Earl of Avon, *Facing the Dictators* (London, 1962) p. 185; K. Middlemass, *Diplomacy of Illusion* (London, 1972), p. 91.

[61] Ralph Wigram seemed to be especially sensitive to this danger of air attack. His wife wrote to Churchill that, after the German reoccupation of the Rhineland in April 1936, 'Ralph said to me, war is now inevitable and it will be the most terrible war there has ever been, wait now for bombs to fall on this little house.' R.W. Thompson, *Generalissimo Churchill* (London 1973), p. 46.

[62] D. C. Watt, *Personalities and Politics*, pp. 102-114.

[63] Prem. 1/252.

During the formative years of 1933-4, however, matters were not so clearly defined. This was not least so because the Foreign Office's assessment of the strategic role of Germany's air power, as well as the pace of her air rearmament, contradicted the evaluation provided by the Secret Service. Vansittart believed his information to be more reliable, probably because it complemented his own ideas concerning Germany's general military plans, and the role of her air force in particular.[64] Referring to the Services' scepticism about his alarmist estimates, he wrote: 'Prophecy is largely a matter of insight. I do not think the Service Departments have enough. On the other hand they might say that I have too much. The answer is that I know the Germans better.'[65] The Permanent Under-Secretary's attitude was reflected in the constant efforts which the Foreign Office made to ensure that its own evaluations prevailed. As will be seen, these efforts exerted an important influence on the decision-making process and, in certain cases, on the actual decisions reached.

On some important points, the Foreign Office's estimates also contradicted those of the Service Departments, all three of which emphasized that the picture conveyed by the Office was grossly exaggerated and, in places, substantially misleading. Their conclusions regarding the date by which Germany might gamble on war, and the importance which she might attach to air bombardment, were based solely on considerations of productive efficiency and military utility. Thus, they all rejected the Foreign Office estimates as to the pace of German rearmament. Hankey echoed this scepticism in a note which he addressed to Vansittart in March 1934:

> I am as much concerned as you are at the German air menace. It is only one of degree or rather of imminence. The Germans are efficient people *but they are not supermen*. They have also to build up a navy and that is not going to be done very quickly.[66]

Furthermore, the three Services unanimously rejected, as improbable, the idea that Germany might risk her air power before completing a substantial part of her comprehensive rearmament programme.[67] 'The menace of German aggression in the west', wrote the Chief of the Imperial General Staff, Montgomery Massingberd, in October 1934, 'is not imminent. Unless Germany goes quite mad she will make no

---

[64] See the interesting correspondence between him and Christie on the subject in Christie Papers 180/1/42.

[65] 5 July 1934, FO 371/17694, C 4297/20/18.

[66] 6 March 1934, Cab. 21/434. Italics added.

[67] Art. 29 of the Defence Requirement Committee's Report, Cab. 16/109.

move in that direction until she is confident of success.'[68] In any case, he explained in April 1935, the 'air danger' was not pressing. 'War cannot be waged by this means alone, and Germany cannot be considered as ready for war until she has a navy, army and air force adequate for this purpose.'[69]

The alleged ability of air power to achieve a decisive knock-out blow was altogether a controversial point. The Admiralty, and the War Office both doubted the ability of an enemy air force not only to inflict severe casualties on the civilian population but also to deliver a crushing strategic blow. This view was clearly expressed in a letter which the First Sea Lord, Chatfield, wrote to the C.I.G.S. in April 1934:

> One of the thoughts which continuously dominate the thoughts [of Ministers] is the danger of the German air menace to England. What I am uncertain about is what is the air menace to this country from Germany and is it vital or not. By a vital menace I mean such a menace as would accrue to this country if a strong naval force was able to occupy the approaches of the Channel which would cause the starvation of the country in a few months, or the danger to this country if it was successfully invaded by an army causing a complete paralysis of the life of the country. Is the air menace whether it is from France or Germany in this category? We cannot be sure that we are not building far reaching plans being swayed by *ignorant* propaganda instead of qualified Judgment.[70]

The same point was put less forcefully by the C.I.G.S. himself:

> I am not going to try and minimize the effect of bombing on large cities or the casualties to civilian population that may be inflicted. But I think we must be careful to realize the limitations of high-performance aeroplanes and the results they can achieve in a national war.[71]

A few months later he enlarged on this issue at a meeting of the C.I.D.

> Personally I am unable to believe that any big scale air attack could be delivered which would so paralyse our whole power that we shall be unable to continue the war. I do not think there are any targets in this country which if heavily attacked would

[68] 4 October 1934, 350 C.O.S. Cab. 53/26.
[69] 27 April 1935, War Office Records London (hereafter W.O.) W.O. 190/824.
[70] 11 April 1934, Cab. 21/388. Italics added.
[71] Massingberd Papers, London Vol. 158.

knock us out from the start and I rather think the same thing will apply to France, Germany and Belgium.[72]

The War Office rejected the idea that the Germans were busy building a huge air force which they intended to use mainly for a strategic bombing offensive. The information in the hands of the Secret Service contradicted that possessed by the Foreign Office.[73] Thus, M.I.3 (Military Intelligence No. 3) noted in November 1934:

> The conclusions of the General Staff are confirmed by reports from the Military Attache in Berlin as to the views of the German General Staff on the future of employment of land and air forces. The German General Staff consider that the action of land and air forces must be complementary and must be directed to the same strategic objectives. They do not contemplate a separate air strategy and hold that air attacks must be followed up by attacks by the field army, otherwise the air effect will be wasted.[74]

The Air Ministry's attitude was somewhat ambivalent. On the one hand, the Air Staff agreed with their military colleagues in considering that the Foreign Office had unduly emphasized the imminence of the German air threat. Thus, criticizing what he regarded as an alarmist estimate by Air Intelligence, the Chief of the Air Staff, Sir Edward Ellington, wrote: 'They [the Germans] cannot achieve the impossible, there is a limit to the emergency measures which can be resorted to under peace conditions.'[75] On the other hand, the Air Ministry took issue with the sister Service Departments, and sided with the Foreign Office, on the decisive effect of an aerial attack. As has already been seen, the belief in this possibility had long since entered the realm of standard Air Ministry doctrine. Throughout this period, the Air Staff continued to urge the Cabinet to recognize that in German schools of strategic thought too, there was a growing belief that the air force would prove decisive in the next war, especially against Great Britain. The Air Staff maintained that to secure a German decision on land against France, assisted by her fortified frontier, would take so long that irretrievable economic ruin would result before any military outcome was achieved. Consequently, according to this assessment, the main German effort would be towards establishing an air force superior to the enemy's and seeking a decision by air attack.

[72] 286 C.I.D., 25 February 1935, Cab. 2/6.

[73] In fact, the former were subsequently proved to be closer to the truth. Christie obtained his information mainly from German Air Ministry circles, a fact which might shed some light on this aspect of his information.

[74] 20 November 1934, W.O. 190/281.

[75] Air 9/69.

The operative implications of this controversy were apparent in 1934 and 1935, when the Cabinet was urged to define its priorities in defence expenditure.[76] In so doing, it had to weigh the assessments of the Foreign Office and Air Ministry regarding the extent of the air danger against the judgments of the War Office and the Admiralty. Since the conflicting estimates implied different allotments of funds, the influence exerted by the fear of aerial bombardment was bound to affect the overall shape of Britain's early rearmament plans. As has been seen, certain prominent politicians themselves tended to adopt the more extreme and pessimistic view of the air peril. Their personal fears necessarily coloured the Cabinet discussions and thereby influenced the decisions arrived at by the Cabinet Disarmament Committee. The precise impact which these fears had on the various stages of the formulation of rearmament plans becomes clear once attention is directed at the process whereby the ultimate decisions were reached.

On 9 November 1933 the Committee of Imperial Defence decided, after considering the serious warnings of the Chiefs of Staff, to establish a committee charged with the preparation of a programme which would repair 'the worst deficiencies' in British defence preparations'.[77] The Defence Requirements Committee, as this body was called, was not inclined to grant the German menace in general, and the danger of air attack in particular, any significant priority over other defence problems. The structure of the Committee in itself was one reason for this attitude. The Committee included the three Chiefs of Staff and any report submitted by such a body had necessarily to reflect something of a compromise. Thus the Admiralty, which for obvious reasons considered the imperial aspect of defence more important than any other, could not agree to a report that depicted the Continental danger as the most ominous.[78] A second factor which determined the Committee's collective view on the German problem

[76] May 1934, 334 C.O.S. Cab. 16/111.

[77] The most comprehensive account of British rearmament during the inter-war period is N. Gibbs, *Grand Strategy,* Vol. I, *Rearmament Policy* (H.M.S.O. London, 1976). For the 1930s see R. Meyers *Britische Sicherheitspolitik 1934-1938,* (Dusseldorf, 1976), J. Dunbabin 'British Rearmament in the 1930s. 'A Chronology and Review' *Historical Journal* XVIII. 3 (1975) pp. 581-609, and J.M. Lippincott, 'The Strategy of Appeasement, The Formulation of British Defence Policy 1934-1939' (unpublished D. Phil. Thesis Oxford 1976). For a useful analysis of the work of the Defence Requirement Committee, see also M. Howard, *The Continental Commitment* (London, 1972), pp. 105-7; P. Dennis, *Decision by Default* (London, 1972), pp. 35-8; K. Middlemas and J. Barnes, *Baldwin, A Biography* (London, 1969), pp. 762-4; S. Roskill, *Hankey, Man of Secrets,* Vol. 3 (London, 1974), pp. 67-121; and S. Roskill, *Naval Policy Between the Wars,* Vol. 2 (London, 1976), pp. 164-84.

[78] See entry in Pownall diary of 4 December 1933, in B. Bond (ed.), *Chief of Staff, the Diaries of Lieutenant-General Sir Henry Pownall,* Vol.I, (London, 1972), p. 27.

was the nature of the available military information on German secret rearmament. The fact that Germany was rearming, and secretly building an air force, had been well known to British Intelligence and to the Foreign Office ever since early in 1933.[79] What had not then been appreciated by the Services was the grandiose scale of German general rearmament, especially as far as the air arm was concerned. Nobody in the Service Departments expected that the German secret air force might rapidly become larger than the Royal Air Force, let alone the French air force. Assessing the German air danger in October 1933, the Chiefs of Staff concluded that 'with France as our ally, we should under existing conditions have *overwhelming* air superiority'.[80] As has been seen, the Chief of the Air Staff himself did stress the serious theoretical implications of a German air attack on Britain; but, early in 1934, he did not consider that danger to be materially imminent.[81]

The Services' representatives planned a comprehensive rearmament scheme based on the recognition of Germany as the 'ultimate' but not the 'close' enemy. The air force was recognized to be Germany's most significant potential threat, and was therefore put forward as the obvious reason for demands to expand the Air Force, enlarge the field force and allocate money for air raid precautions. Yet, even within this context, the serious nature of the danger was minimized. In its report, the Committee confidently predicted that:

> Air attacks are likely to be less frequent than they would be in a war with France for the reason that Germany might be confronted at the same time by the air forces of *France* and perhaps other nations.... For the same reason the period during which intensive attacks are likely to be made should be shorter.[82]

This military appraisal was not accepted by two civilians, Vansittart and Warren Fisher, who participated in the Committee's discussions. They urged that the danger of a continental war in which Britain might be subjected to intensive German air attacks should receive priority in defining defence requirements. Fisher, who seemed

---

[79] See FO 371/16708, C/6099 245/18, FO 361/16707 C/6021/245/18 and R.A.F. Confidential Intelligence Summaries for 1932-1933, Air 8/138. On the German plans to develop military aviation in the period before the Nazis came to power, see K.H. Volker, 'Die Entwicklung der militarischen Luftfahrt in Deutschland 1920-1933', *Beitragne zur Militar — und Kriegsgeschichte*, 3 (Stuttgart: Deutsche Verlags-Anstalt, 1962), pp. 121-292.

[80] 310 C.O.S., Cab. 53/23. Italics added.

[81] Ellington in the Defence Requirements Committee (hereafter D.R.C.), 25 January 1934, Cab. 16/109.

[82] D.R.C. Report, Art. 27, Cab. 16/109. Italics added.

no less obsessed with the danger than Vansittart, told the Committee: 'It appeared that in five years she [Germany] would be in a position to deal us a disastrous blow. The attack might be developed on this country before any attack was made on France.'[83] Vansittart for his part was concerned lest Germany exploit the threat of air attack in order to make some political gains: he also maintained that Britain could not attain security by what he considered to be undue reliance on the French.[84] Both men favoured a rearmament plan based primarily on a recognition of Germany as the immediate as well as the ultimate enemy, and on an appreciation that an air attack was the main danger to be guarded against. In matters of detail, they argued the inadequacy of the Air Ministry's proposal to complete 52 squadrons for home defence. In their view, more intensive air expansion was called for. Furthermore, they considered that far fewer political obstacles would stand in the way of the implementation of a programme which laid the greatest emphasis on the expansion of air defences. Fisher succinctly put both arguments in a subsequent private letter to Chatfield, the Chief of the Naval Staff: 'A large increase in our air defence is the easiest (politically) and the most needed starting point.'[85]

Vansittart and Fisher did not, however, sway the members of the Committee. The only section of the final report to reflect their opinions was that which recommended that the Air Defence of Great Britain (A.D.G.B.) scheme be put on a five-year footing, rather than the eight-year basis originally suggested by the War Office.[86] Otherwise, and on more substantial issues, they received no backing from either the Chief of the Air Staff or his two colleagues — a fact which led to Fisher's sardonic remark that 'it was the civilians [on the Defence Rearmament Committee] . . . that had to act as the Air Staff'.[87] Ellington 'did not consider that Germany would be in a position for many years to come to make heavy and subsequent attacks'.[88] Chatfield naturally concurred and gave Hankey his opinion on what he considered to be Vansittart's undue anxiety about the air peril:

> If there is a real menace we will agree with him and the Air Ministry's normal methods of entry and training must be altered

[83] 4 December 1933, Cab. 16/109.

[84] 30 January 1934, Cab. 16/109.

[85] 11 June 1934, Cab. 21/404.

[86] See discussions on 30 January 1934, Cab. 16/109.

[87] Premier 1/252.

[88] 19 February 1934, Cab. 16/109.

to deal with everything. Our proper advisers are the Air Ministry and on their shoulders only can properly rest the responsibility of assessing the extent of the menace and when it can be materialized. Either we are in danger or we are not. I cannot myself believe we are.[89]

Montgomery Massingberd assured the Committee that 'if the Royal Air Force expanded to 52 squadrons then in alliance with France we should have nothing to fear from Germany'.[90] The report finally agreed upon was submitted to the Cabinet on 28 February 1934. It recommended the spending of £71,323,000 under a five-year plan covering everything the Services considered to be their worst deficiencies.[91]

This report was by no means definitive. As much was abundantly clear to Vansittart, who later informed Simon that he only assented to its air section because he thought that the 'higher authorities' might adopt a different attitude on the matters dealt with, which they would have to reconsider from a point of view other than the professional.[92] More significantly, the report did not present the Government with any clear priorities. As MacDonald put it, 'the Committee had given a catalogue of requirements, not arranged in any particular order of priority or importance'.[93] It was over two months, however, before this matter was dealt with. From March to early May 1934, the Cabinet and the Cabinet Disarmament Committee discussed the dual problems of disarmament and rearmament without any specific reference to the issue of priorities in the D.R.C. report. These discussions were confined mainly to the various British plans designed to save the Disarmament Conference from complete collapse.[94] Notwithstanding the pressures of the Chiefs of Staff and Vansittart, no decision could be taken on rearmament while there was still hope of reaching a disarmament agreement.[95] Londonderry, who continuously pressed the Cabinet to decide on air expansion, was bluntly informed by MacDonald that: 'the Government could not announce a new

[89] 19 February 1934, Cab. 16/109.
[90] 16 March 1934, Cab. 16/109.
[91] See C.P. 63/34 for the detailed plan.
[92] 14 May 1934, Cab. 21/388.
[93] 19 March 1934, Cab. 23/78.
[94] Cabinet conclusion of 19 March 1934, Cab. 23/78, and FO 371/18523, W/4153/98.
[95] See C.P. 113(34) of the C.O.S. Committee and Vansittart memorandum C.P. 116(34).

programme when the question [the British Draft Disarmament Convention of January 1934] was still open'.[96]

During the weeks prior to the final Cabinet discussions, the only aspect of the prospective rearmament programme about which the Government issued a public commitment referred to air parity. Baldwin's announcement to this effect in the Commons on 8 March 1934, was a clear indication of the course the Cabinet was later to choose in dealing with the D.R.C. report. As had already been seen, the significant commitment expressed by this declaration was greatly influenced by the pressure of the Press and Parliament.[97]

In the discussions prior to the actual examination of the D.R.C. report in Cabinet, many Ministers constantly advised their colleagues that the expansion of the R.A.F. would be the most important part of any future rearmament plan. Hoare claimed on 19 March: 'If we decide on parity in the air it could be a tremendous risk for Germany to attack this country. Air parity would mitigate one of the greatest risks'.[98] Halifax disclosed his particular apprehension on 3 May:

> It seemed certain that within the next ten years the speed and range of aircraft would develop very considerably and we think it necessary to consider what effect this development would have on the question of air defence as before long it would be possible for Germany to launch an air attack from her territory.[99]

Neville Chamberlain considered that 'if we possessed an overwhelming Air Force then the air menace would be less serious'.[100] The discussions in March and April made no explicit reference to the D.R.C. report; but the attention given to the importance of Belgium for British strategy, as well as the various proposals for reaching an international pact for security from air attack, show that the Cabinet tended to regard the air peril as significant.[101] The War Office and the Admiralty clearly felt that Ministers took a far more serious view of the danger than they themselves did, and they were understandably disturbed by what Chatfield called the effect of 'ignorant propaganda'

---

[96] 24 April 1934, Cab. 23/79.

[97] See above. p. 50 and Pownall notes in his diary on 13 March 1934. Bond, *Chief of Staff,* p. 38.

[98] Cab. 16/110.

[99] Cab. 16/110.

[100] *Ibid.*

[101] See minutes of the Cabinet Disarmament Committee of 19 and 30 April 1934. Cab. 27/506.

on the prospective discussions of the D.R.C. report.[102] Events were to prove that their apprehensions were justifiable.

On 2 May 1934 the French gave their final negative reply to the British questionnaire on disarmament, making it clear that they would not agree to any convention legitimizing German rearmament. This, as far as the British Government was concerned, was the last nail in the coffin of the Disarmament Conference.[103] Consequently from early May the Cabinet Disarmament Committee devoted all of its time to concrete discussions of the D.R.C. report.

Not surprisingly, the Air section of the report was the first to be selected for debate. The competence of its recommendations to meet the danger of air attack was criticized by Simon and, more forcibly, by Chamberlain. On 15 May, the Air Ministry was asked to prepare a new scheme of expansion, with the significant provision that 'financial limitations need not be taken into account'.[104] The scheme, and with it the whole report, went into the Treasury melting pot. By 21 June, Chamberlain had prepared for the Cabinet Disarmament Committee a plan of his own which drastically altered the balance of the D.R.C. report. Based on the obvious Treasury view of the funds available for rearmament, it took as its points of departure the danger posed by Germany, primarily in the air, and the British public's strong fear of an attack from this quarter. Chamberlain proposed to cut the allocations for the Navy and the Army by about a third and a half respectively, and recommended the provision of 80 fighter squadrons for home defence instead of the 52 which had been asked for by the Air Ministry.[105] It is noteworthy that Fisher consulted Lord Trenchard, Britain's first Chief of the Air Staff, while collaborating with Chamberlain in the preparation of his plan. Fisher shared Trenchard's anxiety about the air danger and their advice seems to have exerted a strong influence on the Chancellor.[106] Chamberlain's political arguments proved to be sound. In the debate of the D.R.C., Simon and Hoare backed the plan and the supporting contentions. They attached particular importance to the public concern about the air peril.

Chamberlain explained that 'to educate the public that war in the Far East constituted a menace as great or even nearly as great as the

---

[102] See Chatfield's letter to the Chief of Imperial General Staff on 10 April 1934, Cab. 21/388.

[103] See minutes in FO 371/18523 W/41531/1/98.

[104] Cab. 16/110.

[105] See details of the plan in D.C. (M) 32 120, Cab. 16/111.

[106] See A. Boyle, *Trenchard* (London 1962), pp. 681-682; on Fisher's activities in preparing the plan, see Cab. 21/902.

Air Defence of this country would be an extremely difficult task, the more so as public opinion was already alive to a considerable extent of our deficiencies in air defence'.[107] Hoare was sure that 'public opinion was deeply concerned over the European situation and the possibility of air attack on Great Britain'. He did not think that 'anything substantially short of the figures proposed by the Chancellor of the Exchequer would satisfy public opinion'.[108] Simon spoke of the menace 'close to our hearts'.[109] Thus although Chamberlain's extreme proposal to abandon the idea of sending the Fleet to Singapore was criticized by Baldwin and MacDonald, and though Eden regarded him as placing undue weight 'on the domestic scene', not one of the politicians seems to have found fault with the main point of his plan: that air expansion for home defence should have priority.

The War Office and the Admiralty representatives on the Cabinet Disarmament Committee rejected the whole scheme. They considered the Chancellor's proposals, based on what they regarded as undue excitement over the air peril, to be mistaken and unbalanced as a defence requirement scheme.[110] In the discussions on rearmament up to the end of June they hammered away at their own points of view. Early in May they presented the Cabinet with their estimates of the strategic use to which Germany intended to put her air force.[111] In June they prevented an Air Ministry paper entitled 'The Potential Menace to this Country from Germany' from being distributed to the Cabinet.[112] It is important to bear in mind that the Chiefs of Staff Committee was under the strong personal influence of Chatfield and that the Chief of the Air Staff had not been able to make his department's views prevail. This was well known to a senior official at the Treasury, who wrote a year later that 'Ellington will not be able to hold his own with his colleagues and air considerations and needs will tend to be watered down or subordinated to the desires and fears of other services'.[113]

[107] 25 June 1934, Cab. 16/110.

[108] *Ibid.*

[109] *Ibid.* On the influence of public opinion see Bond, *Chief of Staff,* p. 49.

[110] See Chief of the Naval Staff's notes in ADM 116/3436, Hodsoll's letter to Hankey, 21 June 1934, Cab. 21/388, and Hankey's letter to Baldwin, 29 June 1934, Cab. 21/434.

[111] 336 C.O.S. Cab. 16/110, Art. No. 7. Their report also presented the conflicting assessment of the Air Ministry.

[112] C.O.S. meetings, 4 May, 27 June 1934, Cab. 53/24.

[113] Bridges's notes in T 172/1830. For the Air Staff's apprehensions about the consequences of too rapid an air expansion which may have been one of their reasons for trying not to over-emphasize the air danger, see, for example, the letter from Charles

The 'other services' criticized both the assumptions of the Air Ministry on the probable nature of German war plans and its calculations respecting the bombload with which Germany might launch an air attack on Britain. Chatfield declared: 'The Chiefs of Staff would be wrong to leave an impression such as given by the press to hold the field without satisfying themselves as to the true position.'[114] Hailsham complained that the War Office had been left as the 'Cinderella of the forces'[115] and Chatfield warned that 'if the Chancellor's views are supported we shall have to come to the parting of the ways as regards imperial defence'.[116]

Nevertheless, the politicians seemed to concur in Baldwin's opinion that the expansion of the Air Force should have priority in action and presentation, and that 'the less that was said about other matters, the better'.[117] The consequent decision, reached on 2 July, to concentrate mainly and above all on the R.A.F. programme was in itself one of the most significant rearmament decisions of the period. The entire air expansion scheme was discussed by a special Cabinet subcommittee which, while slightly altering the Chancellor's suggested allocation of squadrons between home defence and the Far East, still accepted the main idea behind his proposals.[118] The Cabinet's decision provided for the construction of an Air Force for home defence which would consist of 75 squadrons within five years, instead of the 52 which had been suggested by the D.R.C. report. The purpose of the plan was to put as many first-line aircraft as possible on display, to act as a deterrent to any prospective aggressor; it ignored entirely the Air Ministry's demand for adequate reserves for this first line. For as Baldwin put it: 'Any foreign country reading that we proposed to have X squadrons within a certain time would assume that they should be efficient'.[119]

On 18 July the Cabinet Disarmament Committee agreed to make the decision public in the Commons on 30 July. Both the Navy and Army requirements had been subjugated to Chamberlain's plan. Thus

Evans (a senior official at the Air Ministry) to Trenchard, May 1935, Boyle *Trenchard*, pp. 689-690.

[114] 27 June 1934, Cab. 53/4. See also minutes in Air 8/178.

[115] 26 June 1934, Cab. 16/110.

[116] ADM 116/3436, for the services criticism of the way the Disarmament Committee handled defence issues. See Hodsoll's private letter to Brook Popham on 29 October 1934, Brook Popham Papers, London, I/1/5.

[117] 27 June 1934, Cab. 23/79.

[118] See Middlemas and Barnes, *Baldwin,* pp. 772-73.

[119] 6 July 1934, Cab. 21/388.

the Admiralty had to swallow the following:

> Naval construction programme *together* with the deficiencies programme for 1935 should be put forward and considered by the First Sea Lord and the Chancellor of the Exchequer in the *normal* ways. Subsequent programmes should be left undecided pending the results of the forthcoming Naval Conference.[120]

The Army scheme in the D.R.C. report had been cut by half. Significantly, in contrast to the drastic cuts in other aspects of the original Army scheme, the proposals for the completion of the A.D.G.B. plan were largely accepted.[121] The final version of the Defence Requirement Report was agreed to on 31 July 1934.[122] The concluding paragraphs of this report referred in the most explicit terms to the part played by the air anxiety element in the making of the rearmament plans during the first half of 1934:

> On a fresh review of the international outlook we find that, although the situation has fluctuated considerably during our Inquiry, both in the Far East and in Europe, there is no ground for recommending a basic alteration in the general priorities laid down by the Cabinet for the Defence Requirements Committee last November, according to which the expenditures of the Defence Departments are to be governed by the defence of our possessions and interests in the Far East, European commitments and the defence of India. *Our Inquiry, however, has thrown into somewhat higher relief the dangers to this country from air attack by Germany and the importance of the Low Countries from this point of view.* This suggested the desirability of strengthening our air defence with as little delay as possible in order to safeguard the heart of the Empire. *At the same time, the evidence of German intentions to rearm, especially in the air, pointed to the desirability of providing some deterrent to German developments by making it clear that we had no intention of leaving this country so inadequately defended as to invite attack.*
>
> Although currents of more or less uninformed public opinion at home ought never to be a determining factor in defensive preparations, they have to be reckoned with in asking Parliament to approve programmes of expenditure. *In the present case it*

---

[120] Cab. 16/116, italics added.

[121] Compare Arts. 117-121 of the first D.R.C. report and Art. 15 of the Defence Requirement report which had been agreed to in July 1934. See also Hailsham remarks on 17 July in the Cabinet Disarmament Committee, Cab. 16/110; see also M. Postan, *British War Production* (London, 1952), p. 28.

[122] Cab. 24/250.

> *happened that the general trend of public opinion appeared to coincide with our own views as to the desirability of a considerable expansion of the Royal Air Force for home defence. In fact, as already mentioned, the pressure for some statement of the Government's air defence policy before the Parliamentary recess became so strong that we were obliged to anticipate this Report on Imperial Defence as a whole by an interim Report on Air Defence.*[123]

The next stage of the decision-making process on rearmament in Britain, from November 1934 to May 1935, was concerned almost exclusively with the air issue. Committed by Baldwin's undertaking in the House of Commons on 8 March 1934, the Government had to keep abreast of German air rearmament. But this proved to be far more extensive than had been expected, and the revelation created what one official historian termed 'something like panic'.[124]

The Government evinced a notable propensity to go as far as it thought possible in order to meet the air danger. The alacrity with which it did so, despite anxiety concerning the effect of a new rearmament scheme on the forthcoming General Election, contrasted markedly with its reluctance to allocate funds to repair the deficiencies of the Army and Navy and to finance their construction plans. In fact, twice during these seven months, the Government decided to accelerate the expansion of the R.A.F.

The story of the 'air panic' of November 1934-May 1935 has often been told and need not therefore be dealt with in great detail here.[125] But note must be made of some patterns of assessments and decisions during this period which resemble those prevalent in 1934. Both in 1934 and in the following year, the Foreign Office played the role of Cassandra, while the Services tended to present more soothing appraisals of the danger, and the deficiencies which had to be remedied in order to tackle it. Upon weighing the military, financial and internal political considerations involved in an estimate and decision on defence expenditure, the politicians adopted a position somewhere in the centre. They took a more serious view than did the Services, but a less apprehensive approach than did the Foreign

[123] D.R. Report, Arts. 49-50, Cab. 24/250. Italics added.

[124] Sir Charles Webster and Noble Frankland, *The Strategic Air Offensive Against Germany, 1939-1945*, Vol. 1 (London, 1961), p. 69.

[125] On this see, *inter alia*, H. Montgomery Hyde, *British Air Policy Between the Wars 1918-1939* (London, 1976), pp. 326-48: F. Northedge, *The Troubled Giant* (London, 1966), pp. 387-88, and two letters from Londonderry to Baldwin, on 18 May 1936, and on 29 December 1938. Baldwin Papers, Vol. 164, pp. 192-3, Vol. 185, p. 192.

Office. Accordingly, the actual programmes decided upon were in excess of what the Services considered necessary, and beneath the level considered adequate by the Foreign Office. The important difference in circumstances in the two years is, of course, undeniable and will be discussed later, but the resemblances are still remarkable.

In November 1934 the reports on German rearmament became so alarming that the Cabinet decided to appoint a special sub-committee to deal with the required British reaction. From Air Ministry reports this committee learned that for the second stage of her air rearmament, which was to be completed by 1 October 1936, Germany aimed at 1,296 first line aircraft with 100 per cent reserves — instead of the anticipated 1,008 by 1939.[126] This figure was slightly in excess of the first line strength of France's metropolitan air force as well as of Britain's. Although the extent to which Germany could enlarge her aeroplane production was not yet appreciated, the Air Ministry information sounded a loud warning. Despite Chamberlain's contention that there was nothing in that information to justify an acceleration of the R.A.F. programme, it clearly indicated that provided she completed the second stage as planned, by the end of 1936 Germany would obtain slight superiority. These secret reports came at a time when the Government in any case faced mounting attacks in Parliament over the alleged inadequacy of Britain's air defence, which reminded MacDonald of the public hysteria two decades earlier: 'The situation with the air is getting very much what it was with the naval arm before the war'.[128] Samuel Hoare warned Baldwin that unless a frank and careful statement were made about the German air menace 'that is stirring up grave anxiety in the minds of most of our supporters . . . the party would go off the road at a very critical moment in the opening of the session'.[129] The Cabinet therefore decided to accelerate the R.A.F.'s programme to the extent that 32 of the squadrons provided for in the July 1934 plan would be built in two years instead of four.[130]

Addressing the Commons on 28 November, Baldwin stressed the

[126] Air Intelligence Report, 21 November 1934, Air 8/174. See an analysis of this issue in R. Wernham, *The Royal Air Force in Bombing Offensive Against Germany, Prewar Evolution of Bomber Command 1917-1939* (Ministry of Defence, Air Historical Branch, London, 1947), p. 87.

[127] 24 November 1934, Cab. 23/80.

[128] From a private letter to Sir Raymond Beazley, 26 October 1934, MacDonald Papers 2/8.

[129] 19 November 1934, Baldwin Papers, Vol. 1.

[130] Cab. 23/80. On the Influence of Parliamentary pressure, especially Churchill's, see Bond, *Chief of Staff,* p. 54; FO 800/289, p. 397; and Cab. 27/572.

belief that the danger of air attack from Germany could be contained without difficulty:

> Germany can produce the aircraft rapidly if she wants, but a country which has for years possessed no military air force, starts with a very heavy handicap, it would be a considerable time before their efficiency could equal our own. . . . His Majesty's Government is determined on no condition to accept any position of inferiority with regard to what air force may be raised in Germany in the future.[131]

The next stage of decision-making on rearmament stemmed directly from Hitler's boast, made in March 1935, that Germany had already reached air parity with the British and was aiming at reaching parity with the French too.[132] In initiating this stage of the decision-making process, the Foreign Office played a prominent part. The reports which Christie sent to Vansittart from the end of 1934 were alarming. He felt that 'there was a rush to rearm in the air . . . and if Goering could have things his own way Germany would possess 800 heavy bombers'.[133] In fact, as far as 1935 was concerned, Christie's figures were too high; but, not surprisingly, the Foreign Office considered them confirmed by Hitler's declaration. The Department's deepening anxiety was reflected in certain actions which it took independently in order to secure a speedy and adequate reaction by the Cabinet. Without Simon's approval, Vansittart gave Rex Leeper, of the Office's Press Department, permission to leak Hitler's assertion, and the story broke in the *Daily Mail* on 29 March.[134] On 6 April, Vansittart wrote to Simon urging him to take immediate action:

> These figures [German aircraft production and her first line strength] should be known to every member of His Majesty's Government. I beg the Secretary of State to ensure that they are thus known. The number of Service aircraft in Germany is already greater than the number in the United Kingdom.[135]

The Permanent Under-Secretary's concern communicated itself to his Minister, who passed on the figures to MacDonald a few days later with the comment:

> The conclusion that might have to be drawn from the above figures, if they are correct, is that this country is seriously open to

---

[131] Middlemas and Barnes, *Baldwin*, p. 788.

[132] His contention that Germany already possessed a first line force of 2,100 aeroplanes was far from the truth. Eden, *Facing the Dictators*, p. 185.

[133] Conwell-Evans, *None So Blind*, p. 32.

[134] J. Colvin, *Vansittart in Office* (London, 1965), p. 47.

[135] Vansittart Papers, Cambridge, 2/29.

the threat of sudden attack by a Continental power in a degree
which it has not been exposed to for hundreds of years.[136]

On Sunday 7 April Ralph Wigram, the head of the Central Department, paid a secret visit to Churchill. He told him of the great apprehension in the Office, and of the increasing disparity between the facts as known there and as given currency by the Government. This information considerably enriched the ammunition available to Churchill when he attacked the Government towards the end of April.[137]

When Vansittart and Wigram met Charles Medhurst, the Deputy Director of Air Intelligence at the Stresa Conference, they discovered that he took as serious a view of German air rearmament as they did, and that his assessment had not yet been fully accepted by the Air Ministry.[138] As a result, Wigram and Medhurst presented a joint memorandum to MacDonald on 14 April, putting forward their estimates. It put the Foreign Office's specific apprehension in unequivocal terms:

> The Germans must have a very clear impression of present conditions in the British and French Air Forces; and it is not clear that under existing conditions we have during the next year complete security against some wild 'coup de main' by men whose previous acts have shown the nature of their resolution and audacity. In any case, in twelve to eighteen months' time, a greatly increased British Air Force will have to become a vital necessity if we are still to be in a position to pursue an independent foreign policy.[139]

The Air Ministry was apparently fully informed of the Foreign Office's manoeuvre. Possessing its own information and estimates on Germany's most recent secret measures to expand her air force,[140] the Ministry presented to the Cabinet on 15 April its considered views as to the danger and the actions necessary in order to meet it.[141] In his memorandum, Londonderry recalled the figures provided by the Air Ministry in 1934 and justified those forecasts: in numbers, organi-

[136] Air 8/196.

[137] Gilbert, *Churchill,* p. 639.

[138] See Bond, *Chief of Staff,* p. 71. Sir Michael Creswell who, with Wigram and Vansittart, had been the 'air experts' of the Foreign Office, confirmed this in an interview with the writer on 2 October 1973.

[139] FO 371/18836, C 3248/55/18.

[140] On the actual measures taken by Germany at this time, see G.L. Weinberg, *The Foreign Policy of Hitler's Germany,* (Chicago, 1970), p. 205.

[141] C.P. 85(35).

zation and training, Britain was ahead of Germany and would remain so for up to two years. Only the state of the reserves provided cause for disquiet. 'But the future as opposed to the present must cause grave concern . . . there is reason to believe that the organization of the aircraft industry for war purposes in Germany is in advance of that in this country'.[142] The Air Ministry's conclusion was that, to fulfil Baldwin's pledge of air parity, the R.A.F. had to expand gradually to 1,500 first line aircraft by 1940: it did not think that there was a serious possibility that Germany would be ready for an all-out war before 1942.

The Foreign Office did not consider that the Air Ministry memorandum reflected the true state of affairs. Particular criticism was levelled at its two main hypotheses: that Germany would still limit herself to a first-line strength of 1,512 after 1937, and that the danger of air attack could not possibly materialize before 1940, let alone before 1937.[143] When the whole question was put to the Cabinet Disarmament Committee on 30 April 1935, the Committee did not consider the Air Ministry plan for cautious expansion to be adequate. The Foreign Office memorandum clearly influenced the doubts which were cast on the Air Ministry estimates and Londonderry later complained in a private letter to Simon that 'Vansittart's memo had the unfortunate effect of scaring our colleagues'.[144] What worried the Disarmament Committee was not only the military implications of inferiority in the air, but also the increasing criticism in Parliament. These points were made trenchantly by Baldwin at a meeting of the Committee on 30 April:

> In the old days an Englishman thought chiefly about the Navy, and was principally concerned with the question of two keels to one. All the public really cared about was how big our naval margin was over Germany and nothing could cause a panic more quickly than the idea that our naval superiority was in jeopardy. It was as easy to work up a panic today in regard to the Air position and particularly if it was thought that we were inferior. . . . There was no doubt that there was a feeling of uneasiness in the House and in the country on these points. The sooner therefore the statements were made, the better, and the more clearly they were made, the less likelihood of difficulties for the Government.[145]

[142]*Ibid.*
[143]D.C. (M) (32)139.
[144]7 May 1935, FO 800/290, p. 19.
[145]30 April 1935, Cab. 27/508.

Baldwin did not delay in following his own advice. Two days later, on 2 May, he made a firm declaration of adherence to the air parity policy in the Commons, and appointed a special committee to discuss how best to implement the programme.

On 22 May the Cabinet adopted the sub-committee's report, which recommended speeding up the expansion of the R.A.F. to an extent far in excess of that considered necessary by the Chiefs of Staff and at a pace faster than that considered advisable by the Air Ministry.[146] The committee's finding was that Britain's first-line air force of 270 aircraft was inferior to Germany's but that it had more and better trained pilots and greater reserves. Its members agreed with the Air Ministry's estimate that Germany would possess 1,512 first-line aeroplanes by 1937, but proposed that Britain achieve parity by that date, and not by 1940.[147] The conclusion of the sub-committee, that it was essential to do as much as possible as soon as possible, was crystal clear. The Cabinet accordingly decided to make some substantial and very significant changes in the process of aircraft production;[148] the Treasury, which traditionally opposed any large expenditure on defence, appears to have accepted the cost which the programme involved (£30,000,000) without demur.[149] At the time, complementary measures to accelerate the A.D.G.B. plan were not discussed; a large air force was considered to be the best insurance against a possible air attack. In Chamberlain's words: 'Air defence measures for the protection of England did not have the same kind of deterrent effect as the possession of a strong striking force'.[150]

Despite the magnitude of the proposed programme, it was considered inadequate by both the Foreign Office and, for different reasons, the Admiralty and the War Office. To the Services, it represented a substantial alteration in the balanced D.R.C. report; they were particularly troubled by the effect of such an expensive plan

---

[146] See C.O.S. Report, D.C.(M) (32)137.

[147] For details of the report, see Cab. 27/518.

[148] M. Postan and J. Scott, *The Design and Development of Weapons* (London, 1964), pp. 142-143. On British aircraft industry and its problems during this period, see P. Fearon, 'The British Airplane Industry and the State 1918-1935', *Economic History Review* 37 (1974), 236-52; and R. Higham, 'Government, Companies and National Defence, British Aeronautical Experience 1918-1945 as the Basis for a Broad Hypothesis', *Business History Review* 39 (1965), 323-47.

[149] See some minutes by such prominent Treasury officials as Barlow, Bridges, Hopkins and Fisher on the air peril and the urgent need to secure an adequate air force to tackle it in T 172/1830.

[150] Cab. 27/508. See also reference to this point in the Defence (Policy) Requirements Committee on 8 July 1935, Cab. 16/136.

on their prospects of securing funds for their own deficiencies.[151] The Foreign Office, for its part, was haunted by the time factor: what if, as it feared, Germany would be ready to attack before 1937?[152] The alleged inadequacy of Britain's passive air defences was especially criticized.[153] But the Cabinet persisted in its decision, for, in the words of Lord Halifax, 'we should have to satisfy ourselves by tempering what was strategically desirable with limitations of finance and of political possibilities'.[154] Not until early in 1936 did the Cabinet find it necessary to discuss a new, comprehensive defence requirement scheme. The decision of May 1935 may therefore be regarded as the final stage in the first phase of British rearmament.

As has been seen, the debate within the British Government on the pace of German air rearmament, which started during this period and continued up to the outbreak of the Second World War, did not stem exclusively from an acute sensitivity to the danger of aerial bombardment. It was also caused by contradictory assessments of German air power. This much is illustrated by the following anecdote: On one occasion during this period three emissaries of a German resistance group met with a like number of British agents in London, but were disappointed to find that they could elicit little response to their efforts to tell of their aims and plans. Instead, they were persistently interrupted with questions on matters of which they knew very little. So much was this so that one of the Germans finally lost patience. Replying off the top of his head to a query about the size of the Luftwaffe, he gave what seemed to him a patently absurd figure: 'About 20,000 planes'. 'Aha!' exclaimed one of the Englishmen excitedly, 'We have been told that, but we wouldn't believe it'.[155]

A major issue between the Foreign Office — together with Winston Churchill — on the one hand, and the Air Staff on the other during this period, was the supposed strength of the Royal Air Force relative to the Luftwaffe, especially in bombers. It would therefore be of considerable interest to know the actual size of the German Air Force in these years. Recent research has suggested that the varying definitions of what constituted 'first line aircraft', made it extraordinarily difficult to be sure that like was being compared with like.

[151] See discussion in the Cabinet Disarmament Committee on 27 May 1935, Cab. 27/508.

[152] FO 371/18841, C/4104/55/18.

[153] FO 371/18842, C/4174/55/18.

[154] 27 May 1935, Cab. 27/508.

[155] H. Deutsch, *The Conspiracy Against Hitler in the Twilight War* (Minneapolis 1968), pp. 103-104.

However, the suggested conclusion is that the Foreign Office's figures were unrealistically high and must have included converted civil aircraft.[156] However, even more important subjects of contemporary debate were the potential air strength of the two air forces, the provision of reserves and the peace-to-war factory transfer capacity. On each of these points as Gilbert has demonstrated[157] there is a great deal of evidence to show that the Foreign Office were far closer to reality than was the Air Ministry.

As has been shown, it was the problem of the air danger that was paramount in all the discussions on defence in the years 1934-5. In retrospect, the reasons are perhaps not hard to seek. As British defences stood in 1934-5, naval superiority in the Mediterranean appeared to be unchallenged. Before the Abyssinian crisis of late 1935, the possibility of a war in which the Navy would have to fight in two theatres seemed remote. The danger of a war in the Far East was serious, but the prospective naval disarmament conversations still left some hope of an agreement with the U.S.A. and Japan. The danger of air attack, remote as it might be, had to receive attention because of the vulnerability of the heart of the Empire. As a member of the Foreign Office explained it: 'In the air the matter is urgent for here alone we cannot be isolated however isolationist we feel.[158] This, however, still leaves the *extent* of the emphasis on air rearmament largely unexplained. What this chapter has tried to clarify is some of the less 'objective' aspects of the phenomenon by shedding new light on the part played by the fear of an aerial knock-out blow — a fear not confined to the general public, but shared by many politicians and some of the nation's most influential professional advisers.

---

[156] S. Roskill, *Hankey: Man of Secrets,* pp. 234, 263, 664-5.

[157] See *Winston Churchill,* vols. V and VI (Forthcoming).

[158] Allen Leeper notes, 29 November 1933. FO 311/17373 W/13571/40/98.

# 3
## SECURITY BY CONVENTION: (1934-1936)

> If one considers the subjects of security and the dangers to peace, it is quite clear that there has arisen during recent years a new and special danger which is due to the possibility of the misuse of modern developments in the air. Armies have to be mobilized, and however swiftly armies may act, they cannot strike a mortal blow in a very short time. Navies have to be concentrated and move under [certain] conditions, and what they are doing or are likely to do can hardly be kept secret. But this new invention of movement in the air with its latest development of machines and vast range tremendous speed, high power and possibility of rapid and secret manoeuvre, this new development undoubtedly fills many people with a new foreboding of a danger which might conceivably threaten town and country alike.
> (Sir John Simon, The Foreign Secretary In a broadcast, February 1935.)

Following Germany's departure from the Disarmament Conference in October 1933 the British Government reluctantly decided to start rearming on a very moderate scale, limiting its attention almost entirely to the R.A.F. The failure to secure an air disarmament convention at Geneva did not, however, put an end to the search for such an agreement. On the contrary, various additional factors now intruded, which made the attainment of air disarmament seem all the more vital to the British Government. First there was the increase in German air power which, as has already been seen, as early as 1935 appeared to have substantially destroyed the air-power status quo in Europe; second was the gradual realization, following the decisions on rearmament, that Britain might find herself involved in a European war and be liable to air attack from Germany; and third there were the obstacles to all-out British air rearmament. Principle among the latter were the Treasury's reluctance to spend large sums and abrogate the 'business-as-usual' dictum, as well as the technical difficulties involved in expanding fast enough to keep pace with German air expansion.[1]

Though little has been written on this subject, the problem of securing an international agreement that would minimize the danger

---

[1] On German air rearmament in this period see J.R. Overy, 'The German Pre-War Aircraft Production Plans: November 1936 — April 1939', *English Historical Review* 90 (1975), 778-97.

of aerial bombardment preoccupied the British Government throughout the period between 1934 and 1939 and constituted an important issue in its foreign policy. In discussions within the Government following the breakdown of the Disarmament Conference in 1934, and in those that accompanied the three major British efforts to reach a general agreement with Germany — in 1934, 1936 and 1938 — an international air-disarmament agreement constantly emerged as a distinct British aim.

This chapter is concerned with the various British plans for such an agreement during the period 1934-6 and with the fundamental reasons for the successive failure of each of them.

The first phase of the search for an agreement consisted mainly of British efforts to salvage something from the wreckage of the abortive Disarmament Conference. The hope that it might be possible to attain a substantial and all-embracing agreement at Geneva had faded once the Germans walked out;[2] nevertheless, early in 1934 some Ministers continued to believe that the discussions might produce a degree of security from air attack, and were worth pursuing for that reason. Thus in March Baldwin declared in the Commons that should the Disarmanent Conference fail to bring about general agreement, Britain intended to continue to work for an air pact. In this view, even the original objectives still held good. Thus, the various plans for securing an air agreement still stressed the principles of qualitative and quantitative disarmament as fundamental elements. Moreover, both the limitation of air forces and the prohibition of aerial bombardment were repeatedly advocated as the desired bases of an agreement. As far as the British were concerned, the only immediate change caused by the German departure from Geneva was one of scope; rather than seek a global agreement they seem to have become interested in a less ambitious and simpler regional European accord.[3]

In January 1934, the British Government made what it regarded as a last effort to save the Geneva Conference by presenting the antagonists, France and Germany, with a comprehensive disarmament scheme. This still adhered to the principles of the MacDonald plan,[4] but did move slightly in the direction of satisfying the German demand

---

[2]On Germany's change of policy towards the Disarmament Conference, see G. Weinberg, *The Foreign Policy of Hitler's Germany, Diplomatic Revolution in Europe 1933-1936* (Chicago, 1970), pp. 31-52.

[3]On the various proposals see Air 8/201, D.C. (M) (32) 79 and C.P. 255 (33).

[4]The Plan for a disarmament convention, which the British Prime Minister put before the Disarmament Conference on 16 March 1933; see FO 371/17353, W/2883/40/98. See above p. 37.

for *Gleichberechtigung* in matters of air disarmament by cutting down by one half the period during which Germany would not be allowed to possess military aircraft. For that reason there was not much hope that it would prove acceptable to the French.[5] As noted earlier, what turned the whole scheme, and with it the air-disarmament plan, into another historical "might have been" was France's final refusal, in April 1934, to accept any convention that legalized German rearmament.

Meanwhile, and with a view to satisfying Britain's demand for air security by some other means, various efforts were made to attain a different form of international convention. The first proposal in this direction emanated from the Foreign Office early in May 1934, and owed much to Simon's personal eagerness to minimize the country's vulnerability to air attack. Unlike earlier British plans this proposal made no provision for the limitation of air armaments; it aimed only at reducing the chances of aerial bombardment.

The Foreign Office paper described it as a 'positive regional agreement' whereby,

> the States of Europe in respect of territories in Europe would enter into a solemn undertaking not to drop bombs on another person's territory in Europe, either in peace or war, and further, to agree that *if this undertaking was violated, they would all use the whole of their airforces to insist on the due observance of this promise and to punish anyone who required it.*[6]

The new plan, which attracted a great deal of attention in a revised form nine months later, was based on the presumed deterrent effect of the threat of retaliation. It suggested that the fear of collective retaliatory aerial bombardment by its continental neighbours would effectively dissuade any single European country from resorting to unprovoked air attack. The apparent guarantee implied in the plan was superficially attractive, but had to be weighed against two decisive, and insurmountable, criticisms. The first was the traditional objection to any further enlargement of the Locarno military commitment, and especially to what might be regarded as an unrestricted British commitment. The other was that its implementation might delay air rearmament, which by this time was considered to be of prime importance. Understandably, therefore, the Cabinet Disarmament Committee decided not to pursue any further proposals along these lines at this stage.[7] Throughout the remainder of the year the

---

[5] See details of the whole plan in Cab. 24/247.
[6] 8 May 1934, Cab. 23/79 and Cab. 27/507. Italics added.
[7] 17 May, 1934, Cab. 16/110.

Foreign Office therefore made no further effort to secure a regional prohibition of bombing. It appeared impossible to attain that end by agreement —whether it be unilateral in form, or part of a modified convention that would also provide for a numerical limitation of regional air forces, or even for mutual assistance against any state resorting to aerial aggression. The Cabinet was still committed to the cause of general disarmament and continued to foster particular hopes for an air-disarmament agreement;[8] but nothing could be achieved as long as the deadlock on general disarmament remained.

The next stage in the search occurred late in 1934, when the Government initiated steps designed to resolve the deadlock and secure a general disarmament agreement acceptable to both France and Germany. Alarming intelligence reports on intensive German rearmament indicated that Germany would possess as large an air force as Great Britain within a year;[9] late in November the Cabinet decided to make this secret rearmament known to the public.[10] In this manner there emerged a basic theme which pervaded all British discussions on the problem of German rearmament throughout the early and middle 1930s. Britain could not modify German demands by persuasion, neither could she resist them without running the dangerous risk of possible military involvement (sometimes for causes remote from her own primary and direct interests). In the last resort, therefore, she had to try and legitimize them by a negotiated agreement in order to prevent the creation of a dangerous *fait accompli*. Thus, addressing the Commons on 28 November, Baldwin, whilst condemning the level of German rearmament nevertheless accepted its existence as an accomplished fact. In so doing, the Lord President opened the way for negotiations in which the legalization of Germany's rearmament at a reasonable level by the Powers would be balanced by various gestures and guarantees on her part.

As it was taken as axiomatic that Britain and France should co-ordinate their efforts, the next step was to hammer out a joint Anglo-French programme. These negotiations resulted, *inter alia,* in the adoption by the British Government of a French proposal for an anti-bombing agreement known as the air pact. The circumstances in which the decision was reached to commit Britain to the search for such a pact are of particular importance to an understanding of the

---

[8] See Simon's remarks in the Cabinet Disarmament Committee of 17 July, 1934. Cab. 16/110, and Baldwin's of 24 July, 1934, Cab. 16/110.

[9] See Premier 1/155.

[10] Cab. 21/398.

apparent reversal of the decision which the Cabinet took in May 1934 not to pursue a similar plan.

The early history of the air pact was marked by the primary role of the Foreign Office as a fervent advocate of the idea. In part the Department considered this to be an important means of facilitating French cooperation in negotiations with Germany; no less important, in its view, was the substantial contribution which such a pact might make to British security. One constant theme of the discussions within the Foreign Office at the time was the implication of the inadequacy of Britain's air defence, and of her inferiority in air power, for the pursual of a firm foreign policy. The preoccupation with the danger of air attack thus gave expression to Britain's acute awareness of the political significance of this weapon, as well as its military value. This may explain why the Office was so eager to conclude an international disarmament agreement, and with Germany in particular, while there still remained a chance of doing so. As Vansittart told Crozier of the *Manchester Guardian* early in January 1935; 'The sands are running out fast. If we do not get a convention within the next six months, I doubt whether we shall get one at all'.[11] In its efforts to secure Cabinet support for the proposed air pact, the Foreign Office succeeded in out-manoeuvring the opposition of the Services. It also provoked the fierce criticism of some prominent civil servants because of the way it handled the matter; the Foreign Office, they claimed, had taken action on the air pact before the French had formally put the idea forward.[12]

As far as the Government was concerned, the first mention of anything in the nature of an aerial-bombardment pact was contained in a memorandum by Oliver Harvey, First Secretary at the British Embassy in Paris, written (not in Paris but in the Foreign Office) on 25 January 1935.[13] It described conversations between Ronald Campbell, Minister at the Embassy, and Pierre Flandin, the French Prime Minister, and Rene Massigli, of the Quai d'Orsay. During the course of a dinner party and in a more formal subsequent interview, Flandin had hinted that in return for her agreement to drop Clause V of the Treaty of Versailles (i.e. the disarmament of Germany), France would have to demand some understanding with Britain that would provide for rapid aid were she attacked. Massigli had specifically hinted at an aerial bombardment convention.

The memorandum was sent to the Chiefs of Staff and the

[11] A.J.P. Taylor (ed.), *Off the Record, Political Interviews* (London, 1973), p. 30.
[12] See Cab. 21/413.
[13] This account is based on Cab. 21/413.

Committee of Imperial Defence on 28 January, but does not seem to have aroused any particular interest. Hankey, the secretary of the C.I.D., described it as 'the sort of "kites" that were flown before international conferences'. The conversations had been private, and M. Flandin had been expressing his personal views.[14] Talks about the basis for continuing the Anglo-French conversations proceeded without any official mention of the air pact. The Foreign Office provided no information which might have suggested that the memorandum was likely to lead to material proposals, and the subject was not mentioned at the Cabinet meeting on 30 January, even though the Anglo-French conversations were on the agenda.

Nevertheless, the Foreign Office itself would appear to have taken the matter more seriously. A minute written on 28 January, (and later sent to the Prime Minister) strongly recommended acceptance of the proposal for an air pact were the French to put it forward in future discussions. Hitherto, the Foreign Office seems to have been worried by the fact that, in negotiating with the French, Britain had almost nothing to offer them in terms of security which might make their attitude towards the legalization of German rearmament more flexible. Thus, before a decision to recommend acceptance of the fact was taken, Vansittart had written in despair: 'I would agree that the position could be changed if we could make any "security" offer, but what are the chances of that?'[15] Understandably, therefore, the Office regarded acceptance of Flandin's proposal as the proper method to secure French compliance, as well as to further British defence interests. Ralph Wigram referred to this latter point in minuting Oliver Harvey's report:

> Public opinion in this country is well aware of the dangers inherent in German air rearmament; and it is entitled to expect, when the discussions respecting armaments are resumed, that in the final settlement reached, and whilst so many countries are claiming fresh contributions to their security, some contribution will be made to the security of the United Kingdom.
>
> In these circumstances, it is for consideration whether, should the French Ministers raise this question in the forthcoming discussions, the British negotiators should encourage the conclusion of some Air Convention, under which the United Kingdom, Belgium, France and Germany should mutually guarantee one another against attack from the air; and should

---

[14] Cab. 21/413. See also S. Roskill, *Hankey, Man of Secrets,* (Vol. III (London, 1974), pp. 155-164.

[15] FO 371/18825, C 962/55/18.

undertake that if one of their number should be so attacked, the other parties to the agreement should immediately retaliate against the aggressor. Such an agreement would have very considerable advantages for this country, in that whilst not involving for us commitments going beyond those which we have accepted in respect of France and Belgium under the Treaty of Locarno, *it would contain a written provision securing for us the assistance of the French air force in the event of a German attack on the United Kingdom.*[16]

The Foreign Office memorandum was referred to Simon by Vansittart with the following comment: 'We are unanimous in hoping that you and your colleagues will approve its findings'.[17] The Foreign Secretary replied that he agreed with the scheme and 'indeed have for some time been thinking along these lines[18].' He presented the views of the Office to the Prime Minister a day *before* the actual discussions with the French began. On 1 February, the first day of consultations, the French put forward the expected proposal. The vagueness of the terms in which they did so led Hankey, who had not been aware of what had been going on within the Foreign Office, to believe that this was another instance of the pointless and 'usual French bluff[19]', but Simon and MacDonald thought differently.

At the first possible moment after the French proposal had been presented, an informal Cabinet meeting was held at the Foreign Office in order to determine Britain's reaction as quickly as possible. Simon put forward the view that acceptance of the proposal would make it easier for the French to agree to the abrogation of Clause V of the Treaty of Versailles, as part of a general settlement. Besides, in his view, the pact was also inherently sound; it constituted a new and substantial contribution to the efforts to counter the danger of air attack, and thus to British defence. As Simon subsequently emphasized to the King in a private letter:'The proposal would mean that this country for the first time gets the assurance of the immediate help of the French air force if Germany ever attempted to deliver a sudden air attack.'[20] Underlying his recommendation was the claim that, since it was impossible to abolish aerial bombardment altogether, the next best thing would be to create a situation wherein it would not 'pay' for a nation to employ air weaponry as a means of initial aggression. The

[16]See FO 371/18823, C 705/55/18. Italics added.
[17]FO 371/18826, C 1190/55/18.
[18]*Ibid.*
[19]Cab. 21/413.
[20]4 February 1935, FO 800/290.

Office was clearly of the opinion that the advantages of the pact greatly outweighed its disadvantages. In the words of its memorandum:

> While the French commitment to us is plain and new, our obligations under the agreement really are in their nature the same obligations that have already been accepted under Locarno. The difference is that in the event of non-provoked aggression by air on France by Germany, we should be bound to intervene with our air force immediately.[21]

The Chiefs of Staff, who once again opposed anything which might be considered to broaden Britain's military commitment abroad, were caught off guard; unlike the Foreign Office they were not ready to present their case in a well-argued memorandum. The arguments put forward by the Office accordingly decided the issue. Hankey, who vehemently opposed the pact, confided his own feelings (and apparently the Chiefs of Staff's too) to his diary: 'In 24 hours . . . without any proper examination of the proposal, without waiting for the report of the Chiefs of Staff Committee, without giving me an opportunity to be heard the Cabinet . . . has virtually pledged us to the most serious military commitment that we have entered into for centuries, if at all.'[22] Admittedly, the Cabinet did resolve on 2 February to reject the French proposal for the *immediate* announcement of an Anglo-French pact to which the other Locarno powers might subsequently adhere. Nevertheless the Ministers accepted a formula that clearly committed the Government to the search for an air pact that would include France, Germany, Belgium, Italy and Great Britain. They thus reversed the decision of the previous May. The new decision was made public on 3 February, as part of a four-point plan known as the London communiqué.[23] This was accorded a warm reception by many politicians and most of the press, and was considered to be a substantial step towards countering the air peril.[24]

The immediate result was a change in British air disarmament plans. Hitherto, the Government had considered an air limitation agreement to be the only practical way to minimize the danger of air attack within the framework of an international convention. Now, however, attention was also focused on the search for a guarantee

---

[21] C.P. 34(35); and FO 371/18824, C 892/55/18.

[22] Roskill, *Hankey Man of Secrets,* p. 158.

[23] For the formula agreed upon, see FO 371/18824, C 892/55/18.

[24] Kingsley Martin, 'The Air Pact and the British Press', *Political Quarterly* 66, 2(1935), 269-76.

against aerial bombardment. It proved at least as difficult to promote such a pact as it had done to secure the proposed air disarmament agreement of 1932; and ultimately, the result was no different. Several obstacles had to be overcome before agreement could be reached. The Cabinet had to define the exact British interest in any international air agreement yet to be achieved, as well as to discuss once again the whole issue of the anti-bombing pact.[25] When the Cabinet accepted the French proposal for an anti-bombing pact, no clear decision had been reached on its connection with an air limitation agreement as far as British interests were concerned. On 19 February, the Cabinet Disarmament Committee accepted Chamberlain's contention that Britain should strive to secure the anti-bombing pact but ought not to agree to sign it until a convention regulating the size of air forces had been secured. This meant, in effect, that in terms of British policy, it was apparent, even before the revelation of German air rearmament in March-April 1935, that an air limitation agreement was of greater importance than the anti-bombing pact.[26] This position was adhered to until June 1935, when it became clear that Germany had no intention of signing any air limitation agreement whatsoever.

By determining general British policy towards air disarmament, the Cabinet committee did not, however, end the debate on the anti-bombing pact. The Government had to reconsider the proposal, since it was not until late in February, following three meetings of the Chiefs of Staff Committee, that the Services were ready to present the C.I.D. with their views on the advisability of working for such a pact. On the 25th the anti-bombing pact was placed on the agenda of the C.I.D. The Committee did not accept the Services' objections.[27] and confirmed the Cabinet decision on the matter. Cunliffe-Lister, the Colonial Secretary, summed up the dominant opinion when advising that the French proposal should be adhered to, because 'we shall get assistance for the first time under these proposals[28].' At this meeting, the C.I.D. discussed a suggestion by the War Office and the Admiralty that a third element be added to the proposed agreement. The idea was to connect the anti-bombing pact and air limitation agreement with a convention establishing the illegality of the act of

---

[25] In order to prevent unnecessary confusion, the term "anti-bombing pact" will hereafter be used to designate the air pact.

[26] Cab. 27/508.

[27] 268 C.I.D. Air 8/201.

[28] *Ibid.* See also, on these discussions, B. Bond (ed.), *Chief of Staff, The Diaries of Lieutenant-General Sir Henry Pownall* (London, 1972), p. 63.

unrestricted bombing in time of war. As Lord Hailsham, the Secretary of State for War, explained:

> The bombing of London was a real danger which would have the most tremendous moral effect, and was a danger against which it was most necessary to safeguard. The position might be extremely difficult, and perhaps even foolish, unless in this first Air Pact, it was stated plainly that, in the view of the five great Powers concerned, this form of warfare should be outlawed.'[29]

However, as matters stood, the prospect of securing an air limitation agreement and an anti-bombing pact was itself dim enough. Therefore, while recommending that an attempt be made to include in the proposed agreement a prohibition of indiscriminate urban bombing, the C.I.D. declined to make this a *sine qua non*.[30]

The international complications proved to be even more difficult. The Anglo-French communiqué of 3 February, which defined the bases of the prospective negotiations with the Germans, stressed the principle of the simultaneity and indivisibility of all the elements of an agreement. The French did admit that their rigidly negative attitude towards German rearmament could no longer be maintained, but they were prepared to agree to its legalization only on stringent terms: Germany should rejoin the League of Nations; accept the anti-bombing pact and two regional security arrangements in the Eastern[31] and Danubian[32] pacts; and could only rearm to a level which was compatible with French demands. Negotiations could proceed, but nothing could be concluded until agreement was reached on all issues. The Germans had not yet given any clear indication that they might reject the entire arms limitation proposal (even though they had, in January, already secretly reconfirmed their decision to reject any agreement which might limit the level of their rearmament).[33] Neither did the French expressly indicate their opposition to independent Anglo-German *naval* negotiations — an issue noticeably absent from Anglo-French discussions in January-February 1935.[34] Mean-

[29] 268 C.I.D. Air 8/201.

[30] *Ibid*.

[31] On this, see R.E. Radice, 'Negotiations for an Eastern Security Pact, 1933-1936' (Ph.D. thesis, University of London, 1973); W.E. Scott, *Alliance Against Hitler, The Origins of the Franco-Soviet Pact* (Durham, 1962).

[32] On this, see Sz. Ormos, 'Sur les causes de l'echec du pacte danubien (1934-5)', *Acta Historica* (Budapest), 14 1-2 (1968), 21-81.

[33] See Von Neurath's memorandum of 19 January, in Weinberg, *The Foreign Policy of Hitler's Germany*, p. 204.

[34] This fact led the Foreign Office to assume that France had tacitly agreed to such negotiations and the French were informed about intention to enter into discussions on

while, the Foreign Office, in any case, harboured hopes that Hitler might agree to an air arrangement as the price for the legalization of German rearmament.[35] However, the complications introduced by France's insistence on simultaneity were hardly conducive to much optimism in Britain, especially as the Germans were known to have opposed the French plan for the Eastern pact, which had originally been a Russian demand. This in itself made the achievement of a general air settlement most difficult.[36]

In an effort to find a way out of this difficulty, the Foreign Office considered a suggestion that Britain acknowledge a distinction between two separate levels of air arrangement. Basically its idea was to disentangle the negotiations on the proposed anti-bombing pact and the air limitation agreement from the discussions on the other elements of the proposed general settlement. In its view, there were two main arguments for concluding an air agreement with Germany before, and independently of, the proposed general settlement. First, if achieved, it would substantially reduce the German air danger. Second, since the likelihood of securing the general settlement was so small, there was much to be said in favour of striving for a limited separate agreement which the Foreign Office believed would not be strongly opposed in Berlin. The case was put in a Foreign Office memorandum dated 14 February:

> The chances of a "general settlement" are not bright in view of such snags as, for instance, the Eastern Pact. Moreover, Germany is not likely to be willing at this late date to pay much for the legalization of her air force. In these circumstances, if we make the air agreement dependent on the "general settlement" we risk losing it altogether. But assuming the air agreement to be a measure for increasing British security, how can we justify abandoning it because the "general settlement" has not materialized, especially if, as we hope, we succeed in laying the blame for the failure at the door of Germany? The failure, in such circumstances, of a "general settlement" would presumably increase, and not decrease, the existing danger to British security, and would therefore render the conclusion of the air agreement not less but more necessary. If, in these circumstances, we were to say that as there was no 'general settlement' there was not going to be any air agreement, would not the effect be very serious both

the naval issues late in February 1935. See letter to G. Clerk (Paris) from Sir J. Simon, 21 February 1935, in M. Medlicott, D. Dakin and M. Lambert (eds.), *Documents on British Foreign Policy, 1919-1939*, Second Series, Vol. XIII, p. 129 (hereafter *D.B.F.P.*).

[35] See the memorandum on German rearmament of 23 November, 1934 in C 8014/20/18, *D.B.F.P.* II, XII, No. 20, pp. 242-46; W.N. Medlicott, *Britain and Germany, The Search for Agreement 1930-1937* (London, 1969), pp. 12-15.

[36] See Foreign Office minutes in FO 371/18848, C 5453/55/18.

on the French Government and on British public opinion? The French would at once proceed to a Franco-Russian alliance; and as for the British public, would it not be very bewildered if, after having been told of the imminence of the German air danger, H.M. Government were suddenly to withdraw the constructive remedy which they themselves had put forward as a means of meeting it?'[37]

Despite the apparent simplicity of the solution, it clearly conflicted with the attitude adopted by the French. In fact its basic flaw was that the French and British approaches to the issue of a separate anti-bombing pact and air limitation agreement were fundamentally different. A separation might have suited the British well, in view of the growing concern for air defence. But it was totally unacceptable to the French, who viewed it not simply as a question of procedure but as a matter of fundamental policy. In British eyes a separate anti-bombing pact and air limitation agreement between the Western powers would merely provide an instance of the operation of the collective system in a regional form. But as the British realized from the point of view of the French and her allies in the Little Entente, such an arrangement would mark the first step in the disintegration of the united anti-German front; it would initiate a policy of independent action, whereby each country pursued its own immediate interests by coiming to terms with Germany on those matters with which it was itself vitally concerned[38] It was apprehension of the possibility of a break with the French, and the consequences which this would have on the chances of achieving a general settlement, that was mainly responsible for the British decision which seemed to hold until the middle of 1935, not to make an independent move. The Government refused, early in 1935, to embark on a policy that offered the uncertain prospect of an air limitation agreement with Germany at the expense of a general international agreement that would include France.[39]

By the spring a different consideration further militated against the policy of separation. It then became apparent that the approaches of Germany, France and Great Britain to the two basic elements of the proposed air agreement were in conflict. Germany wished to conclude the proposed anti-bombing pact immediately, without dealing with air limitation. Before March 1935 such a step would have provided the Luftwaffe with indirect legality; after Hitler's declaration on Germany rearmament it would have proved Germany's peaceful intentions. At the same time, the anti-bombing pact by itself would not have put any

[37]FO 370/18845, C 4627/55/18.
[38]FO 371/18826, C 1342/55/18.
[39]*Ibid*.

limitation on the extent of her air rearmament. France, while insisting on the principle of the indivisibility of the general settlement, proved from early 1935 to be mainly interested in a bilateral arrangement with Britain, encompassing the implementation of the anti-bombing pact which would satisfy her traditional demand for security. She did not show the same interest in the issue of limitation of air rearmament. Britain regarded both an anti-bombing pact and an air limitation agreement as essential parts of any air agreement. From her point of view the real purpose of the anti-bombing pact was to deter *Germany* from a sudden attack on the United Kingdom. Consequently, a break with France and an agreement with Germany on an anti-bombing pact alone would have been pointless. At the same time, Britain was persistent in her refusal to sign the anti-bombing pact only with France; this would have precluded the possibility of German cooperation in any general settlement that included, *inter alia,* an air limitation agreement. The resultant British policy, which was pursued with minor tactical changes until the middle of 1935, consisted of two main stands: persistent efforts to secure a general settlement and, when this proved impossible, maximum possible pressure for discussions on the vital issue of an air agreement. In the event, this policy failed to bring about the desired results.

The first contacts with the Germans on the subject of the Anglo-French communiqué of 3 February were themselves disheartening. They disclosed that the only proposal acceptable to Germany was the immediate conclusion of the proposed anti-bombing pact, without waiting for the negotiation of an air limitation agreement.[40] Hitler's subsequent demand for air parity with France in any air limitation agreement was far from what the French had envisaged in February. Furthermore, his decision to admit German secret rearmament and to abrogate the military clauses of the Versailles Treaty, in March, diminished the guarded hopes of the Foreign Office that Germany might be ready to 'pay' something for the legalization of her rearmament. Nevertheless the door was still left ajar. Negotiations between Simon and Hitler at the end of March only made it clear that an anti-bombing pact was virtually unattainable as a part of the proposed general settlement. However, Hitler was understood to have hinted that Germany would consider an air treaty should the *naval* talks reach a satisfactory conclusion. That hint, and the optimism to which it gave rise, exerted considerable influence on the shaping of British policy during the coming month. In fact, it is now apparent that the development of the policy of bilateral negotiations

---

[40] See FO 371/18826, C 1216/55/18, 14 February, 1935.

on the naval sphere was greatly motivated by a conviction that these negotiations might promote a solution to the more immediate strategic danger confronting Britain in the air.[41]

Early in March the Foreign Office received alarming reports which indicated that Germany was rearming more quickly than had been assumed. These gave rise to the first sense of urgency within the Office on the need to break the current deadlock in the discussions. A memorandum written on 1 April by Michael Creswell,[42] (a junior officer who specialized in air armaments) and approved by Vansittart, signified and expressed the growing realization within the Foreign Office that a bold initiative had to be taken in order to separate the anti-bombing pact and especially air limitation, from the other issues of the proposed general settlement. Creswell made it clear that the anti-bombing pact would have no deterrent effect on Germany unless Britain succeeded in breaking the deadlock on air limitation and achieved an agreement. Representatives of Italy, France and Britain were to meet at Stresa later that month in order to discuss their collective attitude towards Hitler's announcements, and Creswell suggested that the French be pressed to alter their position. Nevertheless in the Cabinet meetings at which the British attitude at the forthcoming conference was discussed, Simon declined to propose that pressure be exerted on the French to yield on the issue of simultaneity. Instead, the paper which the Foreign Office presented to the Cabinet defined such a course as 'contrary to previous Government intentions' and 'in any case . . . an unattainable object[43].' The need to preserve a united front with the French, and the fact that the extent of German air rearmament was not yet known to the Cabinet as a whole, were the probable reasons for Simon's attitude.[44]

At Stresa, in the second week of April, the French declared their readiness to change the principle of simultaneity only to the point of *negotiating* (but not concluding) the proposed anti-bombing pact before dealing with the other matters.[45] At the same time, they made it

[41] See H.A. Hall III, 'The Foreign Policy Making Process in Britain 1934-1935 and the Origins of the Anglo-German Naval Agreement', *Historical Journal* 19 (1976), 477-99; and J.A. Cross, *Sir Samuel Hoare, A Political Biography* (London, 1977), p. 192.

[42] FO 371/18835, C 3087/55/18. Creswell, together with Wigram and Vansittart, took an active part in the discussion within the Foreign Office on the issue of military aviation. (Information given to the author by Sir Michael Creswell in October 1973.)

[43] C.P. 79(35).

[44] Simon's letter to the Prime Minister drawing attention to the danger of German air rearmament was sent on 14 April. The discussion on the alleged British air inferiority took place only late that month. See above pp. 70-72.

[45] See FO 371/18836, C 3289/55/18.

clear to the British that the anti-bombing pact would be of no interest to France unless supplemented by an Anglo-French bilateral arrangement to ensure its implementation. Although the French demand was regarded by some officials at the Foreign Office as both logical and essential to Britain's own defence interest, such an arrangement was considered certain to preclude any possibility of reaching an agreement with Germany, which was then a distinct aim of British policy.[46] Besides, the French 'offer' did not resolve the major question of the air limitation agreement. The records of the Stresa meeting clearly show that the French and the British, pessimistic about future German developments, were inclined to maintain their previously defined attitudes, in the absence of more viable alternatives.[47]

Between April and June 1935, three events greatly influenced the British search for an air agreement, which seemed to have come to a halt after Simon's talks with Hitler in Berlin in March. These were the disclosure of the extent of German air rearmament, which caused a degree of panic in the Cabinet late in April; the Franco-Soviet pact of early May; and the Anglo-German negotiations which culminated in the famous naval pact of June 1935.

By late April Simon had himself become alarmed at the reports of German air rearmament and at Germany's growing capacity to produce aircraft. He therefore decided to accept a recommendation that had been made by Vansittart early in the month. The latter had then recommended a suggestion to the French that, in view of the growing German air rearmament, it was in their interest as much as Britain's to separate the issue of air disarmament from the proposed general settlement. By this means, Vansittart thought that Britain might attempt to release the deadlock in the air discussion and, at the same time, avoid a break with the French. The Foreign Secretary presented the idea to the Cabinet on 30 April. His memorandum expressed the view that:

> provided that agreement could be reached between the four Powers as to their respective air strengths, the prospects of reaching agreement on the Air Pact would be materially improved, and that we ought to be prepared to contemplate this (assuming that we can carry the others along with us) without making the Air Pact depend upon other matters.[48]

The Cabinet discussed the idea on 1 May and decided to adopt it

---

[46] See Wigram's letter to MacDonald of 14 April, 1935, FO 371/18876, C 3284/55/18; and the C.I.D. meeting of 16 April, 268 C.I.D., Cab. 2/6.

[47] See FO 371/18836, C 3288/55/18.

[48] See C.P. (90), 35.

at its meeting four days later.

Several factors appear to have accounted for this decision. One may have been the discussions in the Cabinet Disarmament Committee on 30 April, which caused increasing concern within the Cabinet as a whole as to the state of British air armaments in comparison with those of Germany.[49] Another was the Franco-Soviet pact of 2 May, which struck a new blow at the tenuous hopes of inducing Germany to accept a general settlement.[50] The Foreign Office still believed that the French might be persuaded. Early in May, Vansittart wrote: 'With care it would be possible, for the French air force is like ours in a poor way compared with the rising efficiency and numbers of Germany, and they [the French] might like a deal.'[51]

The Foreign Office was not altogether sanguine about the attitude of the Germans towards any scheme for an air limitation agreement that was based on the principle of parity. Orme Sargent of the Central Department at the Foreign Office forecast the probable reaction thus:

> If the Germans learn of our inability to accelerate expansion [in air rearmament] — and doubtless they will — will it predispose them to an agreement on a basis of parity? It is only human nature — and certainly German human nature — to stock to the lead they have achieved in the air so long as there is no danger of its being successfully challenged. It is the line which we ourselves took as regards the Navy before the War and which the French have taken since the War as regards land armaments.[52]

Nevertheless, Simon still seems to have harboured hopes of achieving a limitation agreement based on parity, while Vansittart, too, was guardedly optimistic. He expected from Germany 'sufficient goodwill in all directions to make a five power Air Pact possible'.[53] After all, on the eve of the Stresa Conference, Germany had hinted that she would be willing to relax her rigid attitude towards the proposed Eastern pact.[54] Moreover, on 21 May, Hitler declared that the German Government was agreeable to an air convention supplementary to the Locarno Pact, and that 'the German Government's limitation of German air arm to a degree of parity with other individual Western Great Powers, makes possible at any time the fixing of a maximum

---

[49] See above pp. 72-3.

[50] See Medlicott, *Britain and Germany*, p. 12; and Scott, *Alliance Against Hitler*, pp. 243-250. See also FO 371/18836, C 3265/55/18.

[51] FO 371/18836, C 3615/55/18.

[52] *Ibid.*

[53] FO 371/18838, C 3777/55/18.

[54] See FO 371/18838, C 3116/55/18; and FO 371/18839 C 3777/55/18.

which Germany then undertakes to observe'.[55] This placatory speech seemed to vindicate the optimism of the Foreign Office: at the end of May, Neville Chamberlain, the Chancellor of the Exchequer told the Cabinet Disarmament Committee that the programme of R.A.F. expansion should not be accepted as irreversible and that as little as possible should be spent on permanent buildings since 'it might be that we could get Germany to agree to [air] limitation'.[56]

However, British hopes that the French would be equally concerned about the extent of German air rearmament, and would therefore abrogate the principle of simultaneity, proved to be false. Weakened by another of their periodic domestic political crises, the French refused to give a definite answer to the British inquiry, which the Foreign Office understood to be a clear negative response.[57] Vansittart seems to have been disillusioned at last, even though Simon still exhorted the Government to aim at a limitation agreement, which he considered to be the only way to counter Britain's anticipated air inferiority in 1936-7. Minuting a Foreign Office report on German air rearmament on 3 June, he wrote:

> All this, to my mind, increases *the urgency of air limitation between the Locarno Powers*. It is for this very reason that I have been pressing ever since February that, even at the risk of a little temporary disinclination on the part of France, it was essential to get on with this business. I still believe that it is the *only* way in which we can avoid the increasingly dangerous situation in the air which these minutes point out will present itself next year.[58]

By this time, however, it had become abundantly clear that any negotiations held under the shadow of the French insistence on simultaneity would be doomed to failure. In Sargent's words, they would constitute merely 'an academic exercise',[59] with no real prospect of practical results.

In the last week of May the Foreign Office considered the advisability of a stronger demarche in Paris, designed to persuade the French that their attitude towards the proposed air agreement would seriously prejudice Anglo-French relations.[60] The German Ambassador in London was fully aware that this was being considered and,

[55] FO 371/18844, C 4460/55/18. See also Weinberg, *The Foreign Policy of Hitler's Germany*, p. 209.
[56] Cab. 27/508.
[57] FO 371/18846, C 4903/55/18.
[58] FO 371/18847, C 4174/55/18. Italics in Original.
[59] FO 371/18846, C 4694/55/18.
[60] *Ibid.*

after a meeting with Simon on 28 May, reported: 'I have again and again got the impression that political circles and public opinion are exerting strong pressure on the British Government to hasten the conclusion of the Air Pact. . . . The Foreign Secretary is now determined to press forward the question of the Air Pact'.[61] However, a sensational event was about to make any such move ineffective. On 5 June, the Cabinet decided in favour of a naval agreement with Germany.[62] This action clearly reflected the Government's despair of reaching a disarmament agreement by following the French path and was impelled by defence as well as purely internal political considerations. It was taken in the context of continuous pressure from the Admiralty for such an agreement and the Air Ministry's advice that a naval agreement would provide a useful precedent for an air treaty and thus help to reduce Britain's most serious danger. Both the Admiralty and the Air Ministry received encouragement from the Foreign Office. However, the hope that the naval talks might induce Germany to show more responsiveness towards the issue of an air limitation agreement soon proved to be misplaced. During the negotiations preceding the naval pact, the Germans rejected the suggestion of a written 'Gentlemen's Agreement' whereby the naval pact would be followed by an air limitation agreement.[63] The most the British could now hope for was an anti-bombing pact. Meanwhile the general effect of the naval pact on France was disastrous, a fact which was understated if anything by a despatch from Sir G. Clerk in Paris, who informed Sir Samual Hoare that:

> It is generally held, though more in sorrow than in anger, that its conclusion which has developed out of exchange of views between technical experts . . . had dealt a serious blow to the common front of Stresa and is directly contrary to the undertaking entered into by the Franco-British declaration of February 3rd. However stoutly Great Britain may declare that that is not the case, the fact remains that a rude blow has been dealt at all international understanding.[64]

[61] *Documents on German Foreign Policy, 1918-1945* (hereafter *D.G.F.P.*) Series C, IV, 113, pp. 220-221.

[62] On this, see D.C. Watt, 'The Anglo-German Naval Agreement of 1935: An Interim Judgment', *Journal of Modern History* 28 (1956), 155-75; Charles Bloch, 'La Grande'Bretagne face un rearmament allemand et l'accord naval de 1935', *Revue d'histoire de la deuxieme guerre mondiale* 63 (1966), 41-68; Weinberg, *The Foreign Policy of Hitler's Germany*, pp. 210-216; Hines H. Hall III, 'The Foreign Policy Making Process in Britain 1934-1935'. And E.H. Haraszti, *Treaty Breakers or "Realpolitiker", The Anglo-German Naval Agreement of June 1935* (Budapest, 1974).

[63] See K. Middlemas, and J. Barnes, *Baldwin, A Biography* (London, 1969 p. 827 and also FO 371/18846, C 4903/55/18, 13 June, 1935.

[64] 19 June, 1935. *D.B.F.P.*, Second Series, Vol. XIII, p. 437.

The minutes of the Cabinet meeting of 5 June, however, show that the Government was still bent on achieving an air agreement by some means or other. Following the decision to accept the German naval proposals, discussion turned to the air question, and it was decided that an anti-bombing pact and air limitation agreement should be taken up as a separate issue and should no longer be linked to a general settlement.[65]

Between June and August 1935, the British, French and German authorities discussed what proved to be the last British effort of 1935 to break the deadlock on the proposed air agreement. The history of those negotiations need only be outlined here. The British did not abandon all hope of securing the proposed anti-bombing pact in June 1935, even though they were now in a weaker position from which to influence the French to show more flexibility with regard to the question of a separate air agreement. Neither were they totally discouraged by a persistent German refusal to accept any part of the Lonon Communique of 3 February (other than the proposed anti-bombing pact). On 21 June, the Cabinet accepted the recommendation of the Foreign Office and the Air Ministry that:

> If in the course of negotiations it were found that the conclusion of an air limitation agreement were either impossible or indefinitely postponed, then we are clearly of opinion that we ought to go for the conclusion of the Air Pact in order that we may get one positive object at any rate.[66]

In order to secure the proposed anti-bombing pact, French co-operation was clearly a *sine qua non*. Indeed, the crux of the pact, as far as Britain was concerned, was the claim which she would have on immediate French help were Germany to launch a sudden air attack. The French, however, did not show any sign of easing their demand for the indivisibility of the proposed general settlement and on 3 July, the British Government once again found it advisable to concur in principle, even though by doing so it reversed the decision arrived at on 5 June. In effect, the Ministers adopted the Foreign Office's advice to the effect that following the Anglo-German naval pact the 'French must be humoured and not rushed away'.[67] The Cabinet clearly considered that there would be a better chance of the anti-bombing pact materializing once negotiations on this issue were initiated, even though these would commence before the conclusion of the general

[65] FO 371/18846, C 4903/55/18.
[66] C.P. 129 (35).
[67] S. Hoare to G. Clerk (Paris) 20 June 1935, *D.B.F.P.* Second Series, Vol. XIII, p. 441.

settlement.[68] On 3 July, the Cabinet for the first time gave its consent to the French demand that a series of bilateral military arrangements among the Locarno Powers, and specifically between France and Britain, should either accompany or follow the proposed anti-bombing pact, provided Germany agreed.[69] Germany, meanwhile, had been asked to clear the way for the anti-bombing pact by displaying more flexibility as far as the Eastern Pact was concerned.[70]

Ever since Stresa the French had demanded the formulation of a substantial Anglo-French plan which would encompass the eventuality of launching an air attack on Germany from bases on French soil. This was not a proposal to which the British could commit themselves, despite their concession to the French call for a bilateral arrangement of some sort. Any move in that direction would have constituted a drastic departure from the traditional British reluctance to undertake military commitments in Europe. Furthermore, at the time, the British strategic plan was to launch air strikes *from Britain*, unless the length of the flight to certain objectives in Germany demanded otherwise. In so far as cooperation with the French was considered, the Air Ministry intended to do no more than earmark certain aerodromes in France which might be necessary in order to extend the operative radius of bomber squadrons.[71] At the same time, a similar bilateral arrangement with Germany providing for an attack on France from the air was considered pointless. The British were clearly aware that French demands for a bilateral arrangement implied a real undertaking with her and a fictitious one with Germany.[72]

All these difficulties were clear to the Government. However, in giving their qualified consent to the French demand, the British intended to convince the Germans that the bilateral arrangements they were ready to accept would not destroy the equilibrium principle

[68] See Minutes of the Cabinet Meeting of 3 July, Air 8/201 and FO 371/18848, C 5327/55/18.

[69] FO 371/18848, C 5302/55/18.

[70] See *D.G.F.P.*, C, VI, no. 201, for the German reaction.

[71] See Minutes in FO 371/18845, C 4545/55/18 and C 5322/55/18. On the French constant efforts, from the middle 1930s, to tighten the Anglo-French cooperation in matters of air defence, see J. Lecuir and P. Fridenson, 'L'organisation de la cooperation aerienne franco-britanique (1935 — May 1940)', *Revue d'histoire de la seconde guerre mondiale,* No. 73 (1969), 43-75; P. Fridenson, 'Forces et faiblesses des conversations aeriennes franco-britanique' (Paris, 1972); and P. Fridenson and J. Lecuir, *La france et la Grande-Bretagne face aux problèmes aériennes 1935 — mai 1940* (Paris, 1976).

[72] See a very useful memorandum by Sargent on this point in FO 371/18848, C 5327/55/18.

of the anti-bombing pact, and would not amount to an Anglo-French plan for attacking Germany.[73] The condition upon which Britain accepted the French demand for a bilateral arrangement was that *the German Government* agreed to 'the principle of the accompaniment of the anti-bombing pact by such bilateral arrangements between any two parties as those two may judge necessary to render it effective'; it being understood that 'the fact that these bilateral arrangements may be mutually entered upon by any two parties will make it necessary to *limit the scope* of any one arrangement and to a certain extent to preserve the balance between the provisions which each may contain'.[74] The ball was thus thrown to the Germans; but they did not find it necessary to submit an answer on their attitude towards the proposed bilateral arrangement until early in October. When it came, it was a blank refusal.[75]

The failure of the attempt to reach agreement with Germany, after nine months of intensive negotiations, did not discourage Britain for long. Admittedly, the outbreak of the Abyssinian crisis in October (an issue which greatly preoccupied British statesmen until the middle of 1936), did preclude any further effort to reopen the question of an anti-bombing pact for the remainder of 1935. Nevertheless early in 1936 the Cabinet accepted the advice of the Foreign Office to make a new and more thoroughgoing effort to secure a general settlement. The Foreign Office still considered this to be of particular importance in view of the time needed for rearmament; moreover, as one official commented, 'it is dangerous to sit on the safety valve'.[76] Britain continued to hope that such a settlement would include a far-reaching air agreement providing both air limitation and a guarantee against aerial bombardment. But the prospects of achieving a settlement of any kind (particularly in the state of acute international tension caused by Italy's conquest of Abyssinia) were, if anything, less favourable than ever.

Germany continued to put forward the Franco-Russian pact of May 1935 as the main justification for her reluctance to negotiate an air limitation agreement. On 13 December, Hitler publicly rejected

---

[73] See Hoare's telegram to Sir G. Clark of the British Embassy in Paris of 6 July 1935, FO 371/18848, C 5302/55/18, and the report of his conversation with the German Ambassador in London on 1 August, *D.G.F.P.*, C, IV, No. 243.

[74] Foreign Office telegram No. 222 to Paris of 22 July, FO 371/18851, C 7688/55/18. Italics added.

[75] FO 371/18859, C 7698/55/18.

[76] E.H. Carr's minutes in FO 371/17884, C 581/4/18. See an analysis of the background to the quest for an agreement with Germany in 1936 in Medlicott, *Britain and Germany,* pp. 18-22.

any air agreement that did not take into account 'Russia's enormous strength in the air'.[77] He thereby declared an air limitation agreement which included only the Locarno Powers to be unacceptable. However, there was little doubt within the Foreign Office and the Air Ministry that it would be very difficult to persuade Russia to subscribe to any air limitation agreement which did not encompass Japan, her potential enemy in the east. At the same time, Japan herself seemed even less likely to enter into such negotiations unless the United States were also a party to them. Two conceivable solutions to the difficulty were considered: one involved supplementing the proposed air limitation agreement by an escalator clause in order to make allowance for the Russian air force; the other was to seek the inclusion of Japan and the United States in the agreement as well as Russia. Both methods were discussed late in January 1936 by an interdepartmental committee that dealt with the subject of an air agreement. The records of these debates reveal that neither approach was considered to be at all promising.[78]

These discussions made it obvious that efforts to secure an air limitation agreement were doomed to failure. Formally, the British continued to search for such an agreement with Germany throughout 1936; but in effect by February they had already virtually despaired of its attainment.[79] Early that month, Vansittart still seemed to hope that Germany would accept an air limitation agreement as part of the price for British colonial concessions;[80] at the same time, the C.I.G.S. maintained that 'to challenge Germany to a type of war in which we must be in an inferior position would appear to be sheer folly. Air limitation is therefore of infinitely greater importance to our security than the production of superior air forces.' In order to secure Germany's cooperation in negotiating such an agreement he, too, recommended concessions — and suggested the recognition of her right to remilitarize the Rhineland.[81] But on 7 March, German troops unilaterally occupied that area, and thereby dashed even those slender hopes.[82] Ten days later, the Chiefs of Staff Committee

[77] G(36)5, Cab. 27/599.

[78] See the minutes of the interdepartmental committee FO 371/19884, C 682/4/18.

[79] On the German attitude, see Phipps's telegrams of 14 and 17 January to the Foreign Office, FO 371/19893, C 356/4/18 and C 248/4/18. On the despair within the Foreign Office of reaching an air limitation agreement, see FO 371/19884, C 682/4/118 and FO 371/19887, C 1352/4/18.

[80] See C.P. 42(36). 17 February 1936.

[81] Cab. 64/35 and W.O. 190/388, 24 February 1936.

[82] On the reoccupation of the Rhineland, see T. Emmerson, *The Rhineland Crisis,* 7 March 1936, (London, 1977); D.C. Watt, 'German Plans for Reoccupation of the

recommended that efforts at negotiation continue only with respect to the anti-bombing pact; they thus put an end to the search for an international air limitation agreement, the attainment of which would have done so much to quieten British fears of an air attack.

There was still reason to believe that the proposed anti-bombing pact might materialize. From conversations which the British Ambassador in Berlin had with Hitler on 13 December, and with the German Minister for Foreign Affairs on 14 and 17 January, it appeared that Germany was still ready, in principle, to resume negotiations on the pact.[83] Although an anti-bombing pact *without* a complementary air limitation agreement was far less attractive from the military point of view, it nevertheless possessed considerable merit for Britain. It would help her to cope with the increasing difficulties experienced in keeping pace with German air rearmament. It would also ensure immediate French help in the event of a German air attack. As Swinton summed up Cabinet opinion late in February: 'Locarno remains a one-sided agreement and if it be true that Locarno or no Locarno we should be bound to come in in a French war, the converse is not necessarily true, and an Air Pact is *some* insurance'.[84]

Germany's motives for recommending a resumption of negotiations did not seem altogether ingenuous. The Foreign Office suspected that the Germans wished to use their apparent change of attitude to the anti-bombing pact and the air limitation agreement as a ploy with which to enlist British support, and thereby to delay for as long as possible the ratification of the Franco-Russian treaty of the previous May. Vansittart opposed such 'unblushing blackmail,' and the Foreign Office rejected the proposal that Britain cooperate with Germany to the extent of pressing France to delay ratification.[85] Nevertheless, the further declarations of support for an anti-bombing pact Germany made in mid-January, did offer some hope.

In order to encourage a resumption of discussions on the subject, the Foreign Office planned to satisfy both the Germans and the French by agreeing to a separate arrangement with each. The idea was to suggest to both Powers a mutual inspection of their air forces by air attaches to ensure that each party was adequately equipped to

Rhineland: A Note', *Journal of Contemporary History* 1 (1966), 193-99; Max Braubach, *Der einmarschdeutscher Truppen in die entmilitaris ierte Zone am Rhine im Marz 1936* (Cologne, 1956); and Weinberg, *The Foreign Policy of Hitler's Germany,* pp. 239-61.

[83] FO 371/19884, C 581/4/18.

[84] 19 February, 1936, Air 2/1606. Italics added.

[85] See FO 371/19883, C 213/4/18.

render assistance. It was hoped that the Germans would not be able to object that this programme was inconsistent with 'the spirit of Locarno'.[86] On the other hand, the French might be persuaded to accept the arrangement once they had been given to understand the advantages implied — although not openly expressed — in the proposed arrangement. Specifically, the British considered that they were enabling the French to obtain the only advantage which they lacked by including a provision for the use of French aerodromes by British bombers in cases of required operations against Germany.[87]

The prospects of success seemed bright. So much so that in February the Foreign Office included in their comprehensive plan for a general settlement with Germany a proposal for resuming negotiations on an anti-bombing pact.[88] While rejecting some of the suggestions (mainly those concerned with economic aid to Germany), the Cabinet committee which discussed the plan agreed that the anti-bombing pact would indeed be the best starting-point for negotiations.[89] It was not until the end of the first week in March, however, that the Cabinet established initial contact with Germany on the matter. The delay, caused mainly by the Government's preoccupation with the oil sanction crisis at Geneva, certainly reduced the chance that Germany might take seriously Britain's hints about a settlement on the Rhineland issue in exchange for positive negotiations on the anti-bombing pact.[90] By the time the Cabinet made an overt approach, on 6 March, the Germans had already issued the order for the re-occupation of the Rhineland, thus depriving Britain of a very important negotiating lever.[91]

The negotiations dragged on for several months;[92] but the Germans' lack of interest in them was by now only too apparent. On 14 October they finally made their attitude absolutely plain by stating that the guarantee of mutual assistance between France and the United Kingdom, unlike the Anglo-Italian joint guarantee to Germany on the one hand, and to Belgium and France on the other, must be

[86] G(36)4, Cab. 27/599.

[87] *Ibid.*

[88] G(36)3, FO 371/19885, C 1027/4/18.

[89] G(36)3, FO 371/19885, C 1027/4/18.

[90] Medlicott, *Britain and Germany,* p. 23.

[91] FO 371/19890, C 1869/4/18.

[92] See the expressions of the guarded optimism in the Cabinet on the prospects of an air pact in their meeting of 20 May 1936, in FO 371/19906, C 3829/4/18. On later negotiations, see FO 371/19887, C 1480/4/18; FO 371/19913, C 7247/4/18; and FO 371/19913, C 7387/4/18.

excluded.[93] The meaning was clear: Germany would not agree to a general settlement that included a guarantee of French assistance to Britain as part of the proposed anti-bombing pact. This destroyed the last remnant of hope within the British Government, which finally abandoned the intensive search it had begun four years earlier for an agreement which might minimize the danger of a sudden and unprovoked air attack. Thus, at least in one particular sphere, October 1936 marked the end of an era in British diplomacy.

The proposals which Britain put forward at Geneva in 1932 and 1933 for drastic air disarmament had owed their failure primarily to the technical and 'objective' problems of civil aviation. By contrast, the main causes of her inability to secure a substantial air agreement in the years 1934-6 were political complications, which also blocked a general settlement with Germany. Admittedly, the French insistence, throughout 1935, on the principle of simultaneity did not make Britain's task any easier, especially as far as the anti-bombing pact was concerned; but there can be no doubt that it was the Germans who were primarily to blame. Germany had displayed a positive attitude towards an air agreement based on the principle of parity. But she had done so in order to drive a wedge between Britain and France and to convince them that her intentions were peaceable. Fundamentally, she had remained firmly opposed to any external restriction on her air rearmament. Twice during the latter part of the period under consideration — in October 1935 and in October 1936 — she had obstructed the way to negotiations on an anti-bombing pact.

Twice, too, had Germany robbed Britain of a bargaining counter. Until March 1935, Britain had reason to hope that the legalization of German rearmament would smooth the path to an agreement. A year later, to the same end, she considered offering to recognize Germany's right to reoccupy the Rhineland. On both occasions the British were too late. Before the offers could be made they had been pre-empted by German *faits accomplis*.

There now remained only one possible and unexplored means of minimizing the danger of air attack: an international agreement providing for the restriction of bombardment by defining *a code of air warfare*. If attack from the air had to be accepted as inevitable in a war whose portents were gathering ominously on the horizon, then at least every effort had to be made to render such an attack as humane as possible by providing for the protection of the civilian population. It was to this objective that the British Cabinet was now to devote its earnest attention.

[93] See FO 371/19912, C 5951/4/18 and the Cabinet meeting of 21 October, 1936, FO 371/19914, C7493/4/18.

# 4
# AIR WARFARE RULES (1936-1939)

> London will be at once attacked as it was repeatedly on former occasions in exercise of the enemy's air power. To argue otherwise is lunacy especially after the Guernica atrocity in the Basque Province. . . . The enemy would be acting in strict accordance with the higher strategy so that the spirit of resistance of the masses might break the nation's will to war and induce a hurried peace.' (L.E. Charlton, *The Menace of the Clouds* (London, 1937), p. 37.)

The failure to secure both an air limitation agreement and an international guarantee against air attack did not conclude the British Government's search for some other form of international treaty which might minimize the country's liability to air attack. Rather, after 1936, the Government attempted to attain a degree of security from aerial bombardment by concentrating its efforts on yet a third possibility: an international convention 'humanizing' warfare. An analysis of the contemporary arguments adduced in favour of such a convention, as well as a study of the grounds upon which it was criticized, constitute the essential background for any account of a neglected aspect of British foreign policy in the final years before the outbreak of the Second World War. Together they testify to the unique nature of this quest. The record of the lengthy interim debates also provides much of the explanation for the fact that, as late as the first months of 1939, the British Cabinet still found itself in much the same position as it had occupied in 1936. Ministers remained convinced that such a convention would somehow be advantageous but had not yet found a way to bring about its materialization.

The basic principles governing the law of warfare had been laid down before 1914; first among them was the axiom that belligerents shall not inflict on their adversaries harm out of proportion to the legitimate goals of war.[1] The doctrine of the Just War, upon which it was based, further specified that combatants are the main forces of resistance and therefore a legitimate target of military operations; non-combatants shall neither participate nor be subjected to hostilities. This principle implies at least four general requirements: (a) a permanent distinction between belligerents and the civilian population; (b) the immunity of both the civilian population and objects of

---

[1] On this subject see S.D. Bailey, *Prohibitions and Restraints in War* (London, 1972), in particular Chapter 3.

a civilian character to deliberate attacks; (c) the avoidance of any unreasonable damage to the civilian population and objects of a civilian character in attacks on military targets; (d) the avoidance of the use of any weapons or other means and methods of warfare calculated to cause unnecessary or otherwise excessive suffering.[2] After the First World War, these requirements became increasingly difficult to define and almost impossible to apply in practice. This was particularly so since the development of aviation had added a dimension to warfare which had fundamentally modified its physiognomy. As a result of air warfare, the civilian population might suffer from the scourge of war to an extent incomparably greater than ever before. The appearance of the air weapon and the formulation of the doctrine of strategic bombing had taken place in what proved to be the first total war in history.

Subsequent developments, in both military weapons and strategic thought, had rendered the imposition of legal prohibitions and restrictions in a future war almost impossible as far as air warfare was concerned.

Nevertheless the inter-war period witnessed a continuous debate between two camps. One consisted of the 'realists', who claimed that it was pointless and meaningless to make any attempt to define and achieve a code of air warfare rules. The other was made up of 'idealists' who, despite the substantial change in the realm of war, still believed in the supremacy of humanity. Major-General John Fuller placed himself firmly in the first camp. As early as 1923 he taught that a cardinal lesson of the last world war was that whereas: 'a few years ago armies alone went forth to battle; today entire nations go to war; not only as soldiers but as moral and material suppliers of soldiers. This being so we find that while a short time back, it was clearly possible to differentiate between the military and the ethical objectives of nations at war. Today this difference is becoming more and more complex. So much so that both these objectives are likely to coincide and when this takes place to attack the civilian workers of a nation will then be as justifiable as to attack its soldiers'.[3]

A decade later, General Sir George MacDonogh, a former adjutant-general, took the same line. Reviewing the provisions of the draft code for the regulation of air warfare, he commented:

> It is the disease itself and not one of its symptoms which should be attacked. It would seem far wiser and no more difficult to

[2]See F. Kalshoven, *The Law of Warfare* (Geneva, 1973), pp. 28-9.
[3]*The Reformation of War* (London, 1923), p. 70.

> direct the full force of public opinion to the outlawry of war rather than against one of its features. So long as war is permissible it will be the bounden duty of each belligerent to make use of every weapon that may directly lead to victory.... The value of aerial bombardment as a weapon of offence is so great that it seems impossible to lay down any effective rules for the protection of civil population which are likely to be observed and it is submitted that the only effectual means of protecting non-combatant from the horrors of war is by abolishing war itself.[4]

On the other side of the spectrum stood those who refused to believe in the futility of trying to prevent a situation whereby non-combatants would be obliged to accept what a British Admiral defined as 'their share of inhumanity'.[5] Typical was the view of James Garner, the lawyer and humanist, writing on the subject of the international regulation of air warfare in 1932, he said:

> There is no reason to assume that the world is ready to go to the length of totally abandoning the distinction [between combatants and non-combatants] and of recognizing the legitimacy of war directed against both classes of the population equally.... The distinction is fundamental and eternal, it is founded upon consideration of humanity and it would be a singular conception of humanity to abandon it merely because conditions have changed and especially because more powerful instruments of destruction have been invented, by use of which the immediate interests of the belligerent may be better subserved.[6]

Within the British Government, the alignment of the parties to the debate on the subject of a convention governing air warfare was somewhat different. Within this forum, the divergence of views did not revolve around the realist-idealist dichotomy. Instead, during the last portion of the inter-war period, the arguments for and against such a convention were based on contradictory assessments of self-interest and utility. Furthermore the composition of the two parties was itself unique and cannot be assessed on a military-civilian basis. The records of the debate reveal that, within the Government, the representatives of the Services played leading roles as both antagonists and protagonists of an air convention. It is to the reasons for which they did so that attention must now be directed.

Throughout the inter-war period the Air Ministry on the one hand, and the Admiralty and War Office on the other, had maintained

---

[4]Quoted by the Chief of Air Staff on 15 February 1935; FO 371/18827.

[5]Rear Admiral S.S. Hall; Address to the Grutius Society, *Transactions of the Grutius Society,* 5, 1919, p. 3.

[6]'International Regulations of Air Warfare' *Air Law Review,* (April, 1932), pp. 114-115.

divergent positions on the subject of the rules of air warfare. (These differences were not, in fact, reconciled, until the very outbreak of war.) The controversy had already come to a head twice during the 1920s. The first occasion was the 1923 Salisbury Committee debates on the cooperation between the Services.[7] The second was the discussions within the Chiefs of Staff Committee, early in 1928, on the 'proper' function of the air arm (the formal subject on the agenda was the principles of war to be enscribed in the manuals of the three services).[8] Neither debate was, of course, overtly concerned with the framing of a convention governing the rules of air warfare. Yet both gave rise to a discussion of such broad questions as the extent to which the air staff doctrine of strategic bombing violated the 'true' principles of war and, conversely, the degree to which this doctrine aimed at the attainment of victory and therefore constituted a 'correct' use of air power. Central to the discussion on both occasions was whether an air offensive in line with the air staff doctrine was contrary to international law or to the dictates of humanity. Thus Sir C. Madden, Chief of the Naval Staff, wrote that the operations envisaged by the Royal Air Force would endanger civilian life 'to a far greater degree than has ever hitherto been contemplated under international law'.[9] And Sir G. Milne, Chief of the Imperial General Staff, doubted whether His Majesty's Government should accept a doctrine which 'put in plain English amounts to one which advocates unrestricted warfare against the civil population of one's enemy'.[10] Lord Trenchard, on the other hand, was naturally of the opposite opinion. Moreover in 1928 the Chiefs of Staff specifically asked whether it was to Britain's advantage to keep within the accepted codes for the conduct of war as regards the employment of air power. Despite the interest of those debates, the controversy then revealed did not become of immediate and practical importance until almost a decade later. Only when the issue was raised to the level of the C.I.D. and the Cabinet, and even then only when those two bodies commenced urgent and concrete consideration of the 'next war', did it seem vital to weigh the possible advantages and disadvantages of an air convention.

Basically, the argument in favour of a convention on air warfare rules, especially with Germany, was based on a quasi-axiomatic interpretation of Britain's strategic position. The country as a whole,

---

[7] See S. Roskill, *Naval Policy Between the Wars* Vol. I (London, 1968), pp. 372-87.

[8] See C. Webster and N. Frankland, *The Strategic Air Offensive Against Germany 1939-1945, Vol. IV: Annexes and Appendices* (London, 1961), pp. 71-84.

[9] Webster and Frankland, *The Strategic Air Offensive*, p. 82.

[10] *Ibid.*, p. 81.

and London in particular, was understood to be extremely vulnerable to air attack but relatively immune to other weapons of war. Therefore, it was reasoned, it was in Britain's best interest to accept the most drastic restriction of air bombardment which could be devised. Chatfield, who as the Chief of Naval Staff showed a natural interest in saving the Merchant Fleet from air attack, put this point to the C.I.D. early in 1935: 'It was... felt that since the air provided the only way in which we could be attacked in our homes there was tremendous advantage in trying to do something which might avoid unrestricted warfare against the civilian population.'[11] Chatfield, who on this issue enjoyed strong support from successive chiefs of the Imperial General Staff during the late 1930s, was not deluded as to the likelihood of any rules being observed throughout a prolonged war in which national interests were at stake. Nevertheless it was reasoned, that did not imply that any attempt to lay down rules on the subject was futile. Throughout these years, Chatfield and his supporters claimed that as the First World War had itself demonstrated, there were good reasons to assume that at least at the outset of war a belligerent would hesitate before plainly and deliberately violating the code to which he had voluntarily appended his signature not long before. Thus the C.I.D. was reminded in 1935 that 'it had taken Germany two years to make up her mind to proceed with unrestricted submarine warfare which had given us time to make our preparations, if Germany had started in 1914 with that type of war we might have been defeated.'[12] At least one positive and one negative consideration of self interest might make it expedient for Germany to agree to and abide by a convention for air warfare rules. The first, it was claimed, was Germany's heavy dependence on the Ruhr-Rhineland industrial belt for the maintenance of her national life in war. This consideration might induce the Germans to support an international convention which, in a war with Poland and Czechoslovakia would prevent or delay France helping her allies by bombing the area,[13] and, in an Anglo-German conflict, might make Britain hesitant to 'take the gloves off' and hit that target.[14] The presumed negative consideration suggested that the violation of the rules of war would not only alienate world opinion but would have some dangerous and tangible implications for Germany herself. As Lord Hailsham, the Secretary for War, told the C.I.D. 'The example of the United States entry into the last

[11] At the discussion on C.I.D., Paper No. 1163-B, 25 February, 1935. Air 8/201.
[12] *Ibid.*
[13] See For example FO 371/20700, C 6862/148/62.
[14] See for example the arguments of the Joint Planning Committee in October 1938 in Cab. 21/738.

war was a very good one which might be repated again in different circumstances'.[15] Both these arguments seemed to gain in weight from the fact that on various occasions, until early 1938, Germany was apparently remarkably consistent in her expressed interest in a convention for humanizing air warfare. Thus when Simon and Eden visited Berlin in March 1935, Hitler told them that 'the German Government particularly liked the idea of prohibition of indiscriminate bombing of densely populated regions'.[16] In a speech to the Reichstag on 21 May 1935, Hitler said: '... gradual progress is the best way to success. For example there might be prohibition of the dropping of gas, incendiary and explosive bombs outside the real battle zone. This limitation could then be extended to complete international outlawry of all bombing ... should bombing as such be branded as an illegal barbarity, the construction of bombing aeroplanes will soon be abandoned as superfluous and of no purpose'.[17] The German Peace Plan of 31 March 1936, issued after the reoccupation of the Rhineland, similarly suggested that if any international conferences were to be held in the near future, they should point very limited objectives, in order to have any chances of success. The immediate practical objectives of such conferences were defined as the prohibition of the use of poisonous gas or incendiary bombs; and the prohibition of the use of bombs of any kind whatsoever against open localities outside the range of the medium artillery of the fighting forces.[18] Germany seemed to have followed the same pattern in her contacts with Britain late in 1937,[19] and even as late as September 1938. At the height of the Munich Crisis, Hitler told Chamberlain that 'if he had had to use force against the Czechs, he had intended to limit air action to front line zones as a matter of principle he would always try to spare the civilian population and confine himself to military objectives'.[20]

An understanding of the essential nature of Britain's strategic position was also basic to the point of view advanced by the critics of an air convention. Like the advocates of the idea, they too began with the promise that Britain was particularly vulnerable to an air attack. Where they differed, however, was in the entirely conflicting conclusions which they drew. In the view of the Air Staff and of those who

[15] 25 February 1935. Air 8/201.

[16] FO 371/20700, C 8682/148/162.

[17] *Ibid.*

[18] *Ibid.*

[19] See below, pp. 115-16.

[20] FO 371/21629.

joined them in opposing an air convention,[21] the Germans could see the facts of the case as clearly as the British. 'The very fact that we are especially vulnerable to air attack', Sir Edward Ellington wrote to General Montgomery Massingberd early in 1935, 'makes it in the interest of our possible enemies not to limit the use of their most effective weapon.'[22] His statement, in fact, echoed a question put to a C.I.D. committee by his predecessor, as early as 1932; 'Is it seriously to be expected that a nation whose weakness at sea exposed it to the relentless pressure of our naval blockade would not call in the new world [air power] to redress the balance of the old [sea power]?'[23]

A simple consideration of her own national interests made it unlikely that Germany would sign an air convention, and abide by its terms. This calculation would outweigh all others. 'It is necessary to face the fact', indicated an air staff memorandum early in 1938, 'that in war ethical considerations in themselves have ultimately no force. Past experience suggests therefore that the sole criterion by which any method will ultimately be judged is "Will it win the war or at least avert defeat?"'[24] Some British military authorities and a few politicians believed that Germany regarded air power as a definite 'war winning instrument'.

These views in themselves cast doubt on the sincerity of the apparent German attitude towards an air convention. Suspicions were further increased by a report from the Director of Military Operations and Intelligence on his visit to Germany at the end of 1936:

> I asked several of the senior officers their opinion on the question of the abolition of air bombing from the military point of view in connection with Hitler's proposal. None of them believed that it can or will be abolished, nor do they believe in the possibility of limiting bombing to the zone of the armies. Brauchitsch,

---

[21] It should be noted that during the early 1930s, the Air Ministry defended the Hague Convention. Thus, Londonderry wrote to Simon on 25 July 1932, in reference to British proposals made early in that month for the entire prohibition of all air attacks upon the civil population that 'subject to the proviso that the proposed international convention should be based on reasonable and practicable rules for the restriction of bombardment to military objectives these proposals seem to me to be eminently practicable and desirable.' (FO 317/16341.) However, it should be recalled that the air staff were waging a war against the possible abolition of air forces and tried thus to avoid the more drastic solutions.

[22] 15 February 1935. FO 371/18827.

[23] Notes on the proposal to prohibit bombing on sovereign states and shipping. May 1932, Cab. 10/106.

[24] Memorandum by the air staff on the restriction of air warfare, December 1936, Air 8/203.

commanding in East Prussia was ruthless on the subject of the civilian population and said that in the next war anything would be justified in order to make it short, and that civilians might have to suffer as they did in the thirty years war.[25]

In support of these specific contentions, arguments of a more general nature were also adduced. Taking a broad view of the changing pattern of international relations, the critics of an air convention maintained that the 'rules of the game' had been so fundamentally altered that it was futile to strive for an international convention dealing with arms limitation. Not unexpectedly, this contention seems to have gained in strength during the latter half of the decade. Later in 1936, for instance, the Air Staff advised the Government to remember that:

> Conditions today are entirely different from those which prevailed when disarmament discussions at Geneva were actually proceeding. ... The menace of air attack has greatly increased but so have the difficulties of reaching any international agreement. Some Governments are better informed about, and greatly preoccupied with, the problem of air attack and defence but opinions concerning the best method of guarding against air attack are still widely divergent. Other governments seem intent upon achieving their political and territorial aims by force or by the threat of force and show no desire to abide by any international obligations, even by those which they have already assumed. Rearmament has proceeded to lengths previously undreamed of. In these circumstances it appears completely useless to embark upon a unilateral attempt to produce new proposals for the restriction of air warfare unless a favourable political atmosphere can first be produced.[26]

A corollary to this line of reasoning was the contention that the laws of war were subject to the same restraints which governed all legal systems; they were therefore no exception to the rule that the force of law was immensely enhanced if effective penalties were incurred by violation of the law. Yet air warfare appeared remarkably immune to what were considered to be sufficient deterrents in most cases. 'Recent experience', it was suggested, had shown that guarantees of collective action against an aggressor were of 'illusory value';[27] alternatively, neutral opinion, 'certainly would not prevent a desperate belligerent violating any rule if by doing so he might either quickly achieve victory or avert defeat'; retaliation in kind could not be a completely effective deterrent in view of the 'varying degrees of

---

[25] *Ibid.*
[26] *Ibid.*
[27] C.I.D. Paper 1408-B, 1 March 1938. FO 371/21624, C 1704/306/62.

vulnerability of differing social systems resulting in different standards of passive defence' and concentration on air power at the expense of other components of defence.[28]

In fact, ever since the First World War, various attempts to define and codify air law had proved failures. All such efforts had been marred by the inherent difficulties which the issue raised.[29] Broadly speaking, three main groups of proposals had been advanced in an attempt to protect the civilian population by a restriction of air bombardment. The first consisted of a corpus of rules governing air warfare (an example of which was provided by those drafted at the Hague in 1923 in an effort to define the legitimate objects of air attack). The second consisted of proposals for the restriction of bombing to such specified areas as 'the battle zone', (Under this category were the proposals put forward in the first French plan three days after the opening of the Disarmament Conference and the proposals outlined in the German Peace Plan of March 1936). Third, there were proposals made at the Hague for the delimitation of geographical areas which did not contain legitimate military targets and were therefore to be immune from air bombardment. Neither these methods, nor any combination of them, won general acceptance. Admittedly, a commission of jurists from Great Britain, France, Italy, Japan, the Netherlands and the United States, which met in the Hague in 1923, did draft a code of aerial warfare; but it was never ratified. The basic stumbling block proved to be article 24 of their code, which specified that 'aerial bombardment is legitimate only when directed at a military objective'.[30] Neither the jurists themselves, nor anyone else associated with the issue, could possibly define those military targets which would therefore not be immune to this form of attack. After all, entire nations were already organized for war —even in peace-time; others would certainly mobilize the bulk of their population and material resources for military or quasi-military purposes if involved in any major conflict. Under these conditions, it was hard to see which targets could possibly be excluded. Similar

---

[28]*Ibid.*

[29]On the subject, see, *inter alia*, J.M. Spaight, 'Air Bombardment' *British Yearbook of International Law* 4 (1922/3), 21-33; *Air Power and the Cities* (London, 1930); 'The Chaotic State of International Law Governing Bombardment', *Royal Air Force Quarterly* (1938), 24-32; K.V.R.T., 'Aerial Warfare and International Law', *Virginia Law Review* 28 (1942), 518-27; H.S. Leroy, 'Limitations of Air Warefare', *Air Law Review* 12 (1941), 19-33; K.R. Kuhn, 'Aerial Bombardment and the Laws of War as Applied to Food Ships', *American Journal of International Law* (1939), 730-3; and D. Johnson, *Rights in Air Space* (Manchester, 1965), pp. 39-43.

[30]*'General Report of the Commission of Jurists at The Hague 1923'*, *American Journal of International Law* 17 (1923), Supplement, pp. 242-60.

difficulties of definition confronted any attempt to define specific 'safety areas' for the civilian population; they also applied to the limitation of permissible bombing to the battle zone. In a war of movement, that zone might shift daily, or even hourly. The alternative, to limit permissible bombing to the *fighting* zone, would prove even more difficult. Furthermore, both proposals would have operated unequally in the case of different countries.[31] This point was forcefully put in a memorandum submitted to the Foreign Office by the Belgian Government on 19 August, 1935, in connection with the Air Pact.

> Such a limitation has always been strongly opposed by Belgium which has maintained that the determination of the zones in which air bombing would remain authorized could not be effected with sufficient precision and certainty, and would in practice be ineffective. Belgium, in effect on account of the number of built up areas and the density of her road and railway system would to a large extent remain exposed to air bombardment, whereas other belligerents would be better safeguarded.[32]

In view of all these complications, it is not difficult to understand the remark made by Professor Spaight, the British member of the Commission of Jurists which framed the 1923 Code on the regulation of air warfare, and perhaps the best informed of contemporary authorities on the history and methods of air warfare limitation. 'In air warfare', he wrote, 'more than in its elder brethren of the land and sea, the heart and the conscience of the combatant are the guarantee for fair fighting not any rule formulated in a treaty or in a manual'.[33]

Under such circumstances, claimed the opponents of an air convention, it would clearly be folly for the Government to put faith in what could only be an unreliable international agreement. Indeed, claimed the critics, by agreeing and adhering to such a convention, the Government would induce a dangerous sense of false security.[34] More important, it would provide itself with an excuse to neglect the preparation of adequate defences. As one memorandum to the Cabinet put it:

> It may be proved that the public are now alive to the dangers of air attack and are consequently less likely to neglect defence against it than in the past. But the written law commands in England a respect which is unknown to other countries and the

---

[31] Memorandum by the Air Staff on the restriction of Air Warfare, December 1936, Air 8/203.

[32] FO Print 6093/55/18. Quoted in *Ibid*.

[33] 'Air Bombardment', *British Yearbook of International Law*, (1923/4), p. 32.

[34] See for example the correspondence between Ellington and Chatfield early in 1935 on this subject in Cab. 21/739.

English people still retain a measure of confidence in the force of law in the international sphere which unfortunately is unwarranted. It is therefore reasonable to assume that the conclusion of an international agreement would produce a sense of relief and a relaxation of effort which would largely be unjustified. It would be very difficult to combat the resulting urge to get rid of the heavy burden of defence measures. The more so since in this country, unlike the totalitarian states, such measures have to receive the approval of Parliament, and it would be impracticable for His Majesty's Government to declare in Parliament that an international agreement just entered into was not worth the paper on which it was written'.[35]

Even though these difficulties rendered the attainment of an internationally recognized code of air warfare impracticable (if not illusionary), the British Government nevertheless devoted considerable time and effort in an attempt to solve the problems involved. Ultimately, of course, the juridical, political and essentially logical obstacles to an air convention proved to be insuperable. Yet, the fact that this conclusion was not finally accepted until 1939 is itself of considerable importance. The record of the interim debates indicates that no account of the formulation of British defence and foreign policy before the outbreak of war can be complete unless sufficient note is taken of the sincerity, and consistency, with which the Government sought some form of international agreement (indeed, it might be said, *any* form of international agreement) which might minimize the danger of air attack.

In its efforts to deal with the possible restriction of air warfare during the late 1930s, the Cabinet considered two alternative methods. One was to make a unilateral declaration of Britain's intent to observe the draft Hague Rules on the outbreak of war. The second was to propose a new international conference or a bilateral agreement with the object of attaining an agreement on rules of air warfare.

The first of these approaches was suggested by the First Sea Lord at the meeting of the Chiefs of Staff Committee on 13 July, 1936. Its timing seems to have been influenced by the Cabinet's apparent disillusionment with the prospect of attaining either an air pact or an air limitation agreement.[36]

Chatfield proposed that the C.I.D. should recommend to the Cabinet that the plans of the Services for the outbreak of war be based on adherence to the principles of The Hague Rules of air warfare, despite the fundamental difficulties inherent in interpreting them. In

---

[35] C.I.D. paper 1408-B, 1 March 1938, FO 371/21624.
[36] 181 C.O.S. Cab. 53/6.

so doing, he recommended that Britain deliberately desist from the aerial bombardment of a civilian population. In military terms, Chatfield's proposition did not appear controversial. Although the 1923 draft had never reached the stage of an international convention, the special situation of London made it obviously in Britain's interest not to resort to the bombing of civilian targets in the early stages of a war in which she might be involved. This had long been standard British policy, albeit a doctrine to which the C.I.D. had not given its clear and specific adherence. In political terms, however, Chatfield did add a revolutionary rider to his proposal. With the strong support of the C.I.G.S., the First Sea Lord further suggested that Britain should make a public declaration that she accepted article 24 of the 1923 code; this enunciated the guidelines of the policy which His Majesty's Government would adopt at the outbreak of war, without prejudice to action which might be taken were other nations to resort to blatant attacks on the civilian population. In Chatfield's view, a unilateral declaration of that sort would encourage responses in kind from other powers. It would also thereby exercise a restraining effect on an enemy who might be considering the possibility of resorting to unrestricted air bombardment in the early stages of a war. Underlying the proposal was the specific hope that a move of this nature would influence Germany should the latter have to decide whether to 'take the gloves off' and launch an air attack on large British cities. Within this context, Chatfield explained, Germany might herself see the advantage of a positive response. 'It was possible that Germany was not very happy about her industrial districts and the removal of this fear by declaration of our intention might have some advantage'. Such a declaration would serve a further purpose by soothing the air anxiety of the British public 'to declare one's adherence might assist in stopping the general belief and fears that the first thing to happen in war would be the bombing of London'.[37] The Admiralty had earlier made a similar suggestion, during the Ethiopian Crisis, in connection with plans for a possible war with Italy. It then proposed that, since Britain would suffer more than Italy from air attack, she would do well to declare her interpretation of the Hague Rules in regard to indiscriminate bombing in the hope that she might thus be able to effect a restriction on bombing. However, no decision on the question had been reached.[38] Notwithstanding the Air Ministry's natural opposition to this proposal, it was accepted by the Chiefs of Staff Committee

[37] *Ibid.*

[38] C.I.D. paper 1246-B, Cab. 4/24 on the Admiralty's ambivalent assessment of the danger of air attack as far as the Royal Navy was concerned at this time see R. Marder, 'The Royal Navy and the Ethiopian Crisis of 1935-1936', *American Historical Review* 75, (1970), p.1344-5.

which recommended to the C.I.D. that 'there might be something to gain and there should be nothing to lose from the declaration of a policy to which this country binds itself and conceivably it may prove a starting point for the consideration of more practical rules in the future'.[39]

When the suggestion came before the C.I.D. meeting, held a week later, it was rejected. That body did concur with the Services' intention to base their plans on the principle that Britain would not resort to the bombardment of a civilian population. But a public declaration to that effect seemed to be at variance with the Foreign Office's specific programme which, even after the reoccupation of the Rhineland, was designed to test Germany's intentions towards a general settlement.[40] Ultimately, it was to be two years before the British Government would adopt the tactics suggested by the Chiefs of Staff Committee. Not until 1938 did Chamberlain declare in the House of Commons that Britain would only bomb purely military objectives, and even then would take care to avoid civilian casualties in pursuit of three principles: 'It is against international law', he declared, 'to bomb civilians as such and to make deliberate attacks upon the civilian population.' 'Targets which are aimed at from the air must be legitimate military objectives and must be capable of identification.' 'Reasonable care must be taken in attacking these military objectives so that by carelessness a civilian population in the neighbourhood is not bombed.'[41]

Until then the Government had devoted more time to the consideration of the second, and apparently more practical proposal: the restriction of air warfare by direct attempts to secure an international conference with the purpose of attaining an agreement on rules of air warfare, or by bilateral negotiations on this issue. The process in this direction commenced late in 1936, when the C.I.D. defined the promotion of an international convention establishing restrictions on air warfare as a distinct British interest.[42] By that time, the problems arising from Britain's particular vulnerability to air

[39] C.I.D. Paper 1246-B, Cab. 4/24.

[40] 281 C.I.D. Cab. 2/6 and also FO 371/1 912, C 5951/4/18. For an analysis of the Foreign Office's efforts to achieve a general settlement with Germany see W.N. Medlicott, *Britain and Germany: The Search for Agreement 1930-1937* (London, 1969), pp. 30-31.

[41] See R. Wernham, *The Royal Air Force in Bombing Offensive Against Germany: Prewar Evolution of Bomber Command 1917-1939* (Ministry of Defence, Air Historical Branch, 1947), p. 230; and also N. Jones, *The Theory of Strategic Power in the Royal Air Force 1918-1939: Concepts and Capabilities* (Unpublished M.A. thesis, London University, 1968), pp. 169-170.

[42] 284 C.I.D. Cab. 2/6.

attack, and especially the dangers of aerial bombardment on its maritime supply routes and on London, were already being considered by several sub-committees of the C.I.D. At the meeting of the full body on 11 November, Sir Samuel Hoare urged that forum to come to a decision on the code of air warfare. Discussing the desirability of an air convention, he quoted the conclusions reached by the sub-committee on Fuel Supply in Time of War: 'It would be to our general advantage to have an international agreement restricting aerial warfare notwithstanding the doubt that must exist as to whether such laws would in practice be observed.'[43] In the course of the subsequent discussion, it became apparent that the members of the C.I.D. accepted the Foreign Office's opinion that any step towards opening negotiations on such an agreement should await progress in other matters affecting European peace which were to be discussed at a proposed five power conference (Belgium, Italy, France, Germany and Great Britain). Nevertheless, they also approved the Fuel Supply sub-committee's conclusion. The Committee invited Lord Swinton, the Secretary of State for Air (who, surprisingly, had backed the conclusion)[44] to formulate proposals. These were to serve as a basis of an agreement which would be the prerequisite for a consideration of reopening the question with other powers.[45]

For more than a year thereafter, the whole matter lay dormant. One reason was that the Air Staff, which clearly did not share Swinton's ideas as to the desirability of a convention, dragged their feet for several months before formulating British requirements in such a convention.[46] More important was the outbreak of the Spanish Civil War, which greatly preoccupied Britain and all the European powers throughout 1936 and 1937.[47] Finally, the implementation of the C.I.D.'s decision was delayed because the Germans, in their diplomatic dealings with the British from the middle of 1936 until November 1937, did not follow up their earlier suggestion about a

---

[43] *Ibid.*

[44] He told the C.I.D. that he 'felt strongly that an agreement of this nature would be of value even if it only held good for a short time after the outbreak of war', *Ibid.* See also his notes on 14 November, 1937, in Air 9/84.

[45] *Ibid.*

[46] It should be noted that the Air Staff objected in 1935 to the conclusion of the Air Pact lest 'it may lead to its invariable political concomitant — a regional prohibition of bombing'. (April, 1935, Air 8/201.) They remained uncompromising antagonists of such prohibition three years later. (see for example Air Marshal Slessor's notes on 14 January 1938, Air 9/84.

[47] See H. Thomas, *The Spanish Civil War* (London, 1974), and K. Watkins, *Britain Divided, The Effect of the Spanish Civil War on British Political Opinion* (London, 1963).

convention for air warfare rules.[48] However, late in 1937 a British initiative once again seemed expedient. First, the much publicized air attacks on civilian targets in Spain,[49] notably on Guernica, emphasized the need that was recognized by the non-intervention committee for such an air agreement.[50] Secondly, in the course of a conversation with Lord Halifax on 19 November, Hitler hinted that Germany was in favour of reopening negotiations on the subject.[51] The Foreign Office immediately noted that Hitler's suggestion was not an isolated move; throughout November and December, German officials, on various occasions, gave the impression that Germany favoured negotiations on limitation of bombing.[52] Therefore, in the Cabinet discussion on Halifax's report (24 November), it was decided to take up Hitler's suggestion as soon as possible. Chamberlain was sceptical about any understanding restricting aerial bombardment, since 'this would be no more reliable than the gas protocol, which had not saved nations from the cost of anti-gas preparations'.[53] Nevertheless, the majority of Ministers urged the air staff to complete the formulation of British requirement in any convention restricting aerial bombardment.

Meanwhile early in 1938 the House of Commons had been taking a keen interest in the subject of international restrictions on air warfare. This fact lay behind a Cabinet decision, taken on 2 February, to support a private Parliamentary motion dealing with this issue.[54] Thus, Eden referred to the whole question of aerial bombardment in his speech to the Commons on the same day. He stated that he felt sure that 'we could count on Hitler's sympathy and support' in any wider international endeavour to restrict aerial bombardment of defenceless civilians in which 'he felt confidence that the French Government would join'.[55] He also informed the House that an

[48] FO 371/20700, C 7862/148/62.

[49] See Thomas, *The Spanish Civil War*, pp. 537-540. On international periodical literature on this issue see the pioneering research of Goss Milton, 'Civilian Morale Under Aerial Bombardment 1914-1939' (unpublished Ph.D. thesis, Air University, Maxwell, Alabama, 1948), especially pp. 241-65. For reflections on the subject in British non-fiction at that time, see *inter alia*, L.E.O. Charlton, *The Menace of the Sky* (London, 1937); John L. Davies, *Air Raid* (London, 1938); and G.L. Steer, *The Tree of Guernica* (London, 1938); on the newsreel coverage of these events, see F. Aldgate, 'British Newsreels and the Spanish Civil War', *History* 58 (1973), 160-3.

[50] On this Committee, see Dante A. Puzzo, *Spain and the Great Powers 1936-1941* (New York, 1962).

[51] FO 371/20700, C 8682/148/62.

[52] *Ibid.*

[53] Cab. 23/90.

[54] FO 371/21624, C 874/306/62.

[55] *Ibid.*

exhaustive departmental enquiry was under way with a view to preparing the ground and enabling Britain to put forward concrete proposals for an international agreement. Eden's announcement attracted 'more publicity than he anticipated' and was followed by reproaches and enquiries from various governments, notably the French, which seemed to show a great interest in the subject late in 1937 and early in 1938.[56]

While the Cabinet was still awaiting the completion of the Air Ministry plan for restrictions on air warfare, British hopes for achieving something far more substantial than the mere limitation of aerial bombardment grew. On 3 February the foreign policy committee heard a report from the British Ambassador in Berlin, Sir Nevile Henderson, on his meeting with von Ribbentrop on 26 January. Ribbentrop had given the impression that Germany favoured a resumption of negotiations on air disarmament and in particular on the restriction, limitation, and abolition of bombing aircraft.[57] Not surprisingly, the committee considered this to be a highly important offer, especially in view of the allegedly serious British inferiority in air power. Ministers repeated statements made some six years earlier, when the same issue was discussed by the disarmament committee, to the effect of striving for abolition in order to 'regain our insular position'. Chamberlain, in particular, did not hide his enthusiasm for such an agreement. In a prolix exposition, he stated that:

> The great advantage of securing the total abolition of military bombing aeroplanes was that the fighter aeroplanes would be so immeasurably superior in speed etc. to any civil aeroplanes converted into bombers that the latter machines would be unable to do any serious mischief. What was required was an agreement which would in precise terms define a bombing aeroplane and would thus provide that all such aeroplanes should be abolished and that no more should be constructed in the future. It would be an enormous advance and of incalculable value to all concerned. ... We would like to make a start with some limitation on air armaments. This was as important to us as the Colonial question to them.[58]

The apparent German initiative seemed to fit the broad lines of the Prime Minister's appeasement policy,[59] and Henderson returned to Berlin with a clear and straightforward brief: He was to offer 'collaboration in appeasement' in exchange for an agreement on

[56]*Ibid.*

[57]Cab. 27/623.

[58]*Ibid.*

[59]See on this subject K. Middlemas, *Diplomacy of Illusion* (London, 1972), especially pp. 110-57.

colonies and bomber disarmament. The Cabinet considered it possible that Germany would agree to such an 'offer' and called upon the Air Ministry to formulate at once a British desideratum which would cvoer all aspects of air disarmament, including an air limitation agreement and a convention on the restriction of aerial warfare. However, hopes that Hitler might be contemplating an air disarmament agreement were dashed on 20 February 1938. Addressing the Reichstag on that day, the German leader made it clear that Germany would not change her well-known policy with regard to air limitation, declaring that 'it would be a good thing to limit armaments or prohibit bombing but it would be better to muzzle the press'.[60]

This change in Germany's presumed attitude gave rise to serious misgivings within the British Government. Hitler's announcement clearly indicated that air disarmament was out of the question. Consequently, some limited international agreement to 'humanize' air warfare seemed the only immediately practical means of minimizing the air peril. Yet, it was at this stage that all the old misgivings about the value of such a convention reappeared. The Air Ministry, which presented a memorandum on the subject to the Cabinet on 1 March, took a particularly forceful line, claiming that without accompanying limitations on materials and aircraft, a 'humanizing' convention would be positively dangerous.[61]

When asked to comment on the Air Ministry's views, and to advise whether to proceed with the preparation of a convention, the Foreign Office could not present a unanimous opinion. William Strang seemed to doubt the advisability of rejecting the 'one positive proposal that is on the table from the German side',[62] and Sir Alexander Cadogan, the Permanent Under-Secretary, wrote that 'rules of air warfare are useless and maybe dangerous except as an accompaniment of limitation of material,' thus concluding a long minute which showed clearly that the hope of securing the latter agreement did not vanish within the Foreign Office.

> It is a great pity that we cannot have that abolition of military aviation. There are two arguments generally used against it.
> 1. You cannot put the clock back. I am not so sure that this is a fair argument. Opium is invaluable in medicine, but we strive to impose every sort of restriction on its improper and dangerous use without being accused of putting the clock back, and I doubt whether the legitimate use of civil aircraft is half as beneficial as the legitimate use of drugs. ... 2. It was always said (by us) at

[60] FO 371/21656, C 1426/42/18.
[61] FO 371/21624, C 1704/306/12.
[62] 8 March, 1938, *Ibid*.

the Disarmament Conference that if we abolished military aviation we should be at the mercy of the civil aviation of continental countries. At that time that was not untrue; the facilities for developing civil aviation in our small island were restricted, but even at that time some people pointed out that with the increase in range we should be developing our Empire air routes. Also in those days the potential weight of attck to be delivered by a military air force had not developed to the fantastic degree which it has now reached — a degree which could not be approached by any converted civil aviation. Both these anticipations are shown by this report to have been realized. Is it conceivable that any fleet of commerial machines could constitute one tenth of the threat that the existing German bomber fleet represents to us?

And with every week that passes the difference between the threat of the German bomber fleet and German civil aviation increases rapidly. But if we cannot get that abolition we can approach towards it — and should be able to — by limitation. . . . It should do and we ought not to lose sight of it or risk missing any opportunity.[63]

The discussion became rather academic on 3 March, when Henderson reported on a conversation with von Ribbentrop in which the newly appointed Foreign Minister claimed that Germany would now allow herself 'to be cheated by empty provisions [restrictions on air warfare] . . . even if the Soviet Union declared itself ready to refrain from the use of . . . bombs, it would be impossible to place any faith in such a declaration'.[64] It was clear from this report that very little remained of Hitler's previously expressed willingness to proceed with an attempt to prohibit or restrict aerial bombardment. And so far as limitation was concerned he was completely negative. No wonder therefore that when, a week later, the Swiss Government made an enquiry about the British intentions and actions concerning such a convention. Orme Sargent bluntly minuted: 'Has not the time come now for giving up this *farce* of pretending that there is any possibility of reaching agreement on the prohibition in face of the definite attitude which Hitler had adopted?'[65]

Despite the strength of this argument the British Government did not accept Orme Sargent's advice. On the contrary, by the middle of 1938, when the Czechoslovakian crisis was giving rise to increasing fears that Britain might become involved in an armed conflict, it considered there to be an even greater need for an air convention. The fact that the chances of concluding such a convention were slim was

[63]*Ibid.*
[64]FO 371/21656 C 1524/42/18.
[65]FO 371/21627 C 1445/306/62. Italics added.

outweighed by the Cabinet's awareness of Britain's inferiority in air power and of the inadequate state of the country's air defences. Accordingly, late in June, the Government thought it advisable to reopen the discussions on a possible air convention. On this occasion, moreover, the Air Ministry even agreed to withdraw its previous demand that all negotiations on legal restrictions be linked to those on limitations of aircraft.[66] This 'concession' probably owed much to the knowledge that by now not one member of the Government believed that Germany would agree to any kind of air limitation agreement. It seems to have been primarily influenced, however, by the initially unsuccessful nature of the experiments conducted by Bomber Command. These indicated that it was incapable of countering the much feared 'bolt from the blue' by striking directly at the German air bases and thus playing an immediate and major part in the critical stages of defence.[67] A special C.I.D. sub-committee (the Sub-Committee on Limitation of Armaments, consisting of representatives of the Services and the Foreign Office), began discussions on the whole issue on 7 July.[68] This body was unanimous in its view that Britain's interests would best be served by a legal convention, despite its equally unanimous opinion that the convention would not be observed for long after an outbreak of war. Echoing the attitude adopted by the C.I.D. in November 1936, the sub-committee considered the main advantage of a convention to lie in its presumed deterrent effect on an enemy. Moreover, the members seemed to share the opinion of the Secretary of State for War, Leslie Hore-Belisha, that 'anything would be for the good which would make the knock-out blow more remote'.[69] The sub-committee accepted the suggestion of the Foreign Secretary that, in an effort to break the impasse in negotiations with Germany, Britain should work towards a bilateral agreement which, when reached, might induce other Powers to follow suit. In particular, suggested Halifax, such a programme might overcome the disinclination of the Germans to open negotiations on a convention, which seemed to stem from their suspicious attitude towards the Russians.[70] However, before negotiations could commence, the British requirements had to be defined. For this purpose, a special committee, headed by Sir W. Malkin of the Foreign Office, was specifically charged with determining the degree of immunity which Britain

---

[66] fo 371/216 28 c 6072/3061 62.

[67] See Wernham, *The Royal Air Force,* pp. 256-258.

[68] FO 371/21628 C 6580/306/62.

[69] Cab. 16/201.

[70] *Ibid.*

should aim for, and the manner in which she should attempt to improve the draft Hague Rules.[71]

The Committee suggested two principles or methods for restricting aerial bombardment: One was to confine it to certain geographical limits, which might be defined as the area in which fighting on land or sea was actually taking place; the second was to specify the objectives which alone might legitimately be bombarded from the air and the conditions under which a bombardment of this type was permissible. The Committee was unable to predict which alternative was likely to prove more acceptable to the Powers concerned; furthermore, it could not definitely advise which would best serve Britain's own interests.[72] The report was placed before the Limitation of Armaments Sub-Committee on 18 July, and in the discussions which ensued, two important questions were raised.

The first concerned the degree of immunity for which Britain should aim. Within this context, particular reference was made as to whether it would be to Britain's advantage to include factories known to be engaged in the manufacture of arms, ammunition or distinctively military supplies as legitimate military objectives under The Hague Rules. Sir Cyril Newall, the Chief of Air Staff, pointed out that recent investigations into the vulnerability of German industry had shown that Germany's industrial organization was much more exposed to air attack than British military authorities had previously supposed. In particular, the Ruhr, with its dense concentration of war industry and raw materials, contained serious bottlenecks in the system of distribution of electric power and gas. In his view, it was therefore an open question whether or not Britain ought to retain the right to bomb German industrial centres, even if this implied a recognition of Germany's right to bomb similar targets in large British cities. Lord Chatfield thought otherwise. He was clearly opposed to the retention of such a right, and reminded the Committee that the case for prohibiting the bombing of factories was based not only on the protection of the civilian but also on the immunity of merchant ships. His view was that 'once the right to bomb outside the fighting zone was allowed, the whole prospect of protecting the civilian would disappear'.[73]

In consideration of this clash of views, the Limitation of Armaments sub-committee decided not to decide. Instead, it agreed to remit this question for examination and report to the Joint Planning Sub-

[71] Cab. 21/738.
[72] Cab. 21/737.
[73] Cab. 55/13.

Committee, with the assistance of the Board of Trade, the Industrial Intelligence Centre, and the Air Target Sub-Committee.

The second question raised by the Malkin report was of more general interest. It centred on the price Britain might be asked to pay for Germany's cooperation in promoting a convention on air warfare rules. The Malkin Committee's report indicated that any rule proposed by Britain would probably 'be met with a demand that we should, in return, accept such a limitation of belligerent rights at sea as would protect the enemy's civilian population from the suffering resulting from stoppage of seaborne supplies'. The question therefore was whether to agree to the abandonment of some traditional British maritime rights, in particular the interception of foodstuffs, which might be demanded by the Germans as a *quid pro quo*.[74]

Duff Cooper and Vansittart were vehemently opposed to the idea that Britain should agree to such a bargain. The former pointed out that Britain possessed no offensive weapon other than the naval blockade. Should the proposal come from Hitler, he indicated, it would be basically a-symmetric. Hitler would ask 'us to give up the use both of our air force and of our navy in exchange for giving up (*sic*) of the German air force only, meantime the Germans would be free to concentrate the whole of her effort on land operations with every possibility of occupying the channel ports'.[75] Vansittart also considered the idea of a bargain to be 'shortsighted'. It 'would put a premium on the military aggressor in the narrower sense of the word, and, as far as Germany was concerned would give her military predominance over the whole of Europe'.[76] These arguments did not, however, convince the entire Limitation of Armaments Sub-Committee. They were countered by others adduced by those members who favoured the notion of a negotiated bargain. Foremost among the latter was, somewhat surprisingly, Lord Chatfield. His premise was that 'the defence of this country had changed since the last war'. He emphasized that Britain should be ready to pay a high price for a guarantee that her civilian population would not be attacked, which would imply a return to the secure position she enjoyed in 1914. The very fact that Germany might demand a bargain would, in his view, indicate an acknowledgment on her part of the power of the naval blockade as a military weapon. Consequently, the bargain itself

---

[74] For previous occasions on which it was suggested that British maritime rights be the subject of a bargain to secure advantages in other directions, see A.T.B. 196, Cab. 47/6 and N.W. Medlicott, *The Economic Blockade,* Vol. I (London, 1952), pp. 11-12.

[75] Cab. 47/14.

[76] *Ibid.*

would contain a built-in sanction, which would influence Germany to observe her part of the agreement and not bomb Britain. In putting the pros and cons of the suggestion, the Chairman of the Committee, Sir Thomas Inskip, the Minister for Coordinatin of Defence, seemed to concur with Chatfield's contention. He stressed the widespread belief that the main military threat to Britain inherent in an aerial bombardment was the fact that it might cause her to lose a short war. 'Assuming that both sides honoured the agreement,' he said, 'it would mean that whereas it might jeopardize our chances of winning a long war, it would make it impossible for us to lose a short war'.[77] Here, too, the Sub-Committee decided that the question should be examined further, and remitted it for report to the Advisory Committee on Trade Questions in Times of War.[78]

The Joint Planning Committee submitted its report on the Sub-Committee's first question on 24 October. It might legitimately be suggested that its deliberations had been influenced by the intervening Munich crisis.[79] From the point of view of the Air Staff, the experience of September 1938 had been particularly harrowing. Aware that Bomber Command was in no condition to engage in an all-out war, and apprehensive of the damage which the Luftwaffe might inflict on Britain, the Air Staff had been anxious to do as little as possible. The Joint Planning Committee certainly attempted to curtail its operative assignments. That body categorically recommended the abrogation of Britain's right to exert pressure on Germany by aerial bombardment on her industrial centres in the Ruhr, provided the Germans would respond by relinquishing their right to bomb London and British supply systems. The report said:

> Germany depends to an exceptional extent upon the Ruhr-Rhineland industrial area for the maintenance of her national life in war. No similar concentration of industry exists in England, but there is no target in any other country comparable to London in importance and vulnerability. In addition, Germany can find a most profitable objective for her air attack in our supply and distribution system, particularly our ports and shipping. On balance, the retention of the right to exert economic pressure by air attack on industry would not appear to be to our advantage, since it would almost certainly involve attack upon London and our supply system.[80]

The Committee also specified the degree of immunity which it recommended that Britain ought to try to obtain. It regarded as

[77]*Ibid.*
[78]*Ibid.*
[79]Webster and Frankland, *The Strategic Air Offensive,* p. 99.
[80]J.P. 304, Cab. 55/13.

impractical the German proposal to limit air attacks to the 'battle zone'; it would prove difficult to define this area and to obtain a general agreement on the lines of The Hague Rules, which would attempt to specify military objectives and the circumstances under which they might be attacked. The Committee emphasized that most of Britain's industry and a great part of her population must be regarded as part of her 'armament industry' in modern war. It was therefore unlikely that a satisfactory degree of immunity would be obtained by this form of restriction. Instead, it recommended that Britain should require that aerial bombardment outside the 'battle zone' be allowed only in order to *permit air attacks against armed forces.*[81]

Two weeks later the Advisory Committee on Trade Questions in Times of War discussed the second question which had been raised by the Limitation of Armaments Committee, i.e., the possibility of bargaining the restriction of Britain's maritime belligerent rights in return for a German undertaking to avoid air attacks on her civilian population.[82] The Advisory Committee objected strongly to such a bargain, whose practical effect, it held, would be to invite Britain to give up two methods of imposing her will on the enemy in return for one. In its view, the surrender of maritime belligerent rights would neutralize the advantages conferred by naval superiority over army superiority, and would in practice grant exclusive benefits to all of Britain's potential enemies. The Committee was of the opinion that the mere existence of the highly vulnerable Ruhr should render such a bargain unnecessary.

The inadvisability of amending the fundamental principles of maritime belligerent rights was further buttressed by two examples. The Cabinet was reminded that, at the beginning of the First World War, Britain had been strongly pressed by the U.S. Government to abide by the full terms of the Declaration of London, even though the Government had not ratified that document. Only the illegalities committed by the enemy had effectively enabled Britain to escape from the limitations of that Declaration, her agreement to which 'might easily have led to disaster'.[83] Attention was also called to the current investigation into the difficulties resulting from Britain's signature (in 1930) to the Optional Clause and the General Act of the League of Nations, which committed her to submit all disputes on maritime belligerent rights to an international tribunal. Finally, and

[81] *Ibid.*
[82] A.T.B. 196, Cab. 42/6.
[83] *Ibid.*

perhaps most effectively, the Committee pointed out the disastrous results which would ensue, from Britain's point of view, should Germany break her part of the suggested bargain:

> It would always be comparatively easy for an enemy, profiting by the restriction of British right of interception, to build up reserves of commodities during the earlier stages of a war and then to throw over the agreed rules and attempt to secure a decision by unrestricted air attack. The essence of such a move would lie in its quick effect; whereas the sanction of increased economic pressure by naval and diplomatic action would operate very slowly and, indeed, if the enemy's commodity reserves had reached considerable dimensions, would probably have no effect at all for some time.[84]

The unequivocal conclusion of the Committee did not prevent the Cabinet from taking steps to open negotiations with Germany; but it did prevent the use of a very important lever in these negotiations. Moreover, when, early in January 1939, the Limitation of Armaments Committee resumed its discussion on the two reports which it had commissioned the previous July, a definite change of approach was discernible. Sir Kingsley Wood, the Secretary of State for Air, produced some highly effective arguments against continuing the inquiry. He suggested that the international position had altered so much since the Committee was appointed, that were Britain now to come forward with a plan for disarmament, she would appear to do so from a position of weakness. This would have a deplorable effect not only on the British people but on the world in general.[85] The Committee seems to have concurred with Kingsley Wood's opinion, although Pownall's diary indicates that some senior officials within the Services still thought differently. Describing the meeting of the reconvened Committee, he wrote:

> The J.P.C. had produced an excellent report backed by the C.O.S. saying they thought there *was* hope for an agreement to limit air activities ... but Kingsley Wood came out strongly at the meeting that the whole thing was nonsense and a sheer waste of time for busy men to consider. He distinctly jumped the meeting. H.[ore] B.[elisha] who knew nothing about it fell into line with some quite useless remarks. Stanhope [First Lord of the Admiralty] ... let himself, though a little unwittingly be shut up so Inskip did all that was possible by saying he would report to the P.M.[86]

The Committee, however, never met again.

[84] *Ibid.*
[85] Cab. 16/201.
[86] B. Bond (ed.), *Chief of Staff, The Diaries of Lieutenant-General Sir Henry Pownall,* Vol. 1, *1933-1940* (London, 1972), p.181.

Although Inskip shared Pownall's view that 'even if there was a glimmer of a chance of success it was worth trying',[87] and despite the fact that the Prime Minister was also of the opinion that the enquiry should be continued,[88] no further progress was made. The matter became, as one official put it, 'a trifle embarrassing'[89] to the Government, since individual Members of Parliament and some foreign Governments made recurrent approaches to enquire about the progress of the discussions.[90] It appears that early in February 1939 the British Government finally abandoned all hope of attaining the goal for which it had striven since November 1936.

The inconclusive nature of this particular episode must not be allowed to obscure its significance. In searching for an agreement which might somehow 'humanize' air warfare, the British Government gave ample evidence of its sensitivity to the danger of aerial bombardment. The evidence suggests that this fear exercised a dominant influence over British strategic thought throughout the critical period between 1936 and 1939, and supplied a unique (and hitherto neglected) motive in the making of British foreign policy during that period. As has been seen, neither the known technical difficulties inherent in framing an air agreement, nor even the clear indications of Germany's reluctance to cooperate in overcoming them, prevented British Ministers from devoting much time and effort to the project. Indeed, the persistent efforts made to overcome these problems go far towards explaining the lengthy period of apparent inactivity on the British side. They also serve to illustrate the dangerous extent to which British statesmen misconstrued Germany's intentions — a fault which was central to the entire British policy of appeasement.

This is not to imply a complete lack of British realism on the air issue. Admittedly, the Cabinet discussions of 1935-6 were largely abstract; yet those of 1937-8 seem to have been greatly influenced by the very real examples of Guernica and Barcelona. Although the air raids on these towns had been militarily inconclusive, they were psychologically convincing. An Anglo-German war, it was anticipated, would involve attacks on an even larger scale, and avoidance of this horrifying prospect therefore appeared to demand a drastic solution. Unless sufficient account is taken of the conceptual frame-

[87]*Ibid*.

[88]See Chamberlain's comment on Inskip letter of 16 January, 1939, in Prem. 1/318.

[89]Cab. 21/738.

[90]See Chatfield's letter to Halifax on 24 February 1939, in FO 371/24024 W 3624/199/98.

work thus engendered, it is difficult to understand how the Cabinet could have entertained the possibility of bargaining away some of Britain's highly prized naval power in return for a somewhat dubious air convention.

# 5

# THE BOMBER VS. THE EXPEDITIONARY FORCE (1935-1937)

'If we can survive the first two or three weeks, i.e., air attacks, we can win with our long range weapon — the Navy.'
(Warren Fisher, February 1938 (T161 855 S/48439/01/31))

British anxiety concerning the air menace increased in proportion to the degree to which the Nazi regime entrenched itself within Germany and cast a lengthening shadow over Europe. Military studies of British rearmament in Britain between 1935 and 1938 appear to have devoted insufficient attention to the critical influence of that anxiety on the decision to give priority to air over other defence requirements, especially those of the Army. Political historians, too, have frequently failed to note the extent to which it affected the thinking of the Foreign Office and added to the attraction of the policy of appeasement. The present chapter aims to remedy such deficiencies by focussing attention on these issues.

The period 1935-7 was decisive for the consolidation of the knock-out blow concept. During these years, the Government finally accepted the theory that, in a future war, Germany might try to achieve a quick and decisive victory by means of a large-scale and devastating air attack. Although, as has been seen, this theory had been current in various political circles for some time, the military authorities had not hitherto regarded an air attack as the major threat. After 1935, however, various C.I.D. sub-committees came to the conclusion that a German strategic bombing offensive in the early stages of a war against Britain was highly probable, and that its effects would be disastrous. In short, they approved the thesis which the Air Staff had already propagated as vital to any consideration of future defence plans. These professional assessments served to strengthen the by now familiar arguments of the more percipient politicians.

The discussions in the Chiefs of Staff's Committee of the reports on defence requirements (referred to above) were not confined to the subject of plans for war with Germany. In the first report of the D.R.C., the danger of aerial bombardment constituted merely one of a long list of defence problems, the significance and importance of which was presented as secondary.[1] Not even the passage of several

---

[1] See, for example, Articles 27 and 28 of that Report in Cab. 16/109.

months appears to have endowed the issue with any great urgency. Admittedly, the danger was assessed by the Chiefs of Staff in a D.R.C. interim report in July 1935;[2] a second report in November, however, referred to the need to take into consideration the danger of an 'air attack so continuous and concentrated and on such a scale that a few weeks of such an experience might so undermine the morale of any civilian population as to make it difficult for the Government to continue the War'.[3] But there was no detailed evaluation of probable German strategy in a prospective war against Britain and little attention was devoted to the effects of an all-out bombing offensive. Studies of this nature were not commenced until late in 1934, and took two years to complete.

In October 1934, the Chiefs of Staff Committee decided to examine defence plans in the event of war with Germany and furnished the Joint Planning Committee (J.P.C.)[4] with terms of reference for the preparation of a draft report. The C.I.G.S. was of the opinion that 'the menace of German aggression in the West is not imminent'.[5] This pronouncement may perhaps explain the dilatoriness of the J.P.C., which did not complete its first report until August 1935. When it ultimately appeared, however, that document clearly reflected the views of the Air Staff whose representative on the J.P.C., Group-Captain Harris, exercised a strong influence on the entire Committee.[6] Thus, although the report did not envisage a substantial threat from the German fleet, it did make it plain that the greatest danger was an air attack against the British Isles. The report considered the possibility that Germany might attempt to eliminate Britain before undertaking the subjection of France, as an eventuality which represented the 'worst case' in military parlance. It suggested that such a possibility could not be ruled out altogether, although the operational range and speed of the German bomber force did not make an attack of that sort probable within the near future. Sould Germany be contemplating an early war, she was more likely to aim at

[2]D.P.R. 12, Cab.16/138, Article 11.

[3]Cab. 16/112, Article 25(e).

[4]133 C.O.S., 9 October 1934, Cab. 53/26.

[5]4 October 1934, Cab. 53/26.

[6]On this, see R. Wernham, *The Royal Air Force in Bombing Offensive Against Germany: Prewar Evolution of Bomber Command 1917-1939* (London, 1947), p. 145 and Harris's letter to Sir R. Adam, the representative of the General Staff on that Committee, on 24 September 1936, Air 2/1405). It is significant that the Committee's reports of August 1935 and October 1936 reflected many of the ideas which had been embodied in an internal memo of the Air Staff entitled "The Potential dangers to the security of this country and our consequent defence requirements" (15 January 1936, Air 9/2).

occupying the Low Countries first, with the object of developing the maximum weight of her air attack against Britain at the shortest possible range. However, as time went on and the operational range and speed of her bombers increased, an occupation of the Low Countries would decline in importance, and the British Isles could become Germany's first strategic target. 'Neither of these courses may be ruled out', stressed the report.[7] The Chiefs of Staff Committee, which discussed the report late in October, was disinclined to approve it. The controversy over the air peril was clearly reflected in these discussions, which mainly centered on the probability that Germany would resort to an immediate offensive against Britain.[8] Given the opinions which Chatfield and Montgomery Massingberd had expressed on previous occasions, it is not surprising that neither of them showed much enthusiasm for allowing that report to go any further than the Chiefs of Staff Committee itself, especially in view of the forthcoming discussion by the Cabinet of yet a third D.R.C. report. Nor is it surprising that the Air Staff complained that the time being taken over approving the report was 'inordinately prolonged'.[9]

Nevertheless, a further full year elapsed before the J.P.C. submitted its revised and final paper and the Chiefs of Staff Committee recommenced its discussions on the entire subject. The report of October 1936 did not substantially add to the conclusions embodied in that of the previous year. It considered there to be an equal probability that Germany would either move towards the occupation of the Low Countries or choose to try and knock Britain out by extensive air raids during the early stages.[10] Although it did not say so specifically, the emphasis which the report placed on the disastrous effects of such raids indicates a belief amongst its signatories that the latter course was the one more likely to be adopted.

Thus, in their covering note to their report, the members of the J.P.C. stressed that 'our study of this was has brought us to the conclusion that in 1939 Germany would be able to deliver air attacks on this country which if made with the object of demoralizing our people and/or disorganizing our food supplies might well succeed'.[11] The report itself stressed, *inter alia,* that:

> Germany would not initiate a war unless her responsible

[7]Cab. 53/25.
[8]20 October 1935, Cab. 53/5.
[9]Minutes written on 8 January 1936, Air 8/207.
[10]See C.O.S. 513 (J.P.) Cab. 55/8.
[11]*Ibid.*

statesmen believed that she would win. Her prospects of victory would certainly be greatest during the first few months of war. We are therefore convinced that Germany would plan to gain her victory rapidly. Her first attacks would be designed as knock-out blows, and we must anticipate that they would be reinforced by every measure of secret preparation which might effect a surprise. ... It is clear that in a war against us the concentration, from the first day of war, of the whole of German air offensive ruthlessly against Great Britain would be possible. *It would be the most promising way of trying to knock this country out,* and if adopted, would be carried out thoroughly.[12]

The expected effects of such an offensive were put most bluntly and the report was brutally explicit on the question of the civilian population:

> Our civilian population has never been exposed to the horrors of War and the Germany may believe that if our people and particularly our women and children were subject to these horrors ... the majority would insist that surrender was preferable to continuation of attacks.[13]

The Joint Planning Committee recalled that during the First World War there had been some ugly scenes when angry Londoners, incensed by German air raids, had demonstrated against British airmen. A far more serious reaction was to be expected in a future war, and in dealing with security measures, the report considered the possibility of 'angry and frightened mobs of civilians' attempting to sabotage R.A.F. aerodromes.[14] On the basis of Air Staff estimates, casualties of the order of 20,000 persons might be expected in London within the first twenty-four hours of an aerial bombardment; within a week, these might rise to around 150,000.[15] Even H.G. Wells would have had difficulty in conjuring up a more terrifying picture.

The Deputy Chiefs of Staff Committee discussed this final report early in November, and, although endorsing its general conclusion, complained that it placed too much emphasis on the advantages that Germany might gain from an air attack instead of pointing out the difficulties and disadvantages which she might face.[16] The Committee

---

[12]*Ibid.* Italics added.

[13]*Ibid.* This theme was a clear reflection of the Air Staff's much publicized ideas. Compare this part of the report with Trenchard's remarks at a C.I.D. meeting on 26 April 1923, Cab. 21/261.

[14]*Ibid.*

[15]In fact, the *total* civilian casualties in the whole United Kingdom from bombing and other forms of long-range bombardment, including flying bombs, rockets and cross-Channel guns throughout the *whole* of the Second World War, was 146,777. Basil Collier, *The Defence of the United Kingdom* (London, 1957), p. 52.

[16]C.O.S. 540 (D.C.) Cab. 53/29.

recommended that the section of the report devoted to an examination of the probable intensity, character and results of air attacks on Britain should not go further, because work on these matters was not completed. This decision was undoubtedly influenced by Hankey, who served as Chairman of the Deputy Chiefs of Staff Committee and who, throughout the 1930s criticized what he considered to be the Air Staff's exaggerated estimates of the air danger.[17] The Chiefs of Staff Committee endorsed these recommendations; when submitting the major part of the report to the C.I.D. early in January 1937 they made some alterations to the paragraphs referring to the probable impact of air attack. These, although slight, show the continuing lack of consensus among the Government's military advisers. Thus Chatfield and Sir Cyril Deverell, the new C.I.G.S. infsisted on omitting the second part of one paragraph of the original report which said: 'We should anticipate a direct air offensive against the United Kingdom at the outset, *the outcome of which might well govern the ultimate issue of the War'*, and Ellington, the Chief of Air Staff, had to concur.[18] Nevertheless, despite its altered tone, the report as finally submitted to the C.I.D. defined and analysed the air danger in the most definite and specific terms. The Chiefs of Staff Committee considered it probable that a war might commence with a German attempt to achieve a knock-out blow by launching air attacks aimed at disrupting Britain's food supply or at moral and material destruction.[19]

The implications of the hypothesis were not new to the Government. Despite the Chiefs of Staff's suppression of the J.P.C. analysis of air attacks, the C.I.D. and the Cabinet had long been informed of the probable dangers by various papers submitted by many other C.I.D. sub-committees, which had been based upon the estimates of the Air Staff. Thus, in February 1936, almost a year before the C.O.S. submitted their report, one such committee, appointed to consider the location and accommodation of Staff and Government on the outbreak of war, declared that 'casualties in the nature of 50,000 per week was the minimum which could be contemplated'.[20] Its interim report to the C.I.D. further concluded that 'the material danger could hardly be guessed at . . . [but it would be great enough] . . . to put pretty well out of action the administrative machinery of the Government and this assumption applies also to the general life of

---

[17]See the minutes of the Committee in Cab. 54/1 and, on Hankey's opinions, see below pp. 144-5.

[18]192 C.O.S. Cab. 53/6.

[19]See 369 C.O.S. Cab. 53/34, 12 November 1937.

[20]Cab. 16/454.

London in its various aspects'.[21] By the beginning of 1937, therefore, the military authorities had advised the politicians of the full extent of the danger of aerial bombardment. Moreover, both aspects of the knock-out blow concept — the probability of a prospective German strategic bombing offensive against Britain and its almost cataclysmic effect — had been made absolutely clear in various documents presented to the C.I.D.

The apparent clarity and certainty with which these views were presented belies their essentially speculative nature. A study of various departmental minutes and files suggests that the phraseology which the Air Staff employed when communicating with their colleagues conveyed impressions which were far more definite than those actually held within the Air Ministry itself. This is not to cast aspersions on the sincerity of the Air Staff, who seem to have pursued a natural and understandable tendency to present a 'worst cast' analysis to the Cabinet. Yet, this fact serves to illustrate and further emphasize the extraordinary nature of the British fear of an air attack during these years. For that reason, it is worth examining the supposedly rational grounds for that fear in some depth.

The Air Staff possessed little evidence to substantiate its assumption that the Nazi regime had been quick to appreciate the possibilities of a strategic bombing offensive against Britain and, consequently, had formulated plans to launch an air attack. Despite the efforts of Air Intelligence, by early 1935 there was still no definite answer to the question whether German air strategy would be based on a strategic bombing offensive or on close cooperation with the Army.[22] Moreover, the Air Staff analysis of the lessons gleaned from the German air exercise of September 1936, contains no reference to the role of the Luftwaffe as an instrument for a strategic bombing offensive; prominence is given only to its role in cooperating with the Army.[23] Late in 1937, General Stumpff of the Luftwaffe gave the Secretary of State for Air pertinent — and correct — information on German air strategy; but this was not believed because it ran counter not only to the theories of the Air Staff, but to the widespread fear that Germany would try to terrorize the civilian population in order to achieve the desired knock-out blow.[24]

Having been pressed to do so by the Chiefs of Staff Committee, in

[21] C.I.D. Paper 1217-B, 17 March 1936, Cab. 4/24.
[22] Air 2/1405, Notes on 14 January 1935.
[23] Air 9/24.
[24] 21 October 1937, Cab. 21/627.

July 1937 the Air Staff produced a paper entitled 'Principles Governing the Employment of German Air force'.[25] This was the one and only paper of the entire period in which the Air Staff referred specifically to evidence supporting their thesis. According to Hankey, the paper stressed that 'the Germans would conduct air warfare on much the same lines as we should ourselves'.[26] This 'mirror image' of the Luftwaffe was a distortion of contemporary facts and could not possibly have been substantiated by solid and unmistakable evidence from the German side. (Although before 1936 there was a conflict of views in Germany about the role of the German air arm which created stumbling blocks in planning overall aircraft production,[27] there is no question that thereafter the Luftwaffe was rearming for a European war in which it would be used in direct support of advancing ground forces.[28] Not until well into 1938 did the Germans begin to think about strategic bombing offensives against Britain in operational terms. Their assessments indicated that air attacks could have no more than nuisance value; in no circumstances would they exercise a decisive effect on the course of a war.)[29]

At this time, then, British fears of a knock-out blow were quite unfounded. As late as 1939 Hitler privately expressed scepticism about the possibility of any victory through air attack alone, refusing to believe that bombing by itself could completely incapacitate an enemy's war-making potential. He is quoted as saying that 'if the German air force attacks English territory, England will not be forced to capitulate. . . . A country cannot be brought to defeat by an air force'.[30] This attitude had clearly influenced the rearmament of the Luftwaffe and its strategic planning.[31]

---

[25] 198 C.O.S. Cab. 53/7.

[26] 7 July 1937, Cab. 64/15. The paper itself has not been traced at the Public Record Office.

[27] R.J. Overy, 'The German Pre-War Air Production Plans November 1936 — 1939', *English Historical Review* (1975), 788-79.

[28] See J. Killen, *The Luftwaffe, A History* (London, 1967); D. Irving, *The Rise and the Fall of the Luftwaffe, The Life of* Erhard Milch (London, 1974); R. Williams, 'The Development of Luftwaffe Aircraft in the Nazi Era' (Ph.D. thesis, University of Minnesota, 1971); K. Volker, *Die Deutsche Luftwaffe 1933-1939*, (Stuttgart, 1967); R. Suchenwirth, *The Development of the German Air Force 1919-1939* (New York, 1968); and E. Homze, *Arming the Luftwaffe* (Nebraska, 1976).

[29] K. Gundelach, 'Gedenken uber die Fuhrung eines Luftkrieges gegen England bei des Luftflotte 2 in den Jahren 1938/9', *Wehrwissenschaftliche Rundschau,* 1 (1960), pp. 33-46.

[30] *Nazi Conspiracy and Aggression* (Washington, 1946), VII, pp. 852-53.

[31] A. Galland, 'Defeat of the Luftwaffe, Fundamental Causes', *Air University Quarterly Review* 1 (1953), 18-43.

It is understandable, therefore, that British Air Intelligence could not substantiate the Air Staff's thesis; there *was* no tangible proof. It appears to have been able to adduce only two concrete facts to support its arguments. The first was that fighters had a much lower priority than bombers in the various rearmament plans of the Luftwaffe (which gave weight to the view that its plans were substantially for offence);[32] the second was that Germany was putting considerable emphasis on various air defence plans (which might point to preparations to deal with retaliation for a strategic bombing offensive).[33] We now know that the conclusion drawn from the first fact was wrong, since although the Germans stressed the offensive role of the Luftwaffe, they planned at that time to use it mainly in close cooperation with the attacking army. As to the second, the German leadership did not believe in the feasibility of an aerial knock-out blow by any party to a forthcoming war. Nevertheless, Hitler was very anxious altogether to avoid any bombing of Germany, not because he envisaged the kind of total breakdown that London feared, but because he desired to spare Germany all possible wartime hardship.[34]

The estimates which the Air Staff presented to the Government on the probable effects of air raids on Britain were again, merely speculative. As one of the Staff frankly stated: 'the air Ministry could not guess at the probable effects of air attack... it is quite impossible for precise data to be provided when there were so many incalculable factors to be considered.'[35] And the Chief of Air Staff, pressed on the matter by his colleagues at the Chiefs of Staff Committee, explained with limpid simplicity that 'the assessment could not be based on war experience since there was none. . . .'[36]

An admirable summary of the various arguments adduced in support of the prevalent theory is provided in a letter which Colonel Ismay, then secretary to the C.I.D., addressed to Hankey during the

---

[32] See the remarks of Air Vice-Marshall Courtney, Chief of Operations and Intelligence at a meeting of the Deputy Chiefs of Staff Committee on 12 November 1936, Cab. 54/1, and J.P.C. Paper on 29 April 1936, Cab. 53/27.

[33] See a report by the British Air Attache in Berlin on 16 December 1936, Air 9/24.

[34] G. Quester, *Deterrence before Hiroshima* (New York, 1966), pp. 99-100 and R. Dinerstein, 'The Impact of Air Power on the International Scene 1933-9', *Military Affairs* 19, (1955), 65-71. On Hitler's Luftpolitik in the 1930s, see E. Emme 'The Genesis of Nazi Luftpolitik 1933-1935', *Air Power Historian* 6 (1959), 10-24, and 'Emergence of Nazi Luftpolitik as a Weapon in International Affairs 1933-1935', *Air Power Historian* 7 (1960), 92-106.

[35] Wing Commander Saundby at a meeting of the Home Defence Committee on 23 June 1937, Cab. 53/3.

[36] 198 C.O.S. 18 February 1937, Cab. 53/7. See also J. Slessor, *The Central Blue* (London, 1953), pp. 151-152.

autumn of 1936. Since these clearly represented ideas shared by a large group of military experts and politicians, they deserve to be set forth in some detail.[37] Ismay's premise was that the Germans must have planned for a short war, since they could not hope for victory in a long one. From this basic assumption, the following seems to have been simply a natural deduction:

> It seems unlikely that they will attempt to achieve this object by naval operations, since they have voluntarily accepted a drastic limitation of naval armaments. Moreover, they are unlikely to have forgotten the lesson of pre-war years, that any attempt to build a Navy in competition with ours, would be regarded by us as a direct challenge. Nor does it seem likely, in view of the strength of the French defences, that they could hope to achieve a *rapid decision by land operations. The inference to be drawn is that her only chance of a short war lies in the exploitation of air power.* . . .

Ismay went on to put forward the apparent reasons for Germany's choice of Great Britain as the *first* object of attack in any military conflict in which the two countries might be involved:

> The Germans fully appreciate after their experiences of 1914-1918, that the British, if given time, are by far the most formidable of their potential enemies. Their obvious conclusion must be that to fight us at the beginning will be their best, if not their only, chance. In 1914, this was impossible, since we were virtually inaccessible. Today they have the means of striking at the very foundations of our existence within a few hours of the declaration of war, or even before it.
>
> And there is another factor which points to England as the most probable first objective, namely, *the tempting charcter of the target*. The vulnerability of the British Isles in general, and of London in particular, has been elaborated so often that it is unnecessary to say more than that there could scarcely be any more perfect example of "all the eggs in one basket." Germany, on the other hand offers no targets, on which we, or the French, could retaliate with comparable results. Even so, the effect of any retaliatory action that we might take would be discounted to a considerable extent by the elaborate air raid precautions that have been made throughout Germany and by the militant education that has been instilled into the German people.

A point constantly made by those who believed in the feasibility of the knock-out blow by air attack was that, since the Germans seemed to be devout believers in the principle of the concentration of force, they would in a future war against Britain devote *all* their bombing

---

[37] 17 September 1936, Cab. 21/622, from which the subsequent quotations have been extracted (italics added). On Ismay's personal assessment of the danger of aerial bombardment, see Wingate Ronald, *Lord Ismay, A Biography* (London, 1970), p.40.

force to achieve a decisive result. Ismay put the argument thus:

> They may be expected to concentrate practically the whole of their bombers against England, ignoring for the moment France and Belgium, and regardless of any punishment that they themselves may receive, on land or from the air.

He then went on to stress that many persons in Government circles, and especially the Foreign Office, were very nearly convinced that Germany would gamble on a strategic bombing offensive against Britain *before* completing her military preparations for an all-out war.

> There is a tendency to assume that Germany cannot be ready before such and such a date: some say 1942, some say earlier. Any such assumption is not altogether safe, since "readiness" is a relative term. It was, I believe, the general anticipation in pre-war days that Germany would not be ready to strike until 1916. In the event she struck two years earlier. Apart, however, from historical precedent, it is not the practice of Dictators to be slaves to the counsels of perfection that are offered to them by their General Staffs. Mussolini was, I understand, strongly advised by his experts, not to undertake the Abyssinian adventure, and Hitler was warned against what his experts considered a premature occupation of the Rhineland. Consequently, it is unsafe to us to bank on too generous a time margin.

Ismay summed up his whole thesis in one sentence:

> It is certainly possible, and indeed probable, that the dominating feature of the German war plan is the delivery of a knock out blow to England from the air: that this blow will be immediate, continuous, and of an intensity that has not perhaps been visualized; and that it may be delivered earlier than we, at present, have reason to anticipate.

The forecasts of the various C.I.D. sub-committees served to confirm and to strengthen the fears of many Ministers who, as has been seen, were already disturbed at the prospect of attack from the air. Chamberlain often enlarged on the immense and destructive capability of air power;[38] Simon was especially apprehensive about the grave psychological effects of intensive air bombardment on the civilian population;[39] of Hoare's preoccupation with air defence, a C.I.D. official said: 'He has not a thought in his head except anti-aircraft guns; he'd put in a million of them if he could manage it'.[40]

---

[38] See his remarks to the C.I.D. on 14 April 1937, after reading a report on medical arrangements in times of war, and his memorandum on 11 December 1936, C.P. 334(36).

[39] See his remarks at the C.I.D. meeting on 19 April 1937, Cab. 16/181.

[40] Pownall Diary, entry 24 October 1938, in B. Bond, (ed.) *Chief of Staff: The Diaries of Lieutenant-General Sir Henry Pownall* (London, 1972), p. 166.

Sir Thomas Inskip, the lawyer whom Baldwin had, in 1936, appointed Minister for the Coordination of Defence, regarded the danger of air attack as of predominant importance. Late in 1938, he advised the Government to abandon some important blockade rights in times of war in exchange for German cooperation in elaborating a code of air warfare rules.[41] Halifax noted that 'the more realistic view as to how a continental war might develop was not the 1914-18 trench war but war in the air'.[42] In his memoirs, Eden admitted that his particular persistence in matters of air defence and air rearmaments before the War had been the result of 'psychological as well as military' factors.[43]

Perhaps General Ironside exaggerated when observing, late in 1937, that Ministers 'are terrified now of a war being finished in a few weeks by the annihilation of Great Britain, they can see *no other kind of danger than air*'.[44] Nevertheless, Hoare was not alone when contending, early in 1938, that the main defence issue facing Britain was 'how to win the war over London'.[45] In fact he was only voicing the anxieties of a large group of decision makers, which considerably influenced many aspects of the current debate on rearmament and strategy, and many of the decisions taken.

The Government's preoccupation with aerial warfare, and specifically with the danger of aerial bombardment, necessitated that the highest priority be accorded to the means required to counter an air attack. Throughout the long debate on rearmament and strategy during the latter half of the 1930s, many prominent decision-makers repeatedly stressed the argument that this consideration would undermine Britain's ability to intervene by land in military affairs.[46] In terms of strategic planning, the effect of this thesis was to cause marked indecision over the future role of the Army, the debate on which was not seemingly resolved until December 1937. The 'limited liability' formula then adopted determined that Army estimates were henceforth to be drafted on the assumption that British forces would not be committed to a continental land campaign — a fact of which France was to be informed.[47] In terms of specific financial allocations,

[41] Cab. 21/737.

[42] 319 C.I.D. Cab. 2/7.

[43] A. Eden, *Facing the Dictators* (London, 1967), p. 483.

[44] Entry in Diary, 29 December 1937, in R. Macleod and D. Kelly (eds.), *The Ironside Diaries* (London, 1962), p. 42. (Italics added.)

[45] 319 C.I.D., 11 April 1938, Cab. 2/7.

[46] C. Barnett, *The Collapse of British Power* (London, 1972), p. 504.

[47] P. Dennis, *Decision by Default* (London, 1972), pp. 110-114.

the new emphasis on the air danger led to drastic cuts in the Army's overall share of the rearmament budget (to no more than one fifth of the average annual expenditure for the period 1934-37).[48] When alldocating these limited resources, moreover, the Army was to give greater preference to new equipment for anti-aircraft guns than to new equipment for the Field Force.[49]

The argument that Britain dispense with an expeditionary force to the continent, and consequently limit the Army's rearmament, in order to confront the danger of air attack, rested on three considerations. The first was economic and, not surprisingly, was that favoured by the Treasury. This Department's position was that the rearmament plans proposed by the three Services were simply unrealizable in the time considered necessary, unless the country were placed on a semi-war footing. Under present conditions, any attempt to implement them in full might, according to the Treasury's reckoning, endanger the country's economic stability — which was itself considered of primary importance in a prospective long war. Warren Fisher was a constant critic of the Services' 'confusion of paper pounds with resources',[50] Later in 1937 he said that 'while it was important to give no impression of slackening we should be destroying our staying power if we attempted to meet the defence estimates without discrimination.'[51]

Throughout the late 1930s the Treasury urged (generally with success) that the Cabinet scrutinize defence requirements in acordance with a scale of assumed priorities: the basis for discussion was to be the worst menace and the manner in which it might be confronted.[52]

Strategic considerations were further adduced in support of the contention that priority must be given to air rearmament and defence, at the expense of the Field Force. When the case was examined from this aspect, two points appeared relevant. The first concerned the gravity of the danger of aerial bombardment and its implications for rearmament plans; the second referred to the diminishing value of any attempt to prevent the occupation of the Low Countries by Germany in order to minimize the danger of air attacks on Britain. The latter factor seemed to emphasize the overwhelming need for air rearmament,

---

[48] M. Postan, *British War Economy* (London, 1952), p. 28.

[49] See Inskip's letter to Hoare late in September 1936, in Cab. 64/3, and Paper 271 — A, Cab. 3/7, November 1937.

[50] T/161, Box 833, S/48431/01/2.

[51] 7 December 1937, Cab. 64/30.

[52] See manifestation of that idea in Camberlain's memorandum on 20 June, 1934, D.C. (m) (32) 120, Cab. 16/111.

both as a direct defence against the much-feared knock-out blow and as a deterrent which might prevent such a blow altogether. These ideas were predicated on a firm belief in the *decisive* impact of air power on any future military conflict between Britain and Germany, and a consequent reassessment of the role of the air force. Hitherto, the air arm had been primarily regarded as a retaliatory weapon.[53] Now, it was argued, such was the gravity of the air menace that the development of air power was as necessary for Britain as the maintenance of her traditional naval supremacy; both were essential keystones of the country's defence structure. Besides, intensive air rearmament would enable France and Britain to restructure their roles in a collective war effort against Germany. The assumption was that should it fail as a deterrent, a strong offensive Air Force, together with the Navy, would represent Britain's main contribution to concerted action with her continental allies.[54] This line of thought implied that the Army Field Force could be sacrificed for the benefit of the Air Force. As Chamberlain told the Cabinet late in December 1936:

> *The air arm has emerged in recent years as a factor of first rate if not decisive importance.* Shall we not be wiser to exploit these factors to the full and to build up an Air Force which might well *exercise a preponderating influence* than to spread our rearmament on equipping in peace time a military force which could only be small compared with continental armies?[55]

Early in 1937 Inskip presented to the Chiefs of Staff the general opinion of the politicians on the appropriate 'Role of the Army'. He stressed that 'there was no doubt that the Cabinet when the matter was discussed, had had in mind the proposition that air forces would be the most powerful factors in the future and therefore it might not be wise to spend too much on our land forces at the expense of air forces'.[56]

Throughout this period, the protagonists of air power continuously criticized the theory that the establishment of hostile air bases in the Low Countries could best be prevented by an Expeditionary Force. These had been the grounds upon which the C.I.G.S. had hitherto justified his demand for the equipment and rearmament of the Field Force. As early as the first months of 1934, however, Chamberlain asked whether the Expeditionary Force would be able to save the Low

---

[53] See Fisher's correspondence with Hankey in Cab. 21/540 and C.P. 38(36), Cab. 24/260.

[54] See Weir's notes on 9 January 1936. Cab. 64/35.

[55] C.P. 334(36), Cab. 24/265. (Italics added.)

[56] 193 C.O.S. 19 January 1937, Cab. 53/6.

Countries if Germany decided to invade them. Two years later, the Chancellor broadened the scope of the question: could an expeditionary force possibly defend the Low Countries, in view of the time it would need to land on the Continent and the possibility of German air attacks on the ports of embarkation and disembarkation?[57] The C.I.G.S. seems to have given no direct answer. He did supply many reasons for equipping and preparing an expeditionary force; but none of the memoranda which he submitted to the C.I.D. successfully allayed Chamberlain's doubts about its ability to fulfil its task. This as Liddell Hart noted, reflected a basic lack of strategic planning by the General Staff.[58]

Chamberlain was only one source of the arguments advanced against equipping a large Field Force. Another was to be found within the Chiefs of Staff Committee itself. Admittedly, throughout the period between 1934 and 1937, official papers submitted by the Committee continued to advocate an enlarged expeditionary force, largely on the grounds that it would prevent the occupation of the Low Countries by a hostile force. However, a close examination of various Air Staff files indicates that the Committee's unanimity on this subject was (especially after 1936) more apparent than real. The first signs of dissent would appear to have originated with a change of attitude on the part of the Air Staff. As early as May 1934 some members of the Air Staff were questioning the validity of their own Department's recommendation to support the General Staff's advocacy of an Expeditionary Force. Their arguments, although 'unpalatable to the C.I.G.S.', were 'already held by some at least of the Cabinet and by many thinking civilians ...'. 'Our strategy', they stated, 'should be based on a determination not to become involved in a Continental land compaign like the last.'[59]

By 1935 such opinions had become more specific. In that year, Group Captain (later Marshal of the R.A.F.) Harris wrote to Colonel Sir Ronald Adam (of the Directorate of Military Operations and Intelligence at the War Office) that 'the advantages of occupying the Low Countries will become progressively less from the air point of view'.[60] With the introduction of 'the quota system' in rearmament plans, and the consequent inter-services rivalry for defence budgets,

[57] 11 February 1936, C.P. 39(36), Cab. 24/260.

[58] Notes of a conversation with Deverell and Haining, 12 November 1936, Liddell Hart Papers, B2/2.

[59] Notes on C.O.S. 334, 5 May 1934, and C.P. 205(34), Air 9/15. For a full analysis of this episode, see U. Bialer, 'The British Chiefs of Staffs and the 'Limited Liability Formula' of 1938', *Military Affairs* (April 1978).

[60] 17 May 1935, Air 2/1405.

the air force protagonists felt the need to put their case against the Expeditionary Force in a radical manner. Thus, fully two years before Chamberlain enunciated his 'limited liability formula' the members of the air staff felt that the need for an Expeditionary Force to ensure the integrity of the Low Countries was simply a 'Bogey employed to stampede us into maintaining the intention and cadre of a future national army'.[61] In any case, they told each other, the War Office would be bound to experience 'natural difficulties' in obtaining 'sufficient morons willing to be sacrificed in a mud war in Flanders ... [in] endless marching upon short rations with a machine gun bullet in the stomach and a shell hole to lie in as the only possibility of relief'.[62]

Early in 1936, therefore, they suggested that the British army should be trained only for 'protecting our naval and air bases, providing garrisons for the close defence of our frontiers and to assist in the maintaining of internal security'.[63] This clear deviation from the Balance of Power principle, which had traditionally underpinned the Chiefs of Staffs' demands, did not find expression in any of the papers of the C.O.S. Committee or the C.I.D.

The evidence now available suggests that these views were probably withheld in view of the known inadequacy of the R.A.F.'s striking force in 1934: the production of heavy bombers capable of reaching Germany from British bases had yet to begin. This situation had changed by 1937 when Bomber Command began to be equipped entirely with heavy bombers.[64] The change of opinion in the Air Staff in 1936, and even more in 1937,[65] certainly strengthened the convictions of those who favoured the limited liability formula and the concentration in rearmament plans on air defences and on an air striking force. This makes it clear why, in the private notes Montgomery Massingberd left to his successor, he emphasized that:

> I feel that the biggest battle that I have had in the last three years is against the idea that on account of the arrival of air forces as a new arm, the Low Countries are of little value to us and that therefore we need not maintain a military force to assist in holding them. Those belonging to this school of thought desire therefore to concentrate all our efforts on a strong air force firstly to act as a deterrent to Germany, and if that fails as our sole

[61] See a paper entitled 'The Potential Danger to the Security of the British Empire and our Consequent Defence Requirements', 15 January 1936, Air 9/8.

[62] Group Captain A. Harris to Sir E. Ellington, 24 September 1936, Air 9/8.

[63] 'The Potential Danger . . .' 15 January 1936, Air 9/8.

[64] M. Howard, *The Continental Commitment* (London, 1972) p. 117.

[65] See M. Smith, 'The Royal Air Force, Air Power and British Foreign Policy 1932-37', *Journal of Contemporary History* 12, (1977), 166.

contribution towards making good our guarantee under the Treaty of Locarno. The dangers of such a policy and the importance of the Low Countries to us I have put forward again and again, but the elimination of any army commitment on the Continent sounds such a comfortable and cheap policy to those who are ill informed as to its real implications, that from time to time it gains fresh adherents *especially* amongst the air mad.[66]

Such internal opposition probably facilitated a change of stance on the part of the Chiefs of Staff, who early in 1938 finally complied with the limited liability dictum.

Finally, attention must be drawn to the political considerations advanced in support of the argument that the danger of air attack necessitated cuts in the Field Force. Within this context, one basic theme was the emphasis placed on the contrast between public concern with air defence and public opposition to the employment of the Army on the Continent. Throughout the late 1930s, the Rothermere press harped on the need for air rearmament, using the horrors of air attack to fortify their demand.[67] The same course was adopted by various organizations which pressed for air rearmament, and the acceleration of air defence, notably the Air League,[68] and the Air Raid Defence League.[69] The cinema newsreels, then in their formative years, played a prominent part in the spread of this anxiety. By 1938, over half of the population, excluding the very young, was being regaled each week with a view of current events in this form; and a feature of the newsreels was the prominence they gave to the horrors of war.[70] The Spanish Civil War, its atrocities and, especially, the bombardment of civilian areas were extensively exploited by the newsreel producers who wished to drive home their message.[71] At the same time, the Government's publicity of air raid precautions, especially after the introduction of the Air Raid Precautions Bill in July 1937, produced a flood of literature on the dangers of air attack.[72]

[66] n.d. Massingberd Papers, Vol. 158. (Italics added.)

[67] On its activities see H.S.H. Rothermere, *My Fight to Rearm Britain* (London, 1939).

[68] On which see Charles Gibbs Smith, *The Air League 1909-1959*, (London, n.d.).

[69] It included, *inter alia,* Lord Salter, Leo Amery, Liddell Hart, Gilbert Murray, Lord Allen of Hurtwood and others. See Lord Salter, *Memoirs of a Public Servant* (London, 1962), pp. 259-260.

[70] Nicholas Pronay, 'British News Reels in the 1930s, I; Audience and Producers', *History* 56 (1971), 413.

[71] T. Aldgate, 'British Newsreels and the Spanish Civil War', *History* 58 (1973), 60-3.

[72] See the British Museum Subject Index and the International Index to Periodicals

Although the public outcry against preparing a Field Force for action on the Continent abated somewhat, even the War Minister had to admit, late in 1936, that the country at large was adamantly opposed to such a Force.[73] The reasons for this attitude were explained by Liddell Hart, who wrote in a private letter: 'No one who is so placed as I am to hear views of all classes of people can help realizing what lasting harm the memory of the Somme and Passchendaele has done to the cause of defence and attitude of people towards it'.[74] Moreover, isolationist sections in British public opinion regarded the development of air power as an important factor which had removed a decisive argument favouring Continental entanglement. Thus, Beaverbrook wrote late in 1934: the airplane has destroyed the only argument there was for taking part in the quarrels of Europe. A modern airplane can fly across Belgium in twenty minutes. Belgium is no longer of any interest to us.'[75]

It is admittedly difficult to draw exact conclusions about public opinion on the two rearmament issues. However the records show that in their discussions the decision-makers continually enlarged upon the contrast between the public's intense concern with the danger of air attack and its aversion to the preparation of a field force for a Continental war. Early in 1936, for example, Neville Chamberlain clearly appreciated that Parliamentary pressures for the establishment of a Ministry of Defence was primarily based on popular apprehensions concerning the danger of air attack and a generally growing awareness of the implications of air power.[76] As he bluntly told the Defence Requirements Committee: 'There was the political difficulty that proposals for the reconstitution of the Field Force were not likely to get such public support as the proposals for . . . the expansion of the R.A.F.'[77] Similarly, Lord Weir, who in 1935 was appointed special adviser to the Government on rearmament, stressed that the widespread anxiety about air defence had to be considered when allocating defence expenditure: 'In initiation of any new defence policy, our people will certainly require the most effective reassurances on this

(New York, 1949) of the 1935-8 period for books and articles on this issue in Britain. Mass Observation Archive, Sussex University, File 4/S; J.E. Wood, 'The Luftwaffe as a Factor in British Policy 1935-1939', (ph.d. thesis, Tulane University, 1965), and E. Eddy, 'Britain and the Fear of Aerial Bombardment 1935-1939', *Air Power Historian* 13 (1966), pp. 177-85, are useful for public opinion on the subject.

[73]See C.P. 327(36), Cab. 24/265.

[74]Liddell Hart to Deverell, 25 November 1936, Liddell Hart Papers, J/2.

[75]Quoted in A.J.P. Taylor, *Beaverbrook* (London, 1972), p. 349.

[76]C.P. 39(36).

[77]13 January 1936, Cab. 16/123.

issue above all.'⁷⁸ This argument was telling because no one in the Government could deny that there was increasing public apprehension about the prospects of a knock-out blow from the air.⁷⁹

These economic, strategic and political arguments in favour of sacrificing the Field Force in order to expand the air arm prevailed. In some measure, this was due to the prominence and influence of the decision makers who endorsed them. In larger part, however, it was the result of the inherent difficulty of presenting an opposing view.

The C.I.G.S. and his department were especially unequipped to counter the political arguments. Therefore, with the strong backing of Hankey, they rested their case on the strategic view. They advocated the traditional Balance of Power principle in defence planning, and consequently opposed the sacrifice of one Service to another.⁸⁰ In support of their position, they asserted that the decisiveness of aerial bombardment in a future war had been greatly exaggerated: 'undue futurism' about air power (in Hankey's words) could be just as disastrous as unwarranted tardiness in understanding the meaning of other developments in armaments.⁸¹ Furthermore, they claimed, neither the experience of the First World War, nor that of the late 1930s, substantiated the Air Staff's much publicized theories on the impact of air warfare. As Hankey noted late in December 1936, 'to bank on air force is a gamble, since no country has yet achieved complete success by use of air power alone'.⁸² According to the C.I.G.S., the evidence provided by the Japanese air raids against the Chinese at Chapei, and by the Italian actions in Abyssinia, was inconclusive: neither these nor any other air raids of the second half of the 1930s had involved the huge concentration of aircraft that would be available in the event of an Anglo-German war. The validity of the Air Staff's hypotheses could not therefore be tested by reference to contemporary air warfare. This had been apparent to a special investigation of the Air Raid Precautions Department who made on-the-spot observations in Madrid in 1936. It was equally clear to a C.I.D. sub-committee which investigated the lessons of the Spanish Civil War the following year.⁸³

⁷⁸9 January 1936, Cab. 64/35.

⁷⁹See Hoare's remarks in a Cabinet meeting on 29 September 1937, Cab. 28/89.

⁸⁰See an analysis of this principle in Pownall's notes in Cab. 21/509.

⁸¹See Hankey's letter to Baldwin on 15 January 1936, Cab. 21/673. See also his letter to Trenchard in April 1928 in Cab. 21/314.

⁸²Cab. 63/51.

⁸³15 January 1937, Air 2/22022; see Hankey's letter to Inskip of 1 February 1937, Cab. 64/35.

The second reply which the C.I.G.S. made to the Air Staff argument was that German military authorities were not commited to the extreme air warfare strategy. The Nazis certainly regarded the Luftwaffe as a highly important factor in combination with other forms of warfare, but they did not consider it a substitute for them. However, since no evidence about prospective German strategy was ever presented in support of this claim, its effect could not have been very powerful.

The third, and final point made by the C.I.G.S. stressed the need for an efficient and well-equipped Field Force in order to prevent air raids from the Low Countries. The argument here was both strategic and political. Hankey summed it up in January 1936 when stating:

> If we have no efficient army, they [France and Belgium] will feel that we do not mean business. Without some aid from us, France will not help Belgium, Belgium will collapse, London will be exposed to the worst horrors of aerial bombardment and we shall not have an effective base from which to retaliate on Germany. The deterrent effect of our air force will thus be largely reduced.[84]

That argument does not appear to have undermined Chamberlain's repeated conviction that the Field Force would be of dubious *military* value in defending the Low Countries, and in 1936 the C.I.G.S. found himself having to defend his ideas with a *non-military* counter-assertion: 'Our small field force would not make much difference, but that is completely to ignore the *moral* value which such a field force would have, out of all proportions to its size, as we learned in 1914.'[85]

This type of reasoning, however, ceased to have much meaning in the light of the development of British air power and air defence in 1936 and 1937. The growing speed and range of British bombers significantly diminished the value of Belgium as a protection against air attack and as an advance air base for retaliation.[86] In any case, no member of the Government was likely to be in sympathy with the idea that Britain determine her rearmament plans on the basis of certain expectations of her European allies. When, late in 1936, Fisher wrote 'we ourselves must decide how our army can be most usefully employed',[87] he was certainly expressing prevailing opinion.

[84]Letter to Baldwin, 15 January 1936. Cab 21/673.

[85]Massingberd Papers, Vol. 158, n.d.

[86]The development of heavy bombers had been extensively used in 1938 to qualify British reluctance to widen the scope of her air conversations with the French (see minutes of a C.I.D. meeting on 14 February 1938, Cab. 64/121).

[87]Cab. 64/35, 'Notes on the Role of the Army', 23 October 1936.

By early 1938 the outcome of the debate on British strategy (which lasted for four years) was in no doubt. The unmistakable consensus of opinion within the Government was that Britain had to concentrate on air rearmament and on the construction of defences designed to counter the danger of air attack — even if doing so implied foresaking the ability to intervene by land in a European war. In that year, the 'limited liability' formula won general acceptance; priority was given to anti-aircraft defences within the Army's budget; and the concentration on air rearmament was unmistakable. Each of these various decisions signified the adoption of one strategic posture in preference to another. One result was that the extent of air rearmament soon reached the stage predicted by the Chairman of the Treasury inter-services committee at the beginning of 1937: 'The amount to be spent next year is really to be determined by the rate at which progress can be effected.'[88] A second, and complementary, result was no less consequential. On the evidence now available it seems reasonable to suggest that the Government's deep sensitivity to the air threat contributed towards a particular perception of British strategy. The decision to prefer air rearmament, and to oppose the maintenance and deployment of a large army on the continent, ultimately implied an essentially defensive and anti-European strategy. Those members of the Government who opposed this trend, because of its anticipated deleterious effect on Britain's relations with her potential European allies, could now more easily be overruled. On the other hand, the position of those Ministers in Chamberlain's Cabinet who agreed with the Prime Minister's view that this was the correct concept to adopt was now greatly strengthened.

In his *Britain in a Century of Total War,* Arthur Marwick observed: 'British statesmen had a tendency to exaggerate the threat of air attack, but as long as their fear existed, it . . . served as a constraint upon their foreign policy'.[89] The effect of this apprehension on British policy at the time of the Munich crisis has often been cited as a clear example of this thesis.[90] However, a study of the Foreign Office files for the period 1935-7 reveals that the makers of British

[88]Bridges's notes on the Air Ministry Estimates, 15 January 1937, T/161, Box 154, S/35170/3.

[89](London 1968), p. 137.

[90]See, *inter alia,* K. Robbins, *Munich 1938* (London, 1968), p. 201; W.K. Eubank, *Munich 1938* (London, 1963), p. 286; H. Macmillan, *op. cit.*, (London, 1966), p. 575; A.P. Adamthwait, 'French Foreign Policy, April 1938 — September 1939', (unpublished Ph.D. thesis, University of Leeds, 1966), p. 173. K. Middlemass, *Diplomach of Illusion,* (London, 1972) p. 294; and M.P. Sorlin, 'Les perspectives aeronautiques dans la crise tchecoslovaque de 1938', *Forces Aeriennes Francaises* (November, 1958), pp. 601-35.

foreign policy had for some time felt constrained by the danger of air attack. Indeed, such was the nature of their preoccupation with this issue that they had felt bound to point out its political as well as its military implications. Thus, long before the dramatic crisis of 1938, officials had warned of the inadequacy of Britain's air defences and of the effect of air inferiority on the formulation of a firm foreign policy.

In the wider context of overall political strategy, such warnings — and the degree to which they were repeated — had produced two important results. First they reinforced the general opinion within the Cabinet on the priority of rearmament. Indeed, so successful was the Foreign Office in pressing its anxiety from 1934 onwards, that by early 1938 its own officials were criticizing the Government's *exaggerated* concern with the danger of the knock-out blow from the air. Other defence problems, it was claimed, were being dangerously and disproportionately neglected.[91]

Secondly, although the shadow of overwhelming German air superiority was perhaps not the sole, nor even the decisive, reason for the pursuit of agreement with Germany, it clearly influenced those within the Foreign Office who wished to initiate what seemed to them a firmer and more effective policy towards that country. One indication of the Foreign Office's concern with this aspect of the problem — as early as 1934 — is provided by a memorandum on German rearmament which Orme Sargent wrote towards the end of that year. The purpose of the paper was to examine the differences between the long-term danger to Britain of war with Germany after 1938, and the immediate issues raised by any attempt to confront Germany's aggressive (but not military) policy and intimidatory actions before 1938. In a central passage, Sargent wrote:

> There is nothing to show that Hitler, and still less the Reichswehr, are preparing for war of aggression in the near future. Such a policy would indeed be sheer madness, unless Hitler were ready to fight the whole of Europe, and to get Germany into a fit state — military and economically — to do that would be a work, not of a few years but of decades. No: what Hitler, I have little doubt, is aiming at is to accumulate a sufficient amount of military force behind him to enable him to achieve his objectives one by one by the silent threat of force, but without the use, or even the display, of force. In fact, what he intends is an aggressive *policy* and not an aggressive *war,* and there is no reason why at the present rate of Germany's rearmament on the one hand, and of the international disintegration of the rest of Europe on the other, he should not be able to start on this policy in the near future. ...
> Thus Germany would have achieved one of her objectives, not

---

[91] See Strang's notes in F.O. 371/21653, C 3233/37/18.

by fighting but by intimidation, and not because she was in a position to wage a war of aggression, but because her opponent was no longer in a position, without running undue risks, to wage a war of aggression against her.'[92]

During the course of the next three years, the fears of the Foreign Office came to focus increasingly on Germany's potential ability to dictate terms to Britain in Europe; the basis for an aggressive German foreign policy, it was suggested, would be provided by her apparent air superiority over Britain and the latter's inferior air defences. Ralph Wigram made this specific point when commenting on a Foreign Office comparison of the British and German air strengths in 1936.

> But it is legitimate to ask, and those who in the Foreign Office see the extensive information which is available as to the political intentions of Germany cannot help asking, whether further delay and a continuance of what looks very like inadequate measures in matters so vital to us will not expose us in quite a near future to the most terrible demands which we shall not be strong enough to resist.[93]

Late in 1937 when the Air Staff itself had to admit that Britain was two years behind Germany in air rearmament, the Foreign Secretary, Anthony Eden, warned the Cabinet of the far-reaching implications of that fact. He wrote:

> Whatever our foreign policy may be, and whatever our relations with Germany may be, now and in the future, it should be an immutable principle with us that we ought not to be satisfied until we have seen to it that in air strength and air power this country shall no longer be in a position of inferiority to any country within striking distance of our shores. Only by so doing can we be reasonably secure in a world which is becoming more and more dangerous, not only to our security but also to the ideals and ways of life which we cherish; *and only by so doing can we hope to negotiate 'settlements' on terms of equality with either Germany or Italy so as to prevent Europe from falling into that general war which might be our undoing.*[94]

Throughout the years 1935-7, Foreign Office officials devoted a great deal of effort to impressing upon the Government the necessity for air rearmament and the construction of adequate air defences in order to be in a position to counter the growing danger from Germany. They kept a critical eye on the various estimates which the Air Staff produced on the comparative air strengths of Britain and German fearing, in the light of the 1934-5 experience, that this branch tended

---

[92] 31 October 1934, FO 371/17695, C 7088/20/18. (Italics added.)
[93] 19 November 1936. FO 371/19947, C 8249/3928/18.
[94] 25 November 1937, D.P.(P)13, Cab. 16/182. (Italics added.)

149

to minimize the danger of the situation, and were very quick to warn against factual mistakes and erroneous deductions.[95] Similarly, the Foreign Office was wary of the estimates and plans which other defence departments submitted on matters of air defence. Thus, late in July 1935, Ralph Wigram commented in the following manner on the Interim Report of the D.P.R.C., in which the subject of the Air Defence of Great Britain Plan was dealt with:

> When one reads this sort of thing [the D.P.R.C. decision *not* to recommend to the Cabinet the completion of that first stage of its plan by 1940] in an official report, one cannot help being disquieted by the stories one hears from private persons of the treatment they receive from so-called 'Defence' departments when they suggest them taking adequate measures for the protection of their country.[96]

In July 1936 the Foreign Office rejected a German offer to provide the British Air Ministry with full information on German air rearmament,[97] because of the condition that such information should not be used publicly or communicated to Parliament. The Foreign Office was not prepared to make a deal which sealed its lips and undermined its efforts to make the British public more aware of the danger of German air power.[98]

On the other hand, the Foreign Office did provide the C.I.D. with a considerable amount of information on German air rearmament which it had acquired through its own sources, and some of which Air Intelligence described as 'a valuable contribution to our knowledge'.[99] It also compiled some important reports for the C.I.D. on German anti-aircraft defences. One of these, written early in September 1937, emphasized that 'there can be few countries which can anticipate attacks from the air with such comparative confidence as Germany'.[100] This led to an enquiry into Britain's own anti-aircraft defences and the decision to give priority to A.A. defence within the Army's rearmament programme.[101] Eden ceaselessly pressed his colleagues in the Cabinet

[95] See Vansittart's notes on 11 October 1936, FO 371/1947, C 7044/3928/18 and Strang's notes in FO 371/20746, C 5592/1421/18. See also Oliver Harvey's memorandum of 15 February 1937, which stressed the fact that the Air Staff Memorandum seems to have tried not to emphasize the fact that Britain then possessed only 48 long-range bombers against 800 German bombers. FO 371/20701, C 1406/205/62.

[96] FO 371/188848, C 5539/55/18.

[97] 280 C.I.D. Cab. 2/6.

[98] FO 371/19947, C 6879/3928/18.

[99] See correspondence in Vansittart Papers, 3/1.

[100] D.P.R. 219, Cab. 64/14.

[101] See Correspondence between Chamberlain and Weir in Cab. 64/9.

for more intensive air rearmament and adequate air defences,[102] and urged the full implementation of Baldwin's parity pledge.[103] In December 1937 he strongly supported the demands made by Lord Swinton, the Air Minister, for the construction of long-range bombers in numbers which could match those able to reach Britain direct from Germany. He also backed Swinton's plea not to abandon the policy of deterrence.[104]

By the end of 1937 the situation which the Foreign Office had dreaded continuously from 1934 appeared to have become a staggering reality. Germany's considerable air superiority, and the poor condition of Britain's air defences, seemed to have endowed the Nazis with the capability of dictating their will to Britain. It had, therefore, to be admitted that Britain's policy towards Germany would have to be governed by the undeniable factor of her air inferiority. Foreign Office memoranda on rearmament during the late 1930s frequently quoted Lord Grey's famous dictum that 'you must not rely on your foreign policy to protect the United Kingdom'. It was used in a trenchant summing up of Britain's position at the end of 1937 by William Strang, later to become the Permanent Under-Secretary for Foreign Affairs:

> The grave situation revealed ... has not, of course, been a secret to us. What is alarming is that the day of security never comes any nearer, but is successively postponed to a still more distant future. It is now about 4 years ahead, and so far as active ground defence is concerned, even more than that. In ... their memorandum the Air Staff quote Lord Grey: "You must not rely on your foreign policy to protect the United Kingdom." But this is, in fact, what our foreign policy has been trying to do for years; and it now appears that we must go on doing so for some years more. We have no alternative, therefore, but to put on as bold a front as we can, and *play for time*.[105]

And the name of the game, throughout 1938, was to be appeasement.

---

[102] See Eden, *Facing the Dictators*, pp. 482-3, 494-5.

[103] See his correspondence with Vansittart on this issue in Vansittart Papers, 2/33.

[104] See Cabinet Meeting of 22 December 1937, Cab. 23/90/A.

[105] 5 November 1937, FO 371/20734, C 8124/185/18. (Italics added.) It should be noted that the foreign office was discouraged early in 1939 'presumably owing to the insistance of the air ministry' from making any further research into comparative British and German air strength. FO 371/39084 C/5711/148/18.

# EPILOGUE TO AN OBSESSION

'It is only by studying the minds of men', said Professor James Joll in his inaugural lecture at the London School of Economics, 'that we shall understand the causes of anything'.[1] This book has attempted to illuminate one important aspect of the state of mind of the British policy makers during the 1930s: a pervasive fear of a knock-out blow by aerial bombardment which, on the evidence of the records, might not unreasonably be described as an obsession. Ultimately, the Second World War demonstrated beyond all doubt that the British had unduly exaggerated the weight of bombs which Germany could deliver. They had also been particularly mistaken when estimating the probable effect of air attacks on life in the great cities and on the morale of the civilian population. A.J.P. Taylor places the blame for this miscalculation on the British decision-makers, commenting that 'as always, the technical estimates were shaped by non-technical predilections'. In his view, 'this was in everyone's interest: the air chiefs wished to justify their demand for more bombers; the Government wished to justify their demands for more expenditure on rearmaments or on air-raid precautions'.[2] Whether or not the British Government should have relied upon other assumptions must remain an open question. The present analysis has aimed to explain, rather than pass judgment, on the fear of air attack. It suggests that the excessively sensitive apprehensions of British policy-makers concerning that eventuality often went beyond the bounds of rational reflections on the strategic situation. As much is indicated by the continuous and intensive debates on the 'air peril' in 1931-3 — a time when war was hardly considered probable; the intense personal preoccupation of some prominent policy makers with that danger; the impact of relevant public opinion on some of their decisions; the adherence to the search for a convention humanizing air warfare with Germany throughout the late 1930s; and the high price even in military terms, which the Government considered paying for German cooperation in that matter.

Three main factors would appear to have been basically responsible for the extent of the British Government's fear. The first was the concern that the country might lose the inviolability bestowed by its geographical location. This was not a totally recent phenomenon. As recent research has shown, ever since the middle of the nineteenth

---

[1] '1914, The Unspoken Assumption', in H.W. Koch, (ed.), *The Origins of the First World War* (London, 1972), p. 328.

[2] A.J.P. Taylor, *English History 1914-1945* (London, 1965), p. 437.

century the makers of British policy had been disturbed by the threat which the technological advances of the industrial age posed to their country's insular invulnerability. The advent of steam in the 1840s; of ironclads in the 1860s; of rapid mobilization on the German model in the 1870s; and, as a technical possibility, of a Channel tunnel in the 1880s, had each given rise to morbid conjecture concerning the continued preservation of Britain's inviolability to attack from overseas.[3] It is hardly surprising, then, that the policy makers who survived the First World War should have become deeply sensitive to a new form of attack on their own home territory. The formative experience of the bombardment of London in 1917 was itself significant. Not only did the German air raids of that year constitute shattering proof of the loss of insular security; they also demonstrated the particular vulnerability of Britain to this specific form of warfare.[4]

Noble Frankland offers the following explanation for the strong, and seemingly unaccountable, reaction to the death of 150 people and the destruction of Liverpool Street Station by German Gotha bombers in the year which also witnessed the Battle of Passchendaele:

> The fact that the British, nourished by a thousands years of virtual immunity from war (if the Scots and their own quarrels are overlooked), expected to preserve their immunity, and the fact that they had little conception of what was happening to that small percentage of them who were or had been in the trenches perhaps explains the strength of the popular reaction, and the popular reaction, no doubt, in part, accounts for the official one.[5]

In 1931, Anthony Eden addressed the House of Commons as a veteran who had seen active service during the First World War. His speech illustrates the impact of aerial bombardment on the men on the Western Front and stresses the lessons which they learned from that experience:

> Those who have seen war are the least likely to want to see its repetition. . . . Those who saw the first weeks of the last war had a vision of what the next wawr might expect to be. I remember an evening in the last stages of our advance, when we had stopped for our night at Brigade Headquarters in some farmhouse. The night was quiet and there was no shellfire, as was usual at the end of the war, but quite suddenly it began literally to rain bombs for anything from ten minutes to a quarter of an hour. I do not know

---

[3] See H. Moon, 'The Invasion of the United Kingdom: Public Controversy and Official Planning' (unpublished Ph.D. thesis, London University, 1968).

[4] On that experience, see R. Fredette, *The Sky on Fire: The First Battle of Britain* (New York, 1966).

[5] N. Frankland, *The Bombing Offensive Against Germany, Outline and Perspective* (London, 1965), p. 33.

how many bombs fell in that time. But some thing between thirty and forty.I suppose. It seemed to us to be hundreds. What rests in my mind is not only my own personal terror which was quite inexpressible . . . but the comment made when it was over by somebody who said: 'There, now you have had your first taste of the next war'.[6]

Eden's speech touches, too, on the second (and related) cause of the fear of air attack. The twentieth century witnessed a significant flowering of futurological thought, which was reflected in the sudden emergence of literary speculation concerning future wars.[7] This trend was considerably influenced by the philosophy of Social Darwinism, by a conception of 'progress' and, above all, by the rapidly accelerating development of technology. It exerted enormous persuasive power on all levels of opinion, and the politicians of inter-war Britain were no exception.

To an observer living in a supersonic age, the technical advance of civil and military aviation during the inter-war period may seem slow and unimpressive. By the standards of its own time, however, it was considerable. In 1919, the Americans, flying a Curtis D-12, won the Schneider Trophy with a speed of 177 m.p.h.; in 1938 the Germans, flying a Messerschmidt B.F. 109 R, raised the record to 469 m.p.h. In 1920, the Americans captured the altitude record whe flying at 33,000 feet; by 1938, the Italians had reached a height of 56,000 feet. In 1925, a flight of 1,967 miles had proved sufficient to ensure that French pilots would retain the long distance record; in 1938, the British established a new standard when covering 7.158 miles.[8]

These developments in the air stirred the imagination of the makers of British policy no less than the man in the street; but in the case of the former, such advances also carried portentous overtones, and nourished a fear of what may be termed the 'progressive danger.' When privately explaining their grave apprehensions about the possibility of aerial bombardment, British politicians often referred to the prospective increase in the danger. Thus Simon, early in 1932, voiced his deep concern about the evolution of military aviation 'fifty years hence';[9] Vansittart, during the same period, warned the Cabinet about the danger inherent in the 'speed and ease'[10] of its development. Both men gave expression to one of the most important bases of the

---

[6]A. Eden, *Facing the Dictators* (London, 1967), p. 18.

[7]I.F. Clarke, *Voices Prophesying War 1763-1984* (London, 1966), p. 302.

[8]R. Higham, *Air Power, A Concise History* (London, 1972), pp. 78-80.

[9]Above, p. 21.

[10]Above, p. 23.

fear of aerial bombardment which haunted many of their Ministerial colleagues. An essential corollary to the fear of the 'progressive danger' was the need for what might be termed 'advanced thought': an appreciation of the significance of air power indicated that Britain had to keep pace with developments in aviation technology. Samuel Hoare, an ardent air-power protagonist, once criticized the Chiefs of Staff's assessment of the 'next war' on the grounds that it was essentially conservative. 'What had struck me was that we are preparing for a war of exactly the same kind as the last.[11]

Allied to these factors, and indeed exacerbating them, was a third cause which can be seen to have accounted for Britain's particular apprehension concerning aerial bombardment: the inherent difficulty of forecasting the effect of air power on the course and outcome of a future European war. One reason was the unprecedented nature of the supposed danger: 'half the ordinary man's terror of the air war', wrote a prominent British scientist in an unconventional prediction of the impact of aerial bombardment on the eve of the Second World War is due to its novelty. This will disappear in time and if we continue to fight we shall take the threat of bombing in much the same way as people on the continent have accepted the fear of invasion by armies which have only to cross a frontier a few miles away to burn their homes'.[12] Another, more important, cause was the impossibility of drawing definite conclusions from any of the air raids of the inter-war period. In this context, it is instructive to compare the inter-war controversy concerning the effect of air power on strategy and defence with the similar debates associated with the invasion scares of the last 19th century. Before the First World War, Britain's 'navalists' had been able to demonstrate that the fear of invasion, which stemmed from the great strides made in military technology, was grossly exaggerated; these advances had not eliminated the difficulties of invading the island fortress.[13]

By contrast, underlying the history of air power before the Second World War was the crucial fact that in none of the previous military conflicts had any attempt been made to practice large-scale strategic aerial bombardments with the purpose of achieving a knock-out blow (which was how General Douhet, for instance, envisaged the use of air power). The experience of air raids during the inter-war period provided no real clue as to whether intensive aerial bombardment in a major conflict might disrupt an enemy's war-making potential. This

---

[11] Quoted in a personal letter from Hankey to Vansittart, 8 March 1934, Cab. 21/434.

[12] A.M. Low, *Modern Armaments* (London, 1939), p. 201.

[13] Moon, *The Invasion of the United Kingdom,* pp. 639-41.

made it very difficult to challenge successfully those who maintained that a strategic bombing offensive would dictate the result of the 'next war'.

In the absence of reliable information before 1939, however, every level of the nation would appear to have been mesmerized by the slogan culled from Baldwin's warning to the House of Commons in 1932: 'the bomber will always get through'. This belief underlay professional as well as lay attitudes towards defence against air raids until the late 1930s, and largely accounts for the failure of the General and Naval Staffs to persuade the Cabinet that the Air Force's estimates were greatly exaggerated. Moreover, radar, which was to make a substantial contribution to Britain's successes in the aerial battles over London during the Second World War, was not invented until 1935. Several years were to pass before the completion of the chain of radar stations on the East Coast, which provided Britain with the best air defence system in the world. Only on the *very threshold* of war was radar capable of allaying one of the deepest fears of air attack.

During the intervening period, however, the need to preserve the secret of radar as closely as possible, and the fact that it remained until the last year of peace in an experimental stage, had prevented any full revelation of its significance being made to the Cabinet. Thus, writing to Chamberlain on the state of Britain's air defences in July 1937, Hankey referred to radar in the most guarded of tones:

> given a few years more of peace we shall have some nasty shocks for them [the Germans], in the event of aggression. But this is all in *the most secret of spheres,* though in some respects it is on the threshold of actual application in our defensive system.[14]

In any case, the Lord Weir informed Inskip six months later, 'until further experiments have been made, the information by the three Radar stations would have only *a very limited value*'.[15]

No attempt is here made to suggest that during the decade before the outbreak of the Second World War, the British Government was concerned with nothing else except the threat of an air attack. An account of its intense preoccupation with that danger does, however, provide a new perspective which might usefully help to elucidate some of the well-known issues confronting British defence and foreign policy during the late 1930s. Thus, Britain's air anxiety at that time might help to shed new light on the controversy between the Admiralty and the Air Ministry concerning British national strategy.

[14] Cab. 64/15.
[15] Weir Papers 19/8. Italics added.

This debate (which in fact turned on the effect of air power) had commenced during the early 1920s, when the role and status of the Royal Air Force was discussed;[16] it raged throughout the remainder of the inter-war period. As has been shown, the argument became even more heated onced rearmament began and the Government had to decide how the defence budget should be distributed between the three Services. The issue was dangerously over-simplified in the slogan, 'bombers versus battleships', which reflected merely one aspect of the rivalry between the advocates of traditional naval strategy and the supporters of strategic deterrence through air power. The essence of the debate was whether air power had effected such a revolution in warfare as to overthrow the traditional supremacy of naval demands in over-all defence planning. The controversy came to a head on various occasions during this period, one of which was the Abyssinian crisis in 1935, when the Admiralty was disturbed about the danger of an air attack on the Mediterranean Fleet.[17] The same year witnessed a revival of the long-standing quarrel between the Air Ministry and the Admiralty over the Fleet Air Arm.[18]

It was, however, the debates of the C.I.D. sub-committee on the Vulnerability of Capital Ships in 1936 which brought the contention into the open in the most acute fashion. The formal issue before the committee was the extent to which new weapons had increased the vulnerability of naval craft. But the discussions focussed on a wider problem: the value of capital ships in the face of what was popularly termed the air menace. The Committee heard some arguments that the function of capital ship could be carried out at least equally as well by aircraft; that the defence of British territory and trade routes could be accomplished by light naval forces; and that battleships were unecessary as cover for those light forces, since if the enemy possessed battlships, these would be destroyed by British air forces properly deployed in advance to deal with such a situation. Stating the matter in the simplest possible terms, the advocates of the extreme air view urged that the battleship was outdated and that Britain need build no more such ships.[19] It is hardly surprising that the C.I.D. sub-committee declined to accept these views; but in the light of the

---

[16]See G. Till, Airpower and the Battleship in the 1920s ; in B. Ranft (ed.) *Technical Change and British Naval Policy 1860-1939* (London, 1977), pp. 108-22.

[17]See A. Marder, 'The Royal Navy and the Ethiopian Crisis of 1935-6', *American Historical Review* 75 (1970).

[18]See S. Roskill, *British Naval Policy Between the Wars, Vol. II: The Period of Reluctant Rearmament 1930-1939* (London, 1976); and also Roskill, *Hankey, Man of Secrets*, Vol. III, p. 179.

[19]See Cab. 16/147.

widespread fear of air attack revealed by this book, it becomes understandable that in the 1930s, as in the early 1920s, it was still upon the Admiralty and not the Air Ministry that the burden of proof rested. A private letter from Chatfield to Churchill puts the point very simply: 'This country alone is going back mainly due to the fear that has been put into the mind of the public that the day of the Navy is over; that we can defend this country and the Empire much cheaper and better by aircraft'.[20]

The logical corollary, of course, was that Britain also had to be defended *against* aircraft. This is a factor which can be seen to have clearly influenced the Government's policy at the time of the Munich crisis. There can be no doubt that one of the main arguments against going to war in 1938 was the fact that Britain was defenceless against German bombers. She possessed hardly any modern fighters, virtually no air raid precautions, and few means of retaliation. It was this weakness in the air that the Cabinet's military advisers appear, in Setember 1938, to have considered decisive.[21] More important is the fact that Neville Chamberlain shared their awareness of the country's extreme vulnerability to air attack.

The Prime Minister emphasized this aspect of his policy over Czechoslovakia on 24 September, when justifying his policy to the Cabinet after returning from the second of his fateful visits to Hitler. That morning, he told his colleagues:

> he had flown up the river over London. He had imagined a German bomber flying the same course, he had asked himself what degree of protection they could afford for the thousands of homes which he had seen stretched out below him and he had felt that we were in no position to justify waging a war today.[22]

Of course at the time no one realized that German bombers were much less effective at long range than was supposed. In fact the assumed bombing effort of Germany was, until two years later, beyond even the range of her bombing aircraft, let alone their carrying capacity. Neither did anyone then pose the essential strategic question: In the event of Great Britain and France declaring war to help Czechoslovakia, would the Luftwaffe be able to direct its bombers towards England?[23]

[20] 5 May 1935, Chatfield Papers.

[21] See General Ismay's memorandum of 22 September 1938 in Cab. 21/544 and the Chiefs of Staff's report of 24 September 1938, 772 C.O.S.

[22] Cab. 23/95.

[23] Letter from P. Calvocoressi to the Editor of *The Times,* London, 1 August 1970, and P. Calvocoressi and G. Wint, *Total War* (London, 1972), p. 95. For a detailed

Nevertheless, as this book has attempted to show, Munich was not a sudden aberration. Rather, it represented the climax of almost a decade's expection (by the Government and the public) that Britain's 'next war' would be opened by a devastating, almost cataclysmic aerial bombardment against her cities and, especially, her capital. As a result of the intense preoccupation with this issue *before* 1938, this image constituted something more than an idiosyncratic flight of fancy. At the same time, it may also account for a somewhat less 'rational' aspect of the fear and its impact, than is sometimes preferred. This was well emonstrated by the feverish digging of air raid shelters and the filling of sandbags in preparation for a home front in September 1938. Even as sober a writer as Harold Macmillan portrays in blood-chilling words the contemporary atmosphere in his memoirs:

> Among other deterrents of war in 1938, expert advice had indicated that bombing of London and the great cities would lead to casualties of the order of hundreds of thousands or even millions within a few weeks. *We thought of air warfare in 1938 rather as people think of nuclear warfare today.*[24]

Lord Salter had used more highly-coloured language in a Doomsday warning delivered to Parliament a few months before Munich:

> It may be that strangers from distant lands and of alien races will stand upon the desolated site of Westminster and whether in exultation or in sorrow will chant the words of the apocalypse: 'Alas Alas! That great city of Babylon, that mighty city, in one hour thy judgment is come'.[25]

Small wonder that Harold Nicolson should write in his diary on 28 September 1938, the day Neville Chamberlain returned from Munich: 'I find an immense sense of *physical* relief in that I shall not be afraid tonight of the German bombs'.[26]

That this fear continued to exert a powerful influence on British policy, even after Munich, is illustrated by an episode which took place during the very year in which Britain finally went to war. In January 1939, the British Government was thrown into somethng of a

---

analysis of this subject see Williamson Murray, 'German Air Power and the Munich Crisis', in B. Bond and I. Roy (eds.) *War and Society,* vol. II (London, 1977), pp. 107-18.

[24] H. Macmillan, *Winds of Change* (London, 1966), p. 522.

[25] Lord Salter, *Memoirs of a Public Servant* (London, 1962), pp. 260-1.

[26] H. Nicolson, *Diaries and Letters 1930-1939,* ed. Nigel Nicolson, (London, 1966), p. 571. Italics added. For an analysis of the Munich crisis and the fear of air attack see E.S. Smith 'R.A.F. Plans and British Foreign Policy 1935-40' (unpub. Ph.D. thesis, M.I.T. 1966), pp. 134-70.

panic by a 'war scare'. Throughout the previous month various Intelligence sources had reported that the Germans were planning an invasion of the Netherlands, probably coupled with an all-out attack on London, to take place around 21 February.[27] So convincing and so disturbing were the reports that the Government requested Staff talks with the French, something which the Chiefs of Staff had hitherto consistently and vehemently opposed. There is little doubt that the reports were planted by opponents of Hitler — specifically, Admiral Canaris and Colonel Oster — in order to stir Britain into taking a stronger and more resolute attitude towards the Fuhrer than she had been doing in the preceding months. The success of this attempt can now be seen to have been due in large measure to the gnawing fear of the knock-out blow.

As has been seen, British sensitivity to the danger of aerial bombardment had been apparent to the German authorities as far back as 1934,[28] although Hitler himself seems to have been astonished at the reaction caused by his declaration of March 1935. At that time the German Embassy in London was instructed not to stress anything to do with the air.[29] Nevertheless, with the emergence of military force as the decisive arbiter in European affairs during the 1930s, the Luftwaffe, by reason of its loudly proclaimed destructive capability and constantly increasing range, became one of the most effective weapons of persuasion in the arsenal of the Third Reich.[30] The Germans certainly used their Luftpolitik technique, *inter alia*, against Britain during the fevered developments which preceded the Munich crisis. The fact that it was not Hitler himself who applied this threat the following December did not minimize its impact and plausibility. All the circumstances made it only too likely that Britain's worst fears were at last to be realized.

At a quarter past eleven on the morning of Sunday, 3 September 1939, the Prime Minister, Mr. Neville Chamberlain, announced in a broadcast to the nation that Great Britain was at war with Germany for the second time within a generation. A few minutes after he had finished speaking, the warbling note of air raid sirens was heard in

---

[27] D.C. Watt, *Too Serious a Business* (London, 1975), pp. 128-9; and D. Dilks (ed.), *The Diaries of Sir Alexander Cadogan 1938-1945* (London, 1971), pp. 139-44.

[28] See the report of the German Military Attaché in London of 30 July 1934, *Documents on German Foreign Policy 1918-1945* (1962), C, III, No. 138, p. 276.

[29] See G. Schweppenburg, *The Critical Years* (London, 1952), p. 46; and also Sir Eric Phipps's telegram on a conversation with Goering on 3 May 1935, Air 2/1405.

[30] See E. Emme, 'The Genesis of Nazi Luftpolitik 1933-5', and 'Emergence of Nazi Luftpolitik as a Weapon in International Affairs, 1933-5', *Air Power Historian* 6 (1959), 10-24; 7 (1960), 92-106.

London and many other parts of the United Kingdom. On the way down to the shelters of the House of Commons, Sir Samuel Hoare came across Lloyd George, 'very white and greatly excited'. He was soon reassured that there was no German air raid. But 'how strange', Hoare reflected, 'was this great and courageous war leader's fear of air raids. It had become a by-word in the First World War and it seemed to be as strong as ever in the Second'.[31] So often in the past had Lloyd George faithfully reflected the hopes and fears of his countrymen. He was doing no more that anxious Septemmber day. No other scene could provide a better summary to a study of the British obsession with the danger of a 'knock-out blow' by air attack during the second half of the inter-war period.

---

[31] Viscount Templewood, *Nine Troubled Years* (London, 1954), p. 394.

# INDEX

Abyssinia, 75, 96, 144, 156
Adam, Sir Ronald, 140
Adams, Vyvyan, 16
Admiralty: and air disarmament, 24, 28, 31, 103; and rearmament, 43, 57, 59, 63, 65, 67, 73-4; and air power, 155-6, 157
Air Ministry: 5; and air disarmament, 24-5, 28, 30-2, 37, 58-9, 93-5, 103, 112, 117, 119; and rearmament, 61, 64-6, 69, 71-2; and German air power 132; and vulnerability of Capital Ships 155, 157
Anglo-German Naval Treaty (1935), 90, 93-4
Atlee, Clement, 15

Babington, Group Captain, John 19n., 24
Baldwin, Stanley, 41, 69n, 144n; and air disarmament 14, 15, 16, 29, 31, 33, 45, 79; and rearmament, 17, 18, 43, 50, 51, 54, 65, 69-70, 72-3, 77; and fear of air attack, 20-1, 35, 155
Barlow, Sir Thomas, 73n
Barnett, Correlli, 4
Beaverbrook, Lord, 143
Beazley, Sir Raymond, 69n
Belgium, 63, 83, 99, 110, 114, 136, 143, 145
Brauchitsch, Field Marshal Walther von, 107-8
Bridges, Sir Edward, 44, 65n, 73n, 146n
Brook Popham, Sir Robert, 66n
Bullock, Christopher, 6n, 22

Cadogan, Sir Alexander, 10, 38, 117
Campbell, Ronald, 80
Canaris, Admiral Wilhelm, 55
Carr, Edward Hallett, 96n
Cecil of Chelwood, Viscount, 13, 14, 26
Chamberlain, Sir Austen, 16
Chamberlain, Neville, 149n, 158, 159; and fear of air attack 44-5, 136, 143, 157; and rearmament 54-5, 63, 64, 65, 66, 69, 73, 138n, 139-40, 155; and air disarmament 84, 92, 113
Chatfield, Sir Ernle, 64n, 125 n., and German air power 57, 61, 63, 129, 131; and air disarmament 105, 111-2, 121-2; and role of the Navy 157
Chiefs of Staff, 42, 51, 52, 59, 62, 65, 66, 83, 104, 124
China, 144
Christie, Colonel Malcolm, 55, 70

Churchill, Sir Winston, 4, 48-9, 55n, 69n, 71, 74, 157
Clerk, Sir George, 86n, 93n, 96n
Committee of Imperial Defence, 22, 29, 30, 31, 44, 57, 59, 85-6, 104-5, 107, 111-4, 119, 127, 128
Conservative Party, 9, 16, 49
Cooper, Duff, 121
Courtney, Air Vice Marshal Sir Christopher 134n
Creswell, Sir Michael, 55, 71n 89
Crozier, William, 80
Cunliffe Lister, Sir Philip (Later Swinton, Lord), 35, 36, 84

*Daily Mail,* 70
Dawson, Geoffrey, 17
Defence Requirements Committee, 59-67, 127, 128, 129, 143, 149
Deverell, Field Marshal Sir Cyril, 131, 140n, 143n
Dilks, David, 5
Disarmament Conference (Geneve 1932-4) 7-40, 41, 46, 62-3, 77
Douhet Giulio, 154

Eden, Anthony, 11, 37, 65, 115-6, 148, 152
Ellington, Air Marshal Sir Edward, 58, 61, 65, 107, 131, 141n
Eyres Monsell, Sir Bolton, 31
Evans, Charles, 65n

Fisher, Sir Warren, 50-1, 55, 60-1, 64, 73n, 127, 138, 139n, 145
Flandin, Pierre, 80-1
Foreign Office: and air disarmament 10, 22-4, 27-8, 29, 31, 32, 35, 78-83, 86-7, 88, 89, 90, 91, 93, 94, 96, 98, 110, 113-4, 117-8, 119, 120; and rearmament 52-7, 59, 68-75, 127, 136, 146-50
France: Policy at the Disarmament Conference 8, 10, 27, 34, 35, 64, 77-8, 109; Air power, 40, 70, 91; and air disarmament from 1935; 80-3, 85-9, 100, 109, 115-6
Frankland, Noble, 152
Fuller, Major General John, 47, 102

Garner, James, 103
Garvin J., 47
Germany: air attacks on Britain during the First World War 1, 152; air power 4, 20-1, 23, 38, 40, 45-6, 52-9, 60-1, 66, 68, 75, 76, 89, 90, 92, 107, 128-42, 145, 147-50, 157, 159; Policy at the Disarmament Conference 8, 10, 34, 39, 42, 76, 77-8; Secret Rearmament 41, 43, 60, 79; Air disarmament policy from 1935; 87, 88, 89, 91-2, 93, 95, 96, 97-8, 99, 100, 105-9, 112, 114-5
Gibson Hugh, 29

163

Gilbert, Martin, 75
Goering, Hermann, 23
Grey, Lord, 150

Hague, Draft Convention of Air warfare rules, 109-10, 111-2, 120, 123
Hailsham, Lord, 31, 45n, 17, 62n, 121, 85, 105
Haining, General Sir Robert, 140n
Halifax, Viscount, 63, 74, 115, 119, 125n
Halsbury, 2nd Earl of 15
Hankey, Sir Maurice, 52, 53, 134, 139n, 154n; and air disarmament 19-20, 23, 81, 83; and rearmament 43, 51, 65n; and German air power 56, 131, 133, 144, 145, 155
Harris, Air Marshal Arthur, 128, 140, 141n
Harvey, Oliver, 80, 81, 149n
Henderson Arthur 18n
Henderson, Sir Nevile, 116
Hitler, Adolf, 35, 70, 87, 88, 106, 115, 121, 133, 157, 159
Hoare, Sir Samuel, 138n; and disarmament 11, 19, 26, 94n 67, 96n, 114; and air power 22, 137, 144n, 154; and rearmament 44n, 45 n., 63, 65, 69, 136
Hoover, Herbert, 33-4
Hopkins, Sir Richard, 30n, 73n.
Hore Belisha, Leslie, 119, 124

Industrial Intelligence Centre, 54, 121
Inskip, Sir Thomas, 123, 125n, 137, 138n, 139, 144n
Ironside, General William, 137
Irwin, Lord (Later Viscount Halifax), 19, 45n
Ismay, Major Hastings, 134-6, 157n
Italy, 83, 89, 96, 99, 109, 114, 144

James, Robert, 4
Japan, 75, 97, 109, 144
Joll, James, 151

Kyba, John, 46

Labour Party, 8, 9, 15-6, 17, 18
League of Nations, 8, 9, 25, 36, 123
League of Nations Union, 9, 13, 15, 16, 27, 47
Leeper, Allen, 27, 75n, 158
Leeper, Sir Reginald, 70
Liberal Party, 21
Liddell Hart, Sir Basil, 46, 54, 140, 143

Lloyd George, David, 26, 160
Locarno Agreement, 16, 78, 82, 83, 95, 97, 98, 99, 142
Londonderry, Marquess of, 30, 31, 36n, 62, 68n,

Macdonald, Ramsay, 26, 29, 34, 36n, 37, 50, 70, 71, 77, 90 n.;
　　and disarmament 10, 17-8, 20, 21, 33n, 39, 42, 45, 82; and
　　rearmament 43, 62-3, 65, 69
Macdonogh, Sir John, 102
Macmillan, Harold, 158
Madden, Admiral Sir Charles, 104
Malkin, Sir William, 119, 121
*Manchester Guardian,* 80
Martin, Kingsley, 13
Marwick, Arthur, 146
Massigli, Rene, 80
Medhurst, Wing Commander Charles, 54, 74
Milch, Erhardt, 55
Montgomery Massingberd, Sir Archibald, 56, 57, 62, 107, 129,
　　141, 145n
Morton, Major Desmond, 54
Murray, Gilbert, 15n
Munich Crisis, 106, 122, 146, 157-8

Netherlands, 109
Newall, Sir Cyril, 120
*New Statesman,* 13, 14
Nicolson, Sir Harold, 158

*Observer, The,* 47
Ormsby Gore, William, 41, 50

Peace Ballot, 16
Phipps, Sir Eric, 97n
Pownall, Sir Henry, 124, 125

Rhineland, occupation of, 99-100
Ribbentrop, Joachim von, 116
Rothermere, Lord, 142

Salisbury, Marquess of, 104
Salmond, Sir John, 30
Salter, Lord, 158
Samuel, Sir Herbert, 21, 31, 32
Sargent, Sir Orme, 91, 92, 95n, 118, 147-8

Saundby, Air Marshal Sir Robert, 134n
Selborne, 2nd Earl of 43n
Simon, Sir John, 15, 24, 31n, 32, 72, 88, 93, 106; and disarmament: 10n, 18-9, 20, 21, 26, 28, 33-4, 76, 77, 79n, 86 n., 89, 91, 92; and German air power 23, 65, 70-1; and rearmament 45
Slessor, Air Marshal John, 114n
Smith, Howard, 28n
Soviet Union, 86, 90, 96, 97, 118, 119
Spaight, James, 110
Spanish Civil War, 114-5, 142, 144
Stanhope, Earl of, 124
Strang, Sir William, 117, 147n, 150
Stresa Conference, 71, 89-90, 91, 95
Stumpff, Colonel General Hans Jurgen, 132
Swinton, Lord, 98, 114, 150

Taylor, A.J.P., 151
Ten Year Rule, 43
*Times, The*, 15, 48
Treasury, 42, 44, 50, 64, 73, 76, 138
Trenchard, Sir Hugh (later Lord), 22, 64, 104, 130n, 144n
Tyrrell, Lord, 32n

United States, 8, 17, 29, 33, 37, 75, 97, 105, 109, 123

Vansittart, Sir Robert, 19, 150 n.; and disarmament 11, 22n 80, 82, 90, 91, 92, 97, 98, 121; and German air power 23, 52-6, 70, 71, 153; and rearmament 44, 50-1, 60-2, 72, 149n
Versailles, Treaty of, 8, 82, 88

War Office, 24, 28, 31, 58-9, 63, 65, 66, 73-4, 103, 141
Washington Naval Agreement, 8
Watt, Donald C., 44
Weir, Lord, 143
Wells, H.G., 130
Wernham R., 4
Wigram, Clive, 15
Wigram, Ralf, 55, 71, 81, 89n, 90n, 148, 149
Wood, Sir Kingsley, 124

## Other volumes in this series

| | | |
|---|---|---|
| 1 | The Politics of Stability: A Portrait of the Rulers in Elizabethan London | *Frank F. Foster* |
| 2 | The Frankish Church and The Carolingian Reforms, 789-895 | *Rosamond McKitterick* |
| 3 | John Burns | *Kenneth D. Brown* |
| 4 | Revolution and Counter-Revolution in Scotland, 1644-1651 | *David Stevenson* |
| 5 | The Queen's Two Bodies: Drama and the Elizabethan Succession | *Marie Axton* |
| 6 | Great Britain and International Security, 1920-1926 | *Anne Orde* |
| 7 | Legal Records and the Historian | *J. H. Baker (ed.)* |
| 8 | Church and State in Independent Mexico: A Study of the Patronage Debate 1821-1857 | *Michael P. Costeloe* |
| 9 | An Early Welsh Microcosm: Studies in the Llandaff Charters | *Wendy Davies* |
| 10 | The British in Palestine: The Mandatory Government and the Arab-Jewish Conflict | *Bernard Wasserstein* |
| 11 | Order and Equipoise: The Peerage and the House of Lords, 1783-1806 | *Michael McCahill* |
| 12 | Preachers, Peasants and Politics in Southeast Africa 1835-1880: African Christian Communities in Natal, Pondoland and Zululand | *Norman Etherington* |
| 13 | Linlithgow and India: British Policy and the Political Impasse in India 1936-1943 | *S. A. G. Rizvi* |
| 14 | Britain and her Buffer State: The Collapse of the Persian Empire, 1890-1914 | *David McLean* |
| 15 | Guns and Government: The Ordnance Office under the Later Stuarts | *Howard Tomlinson* |
| 16 | Denzil Holles: A Study of his Political Career | *Patricia Crawford* |
| 17 | The Parliamentary Agents: A History | *D. L. Rydz* |

Copies obtainable on order from
Swift Printers (Sales) Ltd., 1-7 Albion Place, Britton Street, London EC1M 5RE